gluten-free flour power

gluten-free flour power

bringing your favorite foods back to the table

Aki Kamozawa

H. Alexander Talbot

W. W. Norton & Company
New York   London

For information about permission to reproduce selections from this book,
write to Permissions, W. W. Norton & Company, Inc.,
500 Fifth Avenue, New York, NY 10110

For information about special discounts for bulk purchases, please contact
W. W. Norton Special Sales at specialsales@wwnorton.com or 800-233-4830

Manufacturing by RR Donnelley, Shenzhen
Book design by Jean Orlebeke
Production manager: Anna Oler

Library of Congress Cataloging-in-Publication Data

Kamozawa, Aki.
   Gluten-free flour power : bringing your favorite foods back to the table /
Aki Kamozawa, H. Alexander Talbot.
      pages cm
   Includes index.
   ISBN 978-0-393-24342-0 (hardcover)
   1. Bread. 2. Pastry. 3. Gluten-free diet—Recipes. I. Talbot, H. Alexander. II. Title.
   TX769.K285 2015
   641.81'5—dc23

                                                                2014037018

W. W. Norton & Company, Inc.
500 Fifth Avenue, New York, N.Y. 10110
www.wwnorton.com

W. W. Norton & Company Ltd.
Castle House, 75/76 Wells Street, London W1T 3QT

1 2 3 4 5 6 7 8 9 0

This book is for our daughter, Amaya,
who taught us that asking questions allows us to make new discoveries.

introduction

*g*luten-free food is not a fad. It's here to stay. For us that is excit-
ing, because we love a challenge. When chefs started calling us to teach
gluten-free workshops, we knew we had to step up our game. It's not
enough to create recipes that are "great—for gluten-free"; we wanted to
create great recipes that just happened to be gluten-free. Leaving out the gluten
was a crucial parameter in developing these recipes, but the defining factors were
taste and flavor.

The definition of the word *diet* is the kind of food that a person, animal, or
community habitually eats. For a variety of reasons, mostly health related, a good
percentage of the population now chooses not to eat gluten. You don't have to
have made that choice yourself to need a few great gluten-free recipes in your back
pocket, you simply have to want to cook for someone who has.

Let's start with the basics. Wheat flour is a hydrocolloid. That means it absorbs
water and creates a gel. Wheat flours, which consist mostly of starch, are classified
by their protein content. The amount of protein in the flour is what dictates the elasticity of your bread or pasta dough. Gluten is formed when two proteins, glutenin
and gliadin, absorb water or another liquid. Gliadin is sticky and stretchy, giving
dough extensibility, and glutenin adds strength and elasticity to a dough. *Elasticity*

refers to the ability of a dough to spring back after it has been stretched. These two proteins work in concert to create gluten.

When gluten absorbs water (a process known as *hydration*), it forms long, stretchy, elastic strands that define the structure of a batter or dough. Then when you cook it, the heat causes the starch granules to swell up, thickening and forming irreversible bonds with the water, the process called *gelatinization*. As the water inside the protein network heats, it changes into steam, which forces the network to expand; this is *steam leavening*. The final step is *coagulation*. Once the proteins reach a high enough temperature (165°F./74°C.), they begin to solidify, setting the structure of the bread or cake.

If you don't develop enough gluten in your bread dough, it won't be able to stretch and the resulting bread will be heavy and dense. If you develop too much gluten in your cake batter, on the other hand, it will become too elastic and the cake will be tough and chewy. Finding the perfect balance with gluten is an art, and replacing gluten with something else entirely can be challenging.

Without the protein in wheat flour, you need to find a new way to build structure in your dough. We do this in our flour blends by using a combination of starches, gums, and proteins that mimics the effects of gluten. We've come up with three different blends to address a variety of dietary needs. Making these blends may seem like an investment because of the number of different flours involved, but you will find that gram for gram, our homemade flour blends are less expensive than the gluten-free flour blends sold in retail outlets. It doesn't take long to whisk them together, and the results are well worth the minimal effort. Our gluten-free blends contain everything you need to re-create your favorite gluten recipes without having to add any other ingredients. They are all-purpose blends made without gluten that can be adapted to any traditional recipe.

We have seen that when people eliminate gluten from their diets, they begin to pay more attention to the effects that food has on their bodies. It's not unusual for people on gluten-free diets to become aware of other food allergies or sensitivities. For that reason, we created three different flour blends. They have all been tested with every recipe in this book and they all work in each one.

When we asked people to taste-test the recipes in this book, we didn't always tell them they were gluten-free. We wanted an honest opinion of flavor and texture without any preconceptions. Anything that did not receive rave reviews was not included here. These are wonderful sweet and savory recipes that you can serve to anyone you love, regardless of whether or not they are eating gluten-free.

gluten-free flour power

our gluten-free pantry

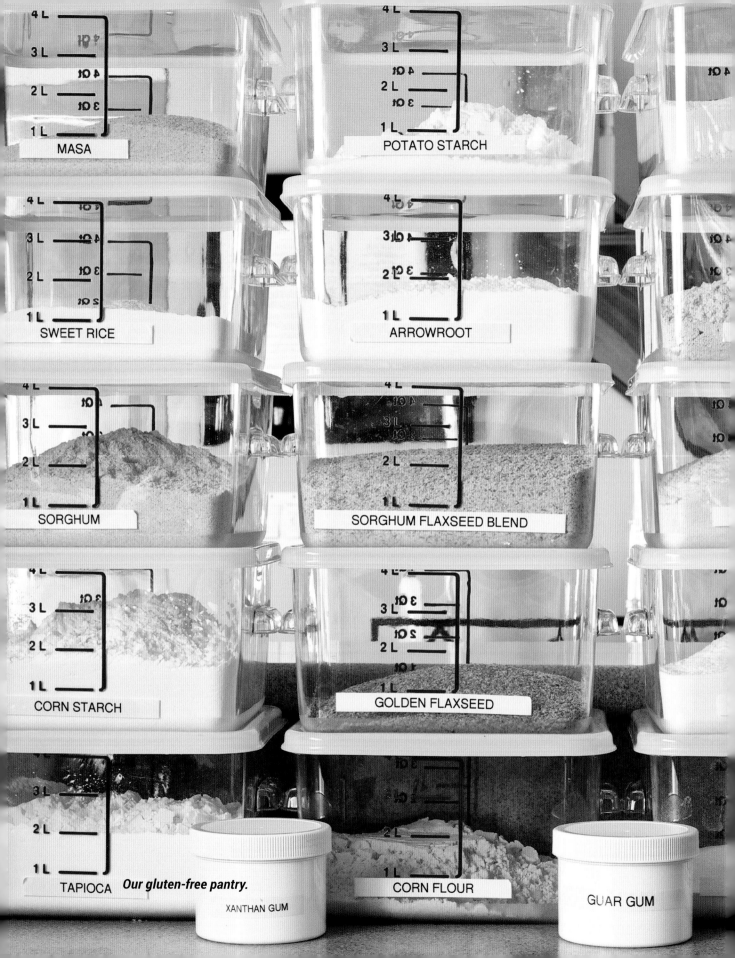

Our gluten-free pantry.

Working with gluten-free flours means putting aside some preconceived notions about how batters and doughs should behave. While some of the recipes in this book will seem remarkably similar to versions you've been making your entire life, others will seem unfamiliar. Bakers are traditionally taught that too much stirring can ruin a delicate cake batter by overdeveloping the gluten, but there's no gluten here. Bread dough will be wet and rise almost completely in the pans before baking instead of the oven. Pie dough will be soft and malleable. It may tear easily but it can simply be pressed back together with no ill effect. Certain textures and techniques will be different. What follows is a little background information on the flours, starches, and proteins we use in this book.

Don't think of gluten-free cooking as restrictive—think of it as changing your perspective. Creativity loves working within new parameters, and this is an opportunity to think outside the box when it comes to recipes that you may have been using for years. You'll find yourself tweaking the tried-and-true recipes that you've always relied on and possibly making them even better than before. Change opens up the imagination, and you may discover flavor combinations that bring new life to old favorites. Exploring different techniques and unfamiliar ingredients is one of the things that makes cooking fun for us.

Gluten-free cooking is easier than you may think. People get hung up on the idea of the vast array of new flours and ingredients that they think they will need, but once you start cooking with gluten-free ingredients, you will likely pick a few that you become very comfortable using. You don't have to use every kind of flour out there to be a good gluten-free cook.

Today there are many companies producing great gluten-free flours and grains, and many of these are readily available in supermarkets. Arrowhead Mills and Bob's Red Mill are two of our favorite producers. We buy these flours and starches in large bags or by the case to save money.

Here's a tip: Nut meals and flours are just finely ground nuts, so most of the time you can make your own. Chill the nuts and grind them in a food processor or blender, pulsing so they don't overheat and turn to nut butter. If you're going to be mixing them with flour or sugar for a recipe, add some of that to the food processor to help grind the nuts into a fine powder without turning them into a paste. It's easy to do and will probably be less expensive, and fresher, than store-bought nut meals or flours. Store any extra nut flour in the refrigerator. If you like, you can substitute up to 50 percent nut flour for the flour called for in most of your favorite recipes. The results will be slightly different, both richer and more delicate in texture, and the added flavor is a bonus. If you love nuts, it's worth experimenting a little bit.

You can also grind your own flour from gluten-free grains. Again, freezing or chilling them first is a good thing, because it helps keep the blender or food processor from getting too warm. You can grind rice into flour or process rolled oats to a fine powder in the food processor. You can make your own flaxseed meal in a spice grinder and turn dehydrated potato flakes into potato flour. Homemade flours will almost always be fresher, better, and less expensive than what you can buy. If you really embrace the process, there is a wide variety of grain mills that you can purchase; there is even a grain-milling attachment available for KitchenAid mixers. The only things you really can't make at home are the starches, such as cornstarch, tapioca starch, or potato starch. Not even we have the equipment for that.

So, what is the difference between a flour and a starch? Starches are present in all flours. Generally speaking, flours are ground grains, seeds, or tubers, cooked or raw, that are dehydrated and then ground whole into flour. A starch, such as cornstarch or potato starch, is isolated from that plant, dried and ground to a powder. Generally flours and starches are not interchangeable. The only exception to this rule is tapioca; for unknown reasons, you may find it labeled either tapioca starch or tapioca flour and both are exactly the same thing.

Arrowroot

Arrowroot is a starch derived from the young rhizomes of the *Maranta arundinacea* plant, which grows in South America, the West Indies, India, Sri Lanka, the Philippines, and Indonesia. Arrowroot often appears in Caribbean and Latin American recipes. It is used as thickener and results in a clear, glossy, odorless gel. It thickens at temperatures ranging from 140° to 187°F. (60° to 86°C.) and has the ability to withstand long cooking times without breaking down. Sauces and puddings thickened with arrowroot can be frozen without negative effects. Arrowroot is best mixed with cold water to form a slurry before blending it into a warm mixtures. Unlike gelatin or cornstarch, it dissolves in cool liquids, and it works well with acidic ingredients. We use arrowroot in our gluten-free flour blends as a thickener and to help retain moisture in the finished breads and cakes.

Cocoa Powder

Chocolate comes from cacao beans. After cacao pods are harvested, they are split open by hand and the seeds are removed and fermented with the pulp that clings to them. During this process, the pulp changes into liquid and the chocolate flavor develops. Then the seeds are dried and cracked, turning them into what are called cocoa nibs. The nibs are roasted, ground, and pressed to remove most of the cocoa butter. The solids that are left after pressing are ground into cocoa powder. It still contains a small amount of cocoa butter, 10 to 12 percent, and it has a very intense chocolate flavor. Dutch-processed cocoa powder, sometimes labeled "alkalized," has been treated with an alkali to increase the pH. This process also blunts the chocolate flavor, so we prefer to use natural cocoa powder in our recipes.

Corn Flour / Cornmeal

Corn flour and cornmeal are both ground from dried corn. The difference between them is the texture. Cornmeal comes in a range from coarse polenta to fine cornmeal, and the texture tends to be sandy rather than fine. Corn flour is the finest grind and is almost powdery in texture. (A note for bakers in England: There the term *corn flour* often refers to cornstarch.) If you need corn flour for a recipe or prefer a finer texture, you can grind cornmeal into flour in the food processor. Pulse it so that it doesn't overheat, and process to a fine, light powder. Don't confuse corn flour with masa harina (see page 11), another dried corn product. Masa harina has a stronger flavor and requires more liquid to hydrate.

Cornstarch

Cornstarch is a powder ground from the endosperm of corn kernels. Cornstarch has something of a bad reputation these days because of the controversy over the safety of genetically modified plants; the corn used for cornstarch is often GMO. There are many who believe that the recent increase in food allergies and sensitivities can be traced back to the widening distribution of genetically modified food supplies. All we can say is choose your cornstarch carefully. As of this writing, anything labeled "organic" in the United States cannot contain genetically modified ingredients.

Cornstarch is used as a thickener, and it is activated at temperatures ranging from 144° to 180°F. (62° to 80°C.). Like arrowroot and tapioca, it dissolves in cold liquids, so it's best to mix it with some cold water to form a slurry before adding it to a warm liquid. It needs to be cooked for 2 to 3 minutes to eliminate its starchy flavor. It forms a firmer gel than tapioca and we usually use it in combination with tapioca in cooked puddings or pie fillings so that they are soft and silky, rather than heavy and gummy. Cornstarch can also be used instead of flour to coat foods to be fried; it forms a light, crisp crust.

Flaxseeds

Flaxseeds are popular as a nutritional supplement. They are a good source of omega-3 fatty acids, lignans (a type of phytoestrogen with antioxidant properties), and fiber. Flaxseeds have a sweet, nutty flavor similar to that of sesame seeds and if you have them, they can be used instead of sesame seeds in recipes. Flaxseeds create a starch-based gel that thickens and emulsifies—that means it can help encourage foaming, thicken liquids, and create structure within batters and doughs. Because of this, flaxseed meal is often used as an egg replacer in vegan recipes. You can grind flaxseeds into a fine meal in a clean coffee or spice grinder, or you can buy them ground. Flaxseed meal is highly perishable and should be stored in the refrigerator or freezer.

flaxseed egg replacer

replaces 1 egg

Used in baking recipes.

3 tablespoons / 42 grams water

1 tablespoon / 7 grams flaxseed meal

Whisk together the water and flaxseed meal in a small bowl and let sit at room temperature for about 10 minutes. It will thicken as it sits.

Guar Gum

Guar gum is derived from the seeds of the cluster bean, an edible plant with pods resembling green beans. It is the ground endosperm of the beans. Guar gum is used primarily as a thickener and has eight times the thickening power of cornstarch. It also increases viscosity as it thickens. Guar gum is soluble in hot or cold liquids, though cold temperatures slow down hydration, lengthening the time it takes to form a gel. Guar gum is notable because it adds a chewy texture as it thickens, in turn, lending a pleasing texture to many baked goods. It is very stable at cold temperatures and discourages the formation of ice crystals in frozen emulsions, making it a favored additive in ice creams and sorbets.

Masa Harina

Masa harina is a type of corn flour, used in Latin American cooking to make tortillas. It is made from dried field corn that is heated in a solution spiked with slaked lime, then rinsed, rubbed to remove the hulls, and dried. Corn that has been treated this way is called *nixtamal*. The whole kernels are sold as hominy and the ground nixtamal is masa harina. Masa has a fine texture and tends to absorb more liquid than cornmeal or corn flour; it has a deep corn flavor and slightly nutty taste. We often cook masa harina and puree it to help add structure to gluten-free bread doughs.

smoked masa harina

makes 2 cups

Cold-smoking grains is a great way to increase flavor. While this recipe is for smoking masa, you can substitute the flour of your choice. Sometimes a touch of smoky flavor is all you need to change up a dish and give it new life. In fact, we discovered that smoked foods actually trigger umami receptors on the palate, making food more savory. We puree smoked masa harina and use it to strengthen the structure of gluten-free baked goods, but you could use it in your favorite tortilla recipe and see what a difference the smoke makes.

2 cups masa harina

Put the masa harina in a shallow container set over a pan of ice. Put it in your smoker and cold-smoke for 1 hour, stirring occasionally. Replace the ice as needed to keep the masa cool. Store in an airtight container.

masa harina puree

makes about 2 cups

This is the basic masa puree that we call for in a few recipes. It's a great thing to have on hand if you are experimenting with creating your own gluten-free bread and pasta doughs. It imports a light, nutty flavor from the corn and helps add viscosity and elasticity to the dough. This puree also makes an appearance in the filling of the Masa Harina Pie (page 293), in our riff on Indian pudding, with a smoother, silkier texture.

2¼ cups / 500 grams water

⅔ cup / 100 grams masa harina or Smoked Masa Harina (page 12)

½ teaspoon / 3 grams fine sea salt

To use a pressure cooker, put the water, masa harina, and salt in a bowl that fits inside your pressure cooker and whisk to blend. Set the bowl on a rack in your pressure cooker, with 2 inches of water in the pot. Cook at high pressure for 20 minutes. Allow the pressure to release naturally.

Remove the bowl from the pressure cooker and stir the masa well; it will look slightly curdled and separated at first and then come together as you mix it. Transfer the bowl to the refrigerator to cool completely.

Alternatively, bring the water to a boil in a medium saucepan and whisk in the masa harina. Bring to a simmer and cook over low heat, stirring often to prevent scorching and sticking, for 40 minutes, or until the masa thickens and is completely cooked through. Pour into a bowl and cool completely in the refrigerator.

Put the cold masa harina in a blender or food processor and puree until smooth; it will be thick and sticky. Masa harina puree will keep in a covered container in the refrigerator for up to a week and can be frozen in an airtight container for up to 3 months. If it separates when you defrost it, simply puree it again before using

Rice Flour

Rice flour is finely milled rice. It can be made from any kind of rice. Brown rice flour is the whole-grain version, containing both the bran and the germ. You can easily make your own rice flour at home. Take some of your favorite white or brown rice, short-, medium-, or long-grain, and grind it into a fine, light powder using a clean coffee or spice grinder, food processor, or high-speed blender.

Rice flour is a staple in Asian cuisines, used to make noodles and sweets. It is also often used in classic shortbread recipes because it adds a pleasingly sandy texture. In gluten-free baking, it add structure to baked goods.

Glutinous rice flour, sometimes labeled sweet rice flour, is milled from glutinous rice; also called sticky rice. It is probably best known for its use in Japanese mochi, glutinous rice cakes. It is very sticky and dense when hydrated and should be added carefully in baking recipes. It contributes moisture and a chewy texture, but in large amounts, it can make cakes and breads dense and compacted.

Nonfat Milk Powder

In its purest form, this is simply powdered dehydrated skim milk. We use it to add protein to our gluten-free flour blends. Sometimes it can be a little clumpy, but if you put it in a blender or food processor, you can fix that in a few seconds flat. We also like to toast it and use the powder in baked goods. Way back in the day, we discovered that if we added nonfat milk powder to brown butter, it would amplify the nutty caramel flavor of the cooked milk solids. Then we figured out that we didn't actually need the butter to get the flavor. Now toasted milk powder is a pantry staple and we use it to add that flavor to many of our favorite things.

toasted milk powder

makes 1½ cups | 100 grams milk powder

*We use this powder to add rich caramelized notes to breads, cookies, and pud-
dings or to bump up the flavor of brown butter. It has a slightly sweet flavor,
with a hint of nuts and caramel, without any actual sugar or fat. We like the
way it gives a bit of depth and complexity to shortbreads and biscuits, pasta
dough, and cake batters. The toasted milk solids don't drown out the other
ingredients, they just make things taste better. Add a couple of tablespoons to
your favorite recipes and see what happens.*

1½ cups / 100 grams nonfat milk powder

Put the milk solids in a microwave-safe bowl and cook them for 30 seconds, then remove
the bowl and stir. Repeat this procedure for a total of 10 minutes, or until the milk solids are
a deep toasted brown. Let cool to room temperature.

Toasted milk powder can be stored in an airtight container at room temperature for up to 6
months.

NOTE: *Alternatively, put the milk solids in a Mason jar. Screw on the lid tightly—you don't want
moisture entering the jar. Set the jar on a rack in a pressure cooker filled with 2 inches of water.
Cook for 1½ hours at high pressure. Let the pressure release naturally before removing the lid and
let the jar cool completely before opening it.*

*Microwaved milk powder—
brown butter solids that help
amplify nutty caramel flavors.*

Oat Flour

Oat flour is a wonderful ingredient. In many ways, it acts like standard wheat flour, adding starch, structure, and moisture to baked goods. It's ground from whole oats, and you can make it yourself by grinding rolled oats in a food processor or blender. Just weigh the oats before you grind so you have exactly the right amount. One caveat: Oats and oat flour are not always guaranteed gluten-free; it's important to read the label.

Oat flour has a fine, light texture and many people simply substitute oat flour for wheat flour with good results. We prefer to blend it with other flours, because it can give baked goods a dense, sticky texture. We use that characteristic to our advantage in some cookies and brownies, like the Peanut Butter Blondies (page 233), but it would be less pleasing in something like a sponge cake.

Potato Flour

Potato flour, ground from dried potatoes, contains everything that the potato has to offer. It is wonderful in baked goods because it holds on to moisture and gives the dough a slightly sticky texture. We use it in all of our gluten-free flour blends. Adding a small amount of potato flour helps keep dough, especially cookie dough, from spreading too much in the oven. One caveat is that it does taste like potatoes, and for that reason, it should be used sparingly unless you want to add that flavor to your cookies and cakes. Potato flour, oat flour, and sweet sorghum flour behave in a similar manner and can be substituted for one another in most recipes.

Potato Starch

Potato starch is the isolated starch extracted from potatoes. Many recipes for latkes call for grating the potatoes and then soaking them in cold water. When you remove them from the liquid, there is usually a small pile of starch in the bottom of the bowl. That is pure potato starch. It is usually used as a thickener, often for sauces and soups, activating at between 136° and 150°F. (58° and 65°C.). It is best added toward the end of the cooking time, because it gels quickly. Potato starch should be dissolved in cold water before it is added to hot liquids.

Potato starch adds structure and moisture to gluten-free baked goods. It is a binder that helps hold everything together. In addition to latkes it can be used for vegetable pancakes and fritters. Potato starch has a fine, soft texture, and it is often used in Asian cooking to dredge ingredients before frying them. It helps batters stick to proteins and vegetables. It can also be used by itself to coat meats, fish, or vegetables for frying. It forms a light, crispy crust that is completely addictive.

japanese fried chicken

makes 6 chicken thighs

One of our favorite uses for potato starch is to coat fried foods. If you've never cooked with potato starch, this recipe will convince you that you must keep it in your pantry at all times. This fried chicken is light, crispy, and full of flavor. Because we couldn't help ourselves, we butterfly the chicken thighs before marinating them. That lets the marinade penetrate more quickly and also promotes even cooking. And it increases the surface area, so you have even more crispy fried goodness to enjoy. The marinade is a blend of Japanese flavors with a bit of American buttermilk to make sure the finished chicken is juicy, tender, and delicious. Once you've tried this, you will never make fried chicken any other way.

marinade

½ cup / 120 grams buttermilk

A 2-inch piece of fresh ginger, peeled and thinly sliced

2 garlic cloves, thinly sliced

3 scallions, white and green parts, thinly sliced

2 tablespoons / 33 grams soy sauce

1 tablespoon / 14 grams Asian sesame oil

1 tablespoon / 13 grams light brown sugar

¼ teaspoon / 1.5 grams fine sea salt

6 medium chicken thighs (about 2¼ pounds / 1 kilo)

3 cups / 552 grams potato starch

Rice bran oil or peanut oil for deep-frying

To make the marinade, put the buttermilk, ginger, garlic, scallions, soy sauce, sesame oil, brown sugar, and salt in a medium bowl and whisk until smooth.

Lay one chicken thigh skin side down on a cutting board, with the bone running vertically, and use a sharp paring knife to cut down the center to the bone, from top to bottom. Gently slide the knife horizontally to the left to butterfly the meat, being careful not to cut all the way through it. Carefully open the flap and lightly score the meat in a crosshatch pattern, being careful not to cut all the way through the meat. Repeat on the right side of the thigh. Add the thigh to the bowl with the marinade, and repeat with the remaining 5 thighs.

Mix the thighs and marinade together, coating each piece thoroughly. Transfer the meat and marinade to a large zip-top bag, press out as much air as possible, and seal the bag. Put the bag in a shallow bowl in the refrigerator and marinate for 12 to 24 hours, turning the bag occasionally to distribute the marinade evenly.

Preheat the oven to 200°F. (95°C.).

Line a baking sheet with parchment paper. Set a wire rack on another baking sheet. Put the potato starch in a large bowl.

Remove one chicken thigh from the marinade, brushing off any pieces of garlic, ginger, or scallion, and add to the potato starch. The marinade clinging to the chicken will help the flour adhere to the meat. Roll the thigh in the potato starch, coating it thoroughly, then put it on the parchment-lined baking sheet. Repeat with the remaining thighs. Then, beginning with the first thigh, dredge each one a second time in the potato starch and return to the parchment-lined pan.

Set a large cast-iron skillet on the stovetop and add 1½ inches of oil. Heat over medium-high heat until the oil reaches 375°F. (190°C.). Once the oil has come to temperature, add 2 or 3 chicken thighs to the skillet, depending on its size (be careful not to crowd the pan), and fry for about 8 minutes, until the bottom side is golden brown. Flip the thighs and cook for another 8 minutes, or until they are a deep golden brown on the other side. Transfer to the rack set over the baking sheet and slide into the oven to keep warm. Fry the remaining chicken thighs, transferring them to the oven as they are done. If not serving immediately, turn off the oven and prop the oven door open a crack so that the thighs remain warm and crisp.

Put the fried chicken on a platter and serve family style, with your favorite accompaniments.

NOTE: *Rice bran oil is one of our favorite oils for frying. Produced from the bran of the rice kernel, it is 20 percent saturated fat and 80 percent unsaturated fat. It has a light nutty flavor and is unlikely to cause allergic reactions. It has long been used in Asia both as cooking oil and for cosmetic purposes. Studies in Japan and the United States have shown that consuming rice bran oil can lower the risk of heart disease. The oil has a high level of nutrients and antioxidants, which gives*

recipe continues

it a unique stability and long shelf life. And its smoke point of 490°F. (255°C.) makes it well suited to frying. Foods fried in rice bran oil tend to absorb up to 20 percent less fat than food cooked in other vegetable oils.

If you can't find rice bran oil, peanut oil is our second choice. It also has a light nutty flavor and doesn't absorb odors from the foods that are fried in it. It also has a relatively high smoke point (450°F./232°C). Lacking either of these, we use blended olive oil. Canola oil is a last resort for frying, because it takes on an unpleasant fishy smell at high temperatures that clings to the fried food.

Butterfly the chicken thighs and score the meat to absorb the marinade and ensure even frying.

Marinated chicken thighs in their first coating of potato starch.

Chicken thighs in a second coating of potato starch, ready for the fryer.

Super-crispy Japanese Fried Chicken thighs cooling on a wire rack.

Sweet Sorghum Flour

Sorghum is a cereal grain that originated in Africa. It is cultivated to produce sorghum syrup, a sweetener, and can also be used to brew beer and other alcohol. Sweet sorghum flour has experienced a rise in popularity as more people have adopted gluten-free diets. It is slightly sweet, with a relatively neutral flavor, and is a good source of protein, iron, and fiber. It is used in bread recipes and for heartier baked goods like pastries and pies.

gluten-free sourdough starter

53 ounces | 1500 grams sourdough starter

We first made a gluten-free sourdough starter with just sorghum flour and water. We combined equal parts (by weight) of the flour and water in a bowl, stirred them, and covered the mix. The following day, we saw bubbles appearing. We discarded half of the starter and added fresh sorghum and water to the mix. This is a common practice when building a sourdough starter, because otherwise you end up with more starter than you know what to do with. If you can't bear to throw away the extra, you can simply fold it into pancake or waffle batter; it will not be sour yet, but it will add the great flavor of the sorghum itself.

By day four, we had an active and healthy starter ready to work with. But sorghum starter on its own did not behave quite like a traditional sourdough starter. Although it had the tang and the yeast activity, it lacked the viscous elasticity of a traditional starter.

We knew we could get extreme elasticity from ground flaxseeds, so we began integrating them into the starter. We figured an equal blend of sorghum to flaxseed meal by weight would give us the correct elasticity, so we tested that. However, we did not count on the water-capturing ability of the flaxseed meal: we quickly discovered that we needed to add twice as much water to create fluid, elastic starter. Once we had our ratio down, we began growing our starter in earnest.

It takes about 4 days to get the starter up and running. At certain times of the year, we crave the tang of Country Sourdough (page 89) or Sourdough Pancakes (page 45), and we've even been known to add a little (½ cup or so) to the yeasted Chocolate Bundt Cake (page 199). But we find that we use it a lot for a while and then discard it. After a few months go by, we get another craving and we simply start a new one.

17.6 ounces / 500 grams sorghum flour

17.6 ounces / 500 grams flaxseed meal

3.5 ounces / 100 grams water, plus additional water for feeding

Put the sorghum flour and flaxseed meal in a bowl and use a whisk to combine. Put 1.76 ounces/50 grams of the starter flour into a bowl, and put the rest of the blend in a zip-top bag and store it in the pantry for future use. Add 3.5 ounces/100 grams of water to the bowl of flour and use a spoon to stir the mixture together into a paste. Cover the bowl with plastic wrap and leave it in a warm space for 24 hours.

The following day, discard half the starter and add 1.76 ounces/50 grams more flour and 3.5 ounces/100 grams water to the remaining starter. Stir the mixture together and cover it again. Continue feeding the starter, discarding half of each before each feeding, for a total of 5 days.

On the fifth day, the starter should have developed a nice sour flavor and show signs of rising yeast bubbles in the mixture. It is now ready to use. Once the starter is alive and well, you can feed it larger amounts of flour and water, keeping them at the ratio of 1 part flour to 2 parts water by weight. Alternatively, as your starter grows, if you are not using it on a regular basis, you can discard some of it prior to its daily feeding. As long as you have 17.6 ounces/500 grams or so, there will be enough food for the yeasts and *Lactobacillus brevis* bacteria to keep reproducing for you.

Sorghum flour, flaxseed meal, and water mixed and ready to ferment into Sourdough Starter.

Using a scale to feed a happy Sourdough Starter.

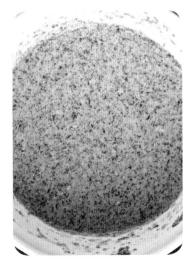

Tapioca Starch | Tapioca Flour

Tapioca starch or flour is derived from the root of the cassava plant. It is colorless when dissolved and has no flavor or odor. Tapioca starch is used as a thickener and tends to create gels with a softer texture than cornstarch. It works more quickly than cornstarch, at temperatures ranging from 126° to 150°F. (52° to 65°C.), and it imparts a glossy sheen as it thickens. Tapioca is a popular thickener for pie fillings and dessert sauces. It remains stable through the freeze-thaw cycle.

sweet-and-spicy ginger cream ice cream

makes about 2 quarts

It's easy to buy high-quality candied ginger, but making it at home is a great way to use up ginger left over from a recipe. Buy ginger that is shiny, with a smooth, thin skin, and feels heavy in your hand. Peel the ginger and thinly slice it with a mandoline or a sharp knife. Cook it in a sugar syrup made with equal parts (by weight) of sugar and water, using enough to cover the ginger slices completely. Bring it to a boil and cook the syrup to 225°F. (107°C.). Let the ginger cool in the syrup and steep overnight. The next day, drain, reserving the syrup, and toss the sliced ginger in sugar. Store in an airtight container at room temperature for as long as it lasts. The ginger syrup can be used to sweeten cocktails, lemonade, iced tea, or sparkling water.

To make the ice cream, we steep the candied ginger in the ice cream base and then puree the mixture to extract the most flavor. The base is made without eggs. Instead, we use tapioca flour as the texturizer. The tapioca gives the ice cream the body you need to make it feel luxurious on the tongue and a little bit of chewiness to make it fun to eat.

5 cups + 6½ tablespoons / 1300 grams half-and-half

1¾ cups + 1 tablespoon / 75 grams nonfat milk powder

1 cup / 200 grams sugar

3 tablespoons / 18 grams tapioca starch

½ teaspoon / 3 grams fine sea salt

3½ ounces / 100 grams candied ginger

Put the half-and-half, nonfat milk powder, sugar, tapioca starch, and salt into a medium pot and whisk them together until smooth. Set over medium heat and cook, stirring with a silicone spatula, until the ice cream base reaches 167°F. (75°C.) to activate the tapioca starch. Add the candied ginger and remove from the heat. Let the ice cream base steep for 30 minutes.

recipe continues

Pour half of the ice cream base into a blender and turn the blender on low. Gradually increase the speed to high and puree until the mixture appears smooth, about 30 seconds. Strain the ice cream base through a fine-mesh sieve into a bowl and repeat with the remaining mixture.

Refrigerate the ice cream base overnight and then freeze in an ice cream maker according to the manufacturer's directions.

Xanthan Gum

Xanthan gum is a thickener created through a fermentation of glucose or sucrose by the *Xanthomonas campestris* bacterium. The xanthan gum manufactured in the United States is often fermented with corn sugars and so should be avoided by anyone with a corn sensitivity. Xanthan gum is one of the easiest thickeners to use because it is soluble in both warm and cold liquids and works almost instantly. It is clear, odorless, and tasteless. It is thixotropic, meaning it has the ability to thin out when agitated and thicken as it stands. It also has a sticky quality that can be attractive in sauces and dressings, allowing them to cling to the foods they are coating. It often used in commercial ice creams because it helps prevent the formation of ice crystals through the freeze-thaw cycle.

Our Gluten-Free Flour Blends

We created three different gluten-free flour blends to address different dietary needs. All three contain a blend of gluten-free flours, starches, and proteins. They all weigh 4½ ounces/130 grams per cup, and can be used interchangeably in the recipes in this book, although the results may differ slightly in texture. So once you decide which one you like the most, you can use it exclusively—or you can play around with blending them.

We are giving you the recipes by weight in grams. All you have to do is whisk everything together and then store the blend in an airtight container in your pantry. You don't need to refrigerate these; treat them as you would regular flour, and all will be well. Occasionally nonfat milk powder can be clumpy—if that happens, pulse it in a food processor before blending it with the other ingredients.

It can be hard to break the habits of a lifetime. Wheat flours are characterized by their protein content because the amount of gluten dictates the structure of the finished bread or cake. Our gluten-free blends have some protein to develop structure but also rely on starches and gums to hold everything together. These combinations dictate the textures of the batters and doughs made with our blends. That said, the differences are only apparent when you taste-test recipes made with different blends side by side. So pick one "all-purpose blend" that you like best and stick with it. Once the choice is made, you can settle in and start cooking.

A canister of What IiF Flour 3.0, ready to be put to use.

what IiF flour 3.0

makes 15½ cups | 2020 grams flour blend

What if you had a gluten-free flour that worked in any recipe as a gram-for-gram substitute for all-purpose flour? That was the question was asked ourselves when we developed this blend. "IiF" stand for Ideas in Food, our blog, where we published the very first version of this recipe. Alex came up with it for fun after reading the ingredient list on Cup4Cup flour (developed by Lena Kwak and chef Thomas Keller), and it worked beautifully. It's gone through a few changes since the original, hence the 3.0, but it remains the easiest gluten-free blend to work with. It mimics all-purpose flour in recipes and for that reason, using a gram-for-gram substitution in any traditional recipe will give you comparable results.

700 grams cornstarch

500 grams tapioca starch

300 grams white rice flour

200 grams brown rice flour

200 grams nonfat milk power

100 grams potato flour

20 grams xanthan gum

Whisk together all the ingredients in a bowl. Store in airtight container at room temperature for up to 6 months.

batch-3 flour

makes 16⅓ cups | 2120 grams flour blend

Our Batch-3 blend gives results that are akin to using whole wheat flour. Breads and cakes made with it tend to have a slightly coarser texture and a more open crumb than those made with the other two blends. We eliminated corn products in this flour, swapping arrowroot for cornstarch to take advantage of its thickening power, added some sorghum flour for its sweet nutty flavor, and we used guar gum instead of xanthan gum to add viscosity and elasticity. This flour has a slightly richer flavor than the What IiF flour and results in a lighter texture than Aki's Blend.

350 grams arrowroot

350 grams sorghum flour

450 grams tapioca starch

450 grams white rice flour (or substitute millet flour)

200 grams brown rice flour (or substitute sorghum flour)

100 grams potato flour

200 grams milk powder

20 grams guar gum

Whisk together all the ingredients in a bowl. Store in airtight container at room temperature for up to 6 months.

aki's low-allergy blend

makes 15⅓ cups | 2000 grams flour blend

Alex named this Aki's Blend because she challenged him to come up with a flour blend without xanthan gum, guar gum, dairy, or soy. It's our low-allergen blend for people with multiple food sensitivities. It doesn't exclude all allergens, but it is as close as we could get to a gluten-free flour blend that just about anyone can use. The texture of baked goods made with it tends to be firmer and slightly chewier than what you get from What IiF Flour and Batch 3.

500 grams tapioca starch

500 grams glutinous rice flour (sweet rice flour)

400 grams arrowroot

300 grams sorghum flour

100 grams potato flour

200 grams golden flaxseed meal

Whisk together all the ingredients in a bowl. Store in airtight container at room temperature for up to 6 months.

Combining gluten-free flours to make Aki's Low-Allergy Blend flour.

breakfast

Blueberry Streusel Muffins cooling on a rack: crisp topping with a hint of the moist cake and berries underneath.

blueberry streusel muffins

makes 12 muffins

These are regular-sized muffins, not the supersized ones you find in many bakeries and bodegas. We like them for their sweet, delicate crumb and healthy dose of fruit. The oatmeal crumb topping gives them more texture and makes them feel indulgent while adding a hint of nuttiness from the oats. You'll see a fair amount of streusel throughout this book, because it adds both texture and flavor to baked goods. We love that little bit of sweetness and hint of crunch contrasting with a tender interior.

streusel

¾ cup / 98 grams Gluten-Free Flour Blend (What IiF Flour 3.0, page 29, Batch-3 Flour, page 30, or Aki's Low-Allergy Blend, page 31)

¾ cup / 75 grams rolled oats

½ cup / 100 grams sugar

½ teaspoon / 3 grams fine sea salt

8 tablespoons / 4 ounces / 113 grams unsalted butter, at room temperature

muffins

1 cup / 130 grams Gluten-Free Flour Blend

¾ cup / 150 grams sugar

½ cup / 65 grams oat flour

2 teaspoons / 12 grams baking powder

½ teaspoon / 3 grams fine sea salt

¼ teaspoon / 0.5 gram ground cinnamon

5 tablespoons / 2⅔ ounces / 75 grams unsalted butter, melted

⅓ cup / 80 grams buttermilk

1 large egg

2 teaspoons / 4 grams pure vanilla extract

1 cup / 137 grams blueberries

recipe continues

Preheat the oven to 400°F. (200°C.). Line a 12-cup muffin tin with cupcake papers.

To make the streusel, put the flour, oats, sugar, and salt in a small bowl and whisk to blend. Add the butter and rub it into the flour mixture with your fingers, or stir with a fork, until the mixture forms coarse crumbs. Cover and refrigerate until needed (up to 5 days).

To make the muffins, put the flour, sugar, oat flour, baking powder, salt, and cinnamon in a medium bowl and whisk to blend.

Put the melted butter, buttermilk, egg, and vanilla in a large measuring cup and mix with a fork to blend. Pour into the flour mixture and mix with a rubber spatula until combined. Fold in the blueberries.

Use a measuring cup or ice cream scoop to portion approximately ⅓ cup batter into each muffin cup. Divide the streusel evenly among the muffins, pressing it gently into the top of the batter.

Bake for 25 minutes, or until the muffins are golden brown and spring back when gently pressed with a finger and a cake tester inserted in the center comes out clean. Let cool for 10 minutes before serving.

Fold fresh berries into blue-berry muffin batter.

Blueberry muffin batter (without streusel) in cupcake papers, ready to be baked.

Freshly baked blueberry muffins.

Warm blueberry muffins (without streusel) bursting with juicy fruit.

strawberry coffee cake

makes one 9-inch cake

This is an easy breakfast cake, perfect for a lazy morning. You can substitute your favorite fruit for the strawberries: bite-sized pieces of bananas, peaches, nectarines, or blueberries all work well here, becoming tender and juicy as they bake. The batter is spread in the pan and then the fruit is scattered over it and topped with the streusel. As the cake bakes, the fruit softens into a rich jammy layer between moist cake and crumbly topping. You can bake it the night before and have it ready to slice in the morning. Serve it by itself or with lightly sweetened yogurt on the side.

streusel

½ cup + 1 tablespoon / 75 grams Gluten-Free Flour Blend (What IiF Flour 3.0, page 29, Batch-3 Flour, page 30, or Aki's Low-Allergy Blend, page 31)

½ cup (packed) / 107 grams light brown sugar

⅛ teaspoon / 0.75 gram fine sea salt

⅛ teaspoon / 0.375 gram grated nutmeg

4 tablespoons / 2 ounces / 56 grams unsalted butter, at room temperature

coffee cake

1 cup + 2 tablespoons / 150 grams Gluten-Free Flour Blend

1 teaspoon / 6 grams baking powder

½ teaspoon / 3 grams fine sea salt

½ teaspoon / 1 gram ground cinnamon

8 tablespoons / 4 ounces / 113 grams unsalted butter, sliced

1 cup / 200 grams sugar

2 large eggs, at room temperature

1 teaspoon / 4 grams vanilla paste or pure vanilla extract

1 pint ripe strawberries, cut lengthwise in half

Preheat the oven to 350°F. (175°C.). Butter a 9-inch springform pan and put it on a baking sheet.

To make the streusel, combine the flour, brown sugar, salt, and nutmeg in a small bowl and whisk to blend thoroughly. Add the butter and use your fingers or a fork to blend the mixture into soft crumbs. Set aside.

To make the coffee cake, combine the flour, baking powder, salt, and cinnamon in a medium bowl and whisk to blend.

Put the butter in a medium saucepan and set it over medium heat. When half the butter has melted, remove from the heat and swirl the pan until all of the butter has melted. Add the sugar, eggs, and vanilla to the pan and stir with a silicone spatula until smooth.

Pour the butter mixture into the flour mixture and stir just until blended. Pour the mixture into the prepared cake pan and tilt the pan to spread the batter evenly. Scatter the strawberries evenly over the batter. Sprinkle the streusel topping evenly over the fruit.

Bake for 55 to 65 minutes, until a cake tester inserted in the center comes out clean (some jammy strawberries may stick to it) and the streusel is golden brown. Let cool for 15 minutes on a rack before removing the sides of the pan, then cool for 10 more minutes and serve warm, or let cool to room temperature.

yeasted pumpkin waffles

makes 12 or so waffles, depending on your waffle iron

Mix the batter for these waffles the night before you plan to make them. The long, slow rest allow the flours to fully hydrate and gives the yeast a chance to activate and multiply. When you wake up in the morning, you will find that the batter has risen and is full of small bubbles. It will be fragrant from the yeast and the spices, and you might even be tempted to stick a spoon in it and give it a taste before you even heat up your waffle iron.

We have been lucky enough to source high-quality ground spices and go through them relatively quickly. Be sure to give yours a sniff before adding them to the batter. If you don't use cardamom on a regular basis, you would be better off grinding whole seeds for the most flavorful result.

We love these fluffy, hearty waffles with butter and maple syrup in the morning, and we love them just as much as the base of a sundae in the evenings. Drenched in Bourbon Caramel Sauce (page 244), with vanilla ice cream and roasted pecans, pumpkin waffles are one of the most decadent desserts we know. If you don't happen to have any pumpkin puree, you could substitute a roasted squash puree, unsweetened applesauce, or sweet potato puree.

3 large eggs

½ cup / 125 grams whole milk

15 ounces / 425 grams canned pumpkin puree

16 tablespoons (2 sticks) / 8 ounces / 225 grams unsalted butter, melted

2⅔ cups / 350 grams Gluten-Free Flour Blend (What IiF Flour 3.0, page 29,
    Batch-3 Flour, page 30, or Aki's Low-Allergy Blend, page 31)

½ cup / 100 grams granulated sugar

¾ teaspoon / 4.5 grams fine sea salt

¾ teaspoon / 1.5 grams grated nutmeg

½ teaspoon / 1 gram ground cinnamon

½ teaspoon / 1 gram ground cardamom

¼ teaspoon / 0.75 grams active dry yeast

2¼ cups / 500 grams raw sugar

Put the eggs, milk, pumpkin puree, and melted butter into a large bowl and whisk to blend.

Whisk together the flour, granulated sugar, salt, nutmeg, cinnamon, cardamom, and yeast in another large bowl. Add the pumpkin mixture and use a rubber spatula to combine. Put the mixture into a 6-quart (6-liter) container, with plenty of room for it to double, cover, and let rise at room temperature for 12 hours.

Stir the batter down and use immediately, or refrigerate for up to 2 days. The batter will continue to slowly ferment in the refrigerator; if it seems to be rising too much, just give it a gentle stir. The flavor will continue to develop, becoming tangier with a pronounced yeasty flavor. If it's been refrigerated, let the batter come to room temperature for at least 2 hours before using.

Heat a waffle iron. Add enough batter for one waffle to the iron, sprinkle generously with raw sugar, and cook according to the manufacturer's directions. Serve warm, and continue making waffles. If you end up with more waffles than you need you can freeze the extras and warm them up in a toaster or cut them up to use in your favorite bread pudding recipe.

Peach Breakfast Cake straight from the oven. Everything has come together into a sweet, tender cake studded with juicy roasted peaches.

peach breakfast cake

We like to serve slices of this breakfast cake with lightly sweetened yogurt and granola. The tender, delicious cake is best eaten with a spoon. Served warm with a dollop of sweetened sour cream and a drizzle of honey, it could also be served for dessert. The directions may seem a little odd: a layer of melted butter followed by a layer of batter and then a layer of fruit. Keep the faith—everything comes together in the heat of the oven. This cake works beautifully with any fresh or frozen fruit. In the wintertime, we make it with frozen peaches, transferring them to refrigerator the night before so they can slowly defrost. As the ice crystals melt out of the fruit, they leave microscopic holes behind that tenderize the peaches, helping them release even more juicy flavor into the cake.

In a pinch, you can substitute buttermilk, heavy cream, or even plain yogurt for the milk.

8 tablespoons / 4 ounces / 113 grams unsalted butter, sliced

1 cup / 260 grams whole milk, at room temperature

1 large egg, at room temperature

1 teaspoon / 4 grams pure vanilla extract

1 cup / 200 grams sugar

1 cup + 2 tablespoons / 150 grams Gluten-Free Flour Blend (What Iif Flour 3.0, page 29, Batch-3 Flour, page 30, or Aki's Low-Allergy Blend, page 31)

1 teaspoon / 6 grams baking powder

½ teaspoon / 3 grams fine sea salt

4 cups sliced fresh fruit or berries or defrosted sliced fruit or berries (about 1 pound/455 grams)

recipe continues

Preheat the oven to 375°F. (190°C.).

Put the butter in a 9-by-13-inch baking dish and put it in the oven for 5 minutes, or just until the butter melts. Remove from oven and leave it on the stovetop while you prepare the batter.

Put the milk, egg, and vanilla in a large measuring cup and mix thoroughly. Put the sugar, flour, baking powder, and salt in a medium bowl and whisk to blend. Pour the milk mixture into the flour and mix with a rubber spatula to blend.

Pour the batter into the baking dish over the butter. You will have two distinct layers of melted butter and batter: do not mix them together. Lay the fruit over the top of the batter.

Bake for 45 to 50 minutes, until the top is a deep golden brown. Let cool for 10 minutes and serve warm, or let cool to room temperature.

Peach Breakfast Cake begins with a messy pan of melted butter.

Pour the batter into the melted butter. The butter will rise to the top, and the layers will remain separate and look wrong.

Arrange peaches over the top of the separated batter.

sourdough pancakes

makes 16 medium pancakes

Pancakes are one of our favorite breakfasts. It's easy to whip up a batch first thing in the morning, and you can have a skillet of bacon or ham cooking as you make them on your griddle. This recipe makes pancakes that are light and fluffy, easily absorbing a healthy slather of butter and a drizzle of warm maple syrup. The sourdough imparts a tangy flavor that contrasts nicely with the sweetness of syrup. The baking soda reacts with the buttermilk, slightly neutralizing the acidity of both it and the starter while providing a little extra lift for the cakes.

2 cups / 260 grams Gluten-Free Flour Blend (What IiF Flour 3.0, page 29, Batch-3 Flour, page 30, or Aki's Low-Allergy Blend, page 31)

1 teaspoon / 6 grams baking powder

¾ teaspoon / 4.5 grams fine sea salt

½ teaspoon / 2.5 gram baking soda

2 cups / 480 grams buttermilk

½ cup / 90 grams Gluten-Free Sourdough Starter (page 22)

2 large eggs, lightly beaten

2 tablespoons / 30 grams sugar

2 tablespoons / 1 ounce / 28 grams unsalted butter, melted

Butter and maple syrup for serving

Put the flour, baking powder, salt, and baking soda in a medium bowl and whisk to blend. Add the buttermilk, sourdough starter, eggs, and sugar and stir everything together with a rubber spatula until almost fully mixed. Add the melted butter and stir until the batter is smooth and homogenous; don't fret about overmixing, because there's no gluten to worry about.

Heat a nonstick electric griddle to 350°F. (175°C.) or set a cast-iron griddle or heavy skillet over medium heat. Once hot, use a 2-ounce ladle to spoon the pancakes onto the griddle. Let them cook until the bottoms are set and bubbles appear on the surface. Flip the pancakes and cook until deep golden brown on both sides. Serve immediately, with butter and maple syrup, or keep warm in a low oven while you make the remaining pancakes.

sunbutter and jelly crumble cake

makes one 9-inch cake

SunButter is a great alternative to peanut butter. It's a lightly sweetened spread made with sunflower seeds, available in most supermarkets and health food stores. It is delicious—with a light, earthy flavor, and a soft nuttiness on the finish. If you don't love sunflower seeds, use peanut or almond butter instead.

Most breakfast cakes take so long to mix and bake that the cook has to be up early to get one on the table in time. On lazy days, our solution is to use a scone dough. It mixes up in a few minutes in a food processor, takes well to additions and extra flavors, and bakes relatively quickly. We roll the dough out into two rounds, spread SunButter between them and jelly over the top layer, and add a final layer of streusel on top of that. The cake bakes in less than half an hour and makes any breakfast table look festive and inviting.

streusel

½ cup / 65 grams Gluten-Free Flour Blend (What IiF Flour 3.0, page 29,
   Batch-3 Flour, page 30, or Aki's Low-Allergy Blend, page 31)

¼ cup (packed) / 53 grams light brown sugar

4 tablespoons / 2 ounces / 56 grams unsalted butter, diced, at room temperature

scone cake

3½ cups / 450 grams Gluten-Free Flour Blend

½ cup / 100 grams sugar

2 teaspoons / 12 grams baking powder

½ teaspoon / 3 grams fine sea salt

½ teaspoon / 2.5 grams baking soda

8 tablespoons / 4 ounces / 113 grams cold unsalted butter, diced

1 cup / 240 grams buttermilk

½ cup / 140 grams SunButter (or peanut butter or almond butter)

½ cup / 170 grams strawberry jelly

Preheat the oven to 400°F. (200°C.). Line a baking sheet with parchment paper.

To make the streusel, put the flour and brown sugar in a small bowl. Mix well with a fork, then add the butter and mix with the fork or your fingertips until the mixture comes together in small crumbs. Cover and refrigerate.

To make the cake, put the flour, sugar, baking powder, salt, and baking soda in a food processor and pulse a few times to blend. Add the butter and pulse to blend; the mixture should look like crumbs. Add the buttermilk and pulse until the dough begins to clump together.

Turn the dough out onto a lightly floured surface and knead it a couple of times just until it is smooth. Divide the dough in half and use your hands to shape each half into an 8-inch round.

Put one round on the prepared baking sheet. Spread the SunButter evenly over the top, leaving a ¼-inch border all around. Top with the other round of dough and gently press them together, making sure the sides are even and clean—use a butter knife or spatula to scrape off any oozing SunButter so it doesn't burn in the oven. Spread the strawberry jelly evenly over the top, from edge to edge. Sprinkle the streusel evenly over the jelly.

Bake for 20 minutes, or until a cake tester inserted in the center comes out clean and the sides are golden brown. Let the cake cool on the baking sheet for 10 minutes before serving.

breakfast bars

makes 16 bars

These portable pastries are reminiscent of Toaster Strudels, but so much better. They are just right for breakfast on the run. The dough is made with a combination of butter and sour cream, giving it a balanced flavor that complements the fruit filling. We created this in the wintertime, when fresh fruit was scarce, so we looked to the pantry and our collection of dried fruit. You don't need as much dried fruit as you would fresh, because the dehydration process concentrates the flavor. The pastry is rich and flaky, the sugar on top of the dough adds crunch and a little extra sweetness, and the dried berries gives the bars a bright, fruity flavor.

2½ cups / 325 grams Gluten-Free Flour Blend (What IiF Flour 3.0, page 29, Batch-3 Flour, page 30, or Aki's Low-Allergy Blend, page 31)

½ teaspoon / 3 grams fine sea salt

16 tablespoons (2 sticks) / 8 ounces / 225 grams unsalted butter, diced, at room temperature

1 cup / 240 grams sour cream, at room temperature

½ cup / 100 grams raw sugar, plus more for the tops

1 cup / 145 grams dried blueberries, cherries, or cranberries

Put the flour and salt in the bowl of a stand mixer fitted with the paddle attachment (or use a hand mixer) and mix on low to blend. Add the butter and sour cream and mix on low just until a smooth dough forms. Turn the dough out, wrap in plastic wrap, and chill for at least 4 hours.

Unwrap the chilled dough and divide it into 4 equal pieces. Lay two 18-inch-long sheets of plastic wrap overlapping them on the counter, so they form a 13-by-18-inch rectangle. Put a piece of dough in the center of the plastic wrap and cover with two more sheets of plastic wrap. Roll the dough into a 9-by-12-inch rectangle. Remove the top layer of plastic wrap. Dust the top surface of the dough with 2 tablespoons of the raw sugar. Sprinkle ¼ cup of the dried blueberries over the dough. Starting from a long side, use the plastic wrap to roll the dough over itself 3 times so you have a cylinder approximately 12 inches long and 2½ inches wide. Gently roll the dough into a bar approximately ½ inch thick, and wrap in the plastic wrap. Repeat with the remaining dough, sugar, and berries to make 3 more bars. Refrigerate for at least 1 hour.

Preheat the oven to 350°F. (175°C.). Line two large baking sheets with parchment paper.

Remove the bars from the refrigerator and cut each one into 4 equal pieces. Sprinkle raw sugar over the top of each one. Arrange them on the prepared pans, leaving at least 2 inches of space between them. Bake the bars for 20 minutes, or until they are browning on the edges and the tops have begun to split. Let cool for at least 15 minutes and enjoy warm, or cool to room temperature and store in a covered container for up to 3 days.

quick breads

Easiest Buttermilk Drop Biscuits and honey.

easiest buttermilk drop biscuits

makes 6 biscuits

These are quite possibly the easiest biscuits to make in the world. You don't even have to roll them out—just scoop the dough out of the food processor onto a sheet pan and bake. The little bits of butter in the batter melt as the biscuits bake, providing a little steam leavening as the water evaporates, and leaving behind small butter-soaked holes that give the biscuits a moist, tender texture. Their rustic appearance tells everyone that you made them yourself with the best ingredients and a little bit of love. Add some sausage gravy or a few slices of country ham, and you have the perfect breakfast for a cold winter morning.

2⅓ cups / 300 grams Gluten-Free Flour Blend (What IiF Flour 3.0, page 29, Batch-3 Flour, page 30, or Aki's Low-Allergy Blend, page 31)

2 teaspoons / 12 grams baking powder

1 teaspoon / 4 grams sugar

½ teaspoon / 3 grams fine sea salt

8 tablespoons / 4 ounces / 113 grams cold unsalted butter, diced

1 cup / 240 grams buttermilk

Preheat the oven to 400°F. (200°C.).

Put the flour, baking powder, sugar, and salt in a food processor and pulse to blend. Add the butter and pulse 2 or 3 times; there should still be small chunks of butter in the mix. Add the buttermilk and pulse until the dough comes together; it will be a wet dough.

recipe continues

Remove the blade and portion out about ½ cup of dough per biscuit (you can use a 4-ounce ice cream scoop if you have one), dropping them onto the prepared pan and leaving 3 inches of space between them; these will spread as they bake. Bake for 18 to 20 minutes, until golden brown. Let cool for 5 minutes before serving.

Use a large ice-cream scoop to portion the biscuits

Just-baked Easiest Buttermilk Drop Biscuits.

honey-glazed break-apart biscuits

makes 9 biscuits

These were inspired by Shirley Corriher's famous Touch of Grace biscuits. We like the way she combines cream and buttermilk to get both richness and tang. The cream adds liquid fat to the dough and the buttermilk brings acidity to balance the richness. For this recipe, we work the butter completely into the flour to thoroughly coat the starch, resulting in very tender, uniformly textured biscuits. We especially love the way the honey and cinnamon combination brings out the nutty flavors of the crust, while at the same eliminating any residual bitterness from the baking powder. We serve these biscuits with Japanese Fried Chicken (page 18).

biscuits

2⅓ cups / 300 grams Gluten-Free Flour Blend (What IiF Flour 3.0, page 29, Batch-3 Flour, page 30, or Aki's Low-Allergy Blend, page 31)

¼ cup / 50 grams sugar

2 teaspoons / 12 grams baking powder

1½ teaspoons / 9 grams fine sea salt

4 tablespoons / 2 ounces / 56 grams cold unsalted butter, finely diced

¾ cup / 180 grams buttermilk

⅔ cup /160 grams heavy cream

glaze

2 tablespoons / 1 ounce / 28 grams unsalted butter

2 tablespoons / 33 grams honey

¼ teaspoon / 0.5 gram ground cinnamon

recipe continues

Preheat the oven to 425 degrees F. (220°C.). Spray a 9-inch round cake pan with nonstick cooking spray.

Put the flour, sugar, baking powder, and salt in a bowl and whisk to combine. Add the butter and use your fingers to work it into the flour until there are no lumps and the mixture looks sandy. Stir in the buttermilk and heavy cream. The dough will be very sticky.

Use a large spoon or ice cream scoop to dollop 9 biscuits into the prepared pan. Bake until lightly browned, about 25 minutes.

Meanwhile, make the glaze: Melt the butter and honey with the cinnamon in a small saucepan; remove from the heat.

Remove the biscuits from the oven and brush with the glaze. Return to the oven and bake for 3 more minutes. The biscuits will absorb the glaze and become a deep golden brown. Remove from the oven and let them rest for 5 minutes.

Run a butter knife or small spatula around the inside of the pan to loosen the biscuits and transfer to a bread basket lined with a napkin. Serve warm.

cheddar jalapeño corn biscuits

makes at least 1 dozen biscuits

Rich from the cheddar cheese, with a bit of kick from the jalapeño, these biscuits are practically a meal on their own. We like a little kick from the pepper, so we use the whole chile. Most of the heat is contained in the seeds and the membranes. An easy way to remove them is to cut the bottom off the jalapeño pepper so you can stand it up on your cutting board, holding the stem. Then use a small paring knife to slice the flesh of the pepper away from the membranes and seeds, cutting from top to bottom and rotating the pepper as you go. You will end up with long slices of pepper flesh and the seeds and membranes will remain attached to the stem; discard them.

Fleur de sel is a crunchy finishing salt with a light texture and clean flavor. It is produced by harvesting the thin layer of crystallized salt that rises to the tops of pools of seawater in coastal areas of France, mainly in Brittany. We sprinkle it on the biscuits to add a salty, crunchy accent that makes the overall experience of eating them a little bit more fun and flavorful.

2 cups / 260 grams Gluten-Free Flour Blend (What IiF Flour 3.0, page 29, Batch-3 Flour, page 30, or Aki's Low-Allergy Blend, page 31)

1 cup / 116 grams corn flour

2 teaspoons / 12 grams baking powder

½ teaspoon / 2.5 grams baking soda

½ teaspoon / 3 grams fine sea salt

1 jalapeño pepper, thinly sliced (remove the seeds and membranes if you don't want too much heat; see headnote)

8 tablespoons / 4 ounces / 113 grams cold unsalted butter

4 ounces / 113 grams sharp cheddar cheese, cut into small dice

1 cup / 240 grams buttermilk

Heavy cream for brushing the biscuits

Fleur de sel

recipe continues

Preheat the oven to 400°F. (200°C.). Line a baking sheet with parchment paper.

Put the flour, corn flour, baking powder, baking soda, salt, and jalapeño in a food processor and pulse to blend and chop the chile. Add the butter and cheese and pulse 2 or 3 times to blend. Add the buttermilk and process just until the dough comes together.

Turn the dough out onto a lightly floured countertop and knead it a few times. Using a rolling pin roll the dough out about an inch thick. Use a 1½- to 2-inch round biscuit cutter to cut out biscuits and arrange 2 inches apart on the prepared baking sheet. Pull the scraps together, reroll, and cut out more biscuits.

Brush the biscuits with heavy cream and sprinkle fleur de sel over the tops. Bake for 15 to 18 minutes, or until the biscuits are a deep golden brown. Let cool for 5 minutes before serving.

crunchy upside-down bacon corn bread

makes one 10-inch round bread

We use masa harina instead of cornmeal in the batter for this bread. It has a finer texture that will appeal to anyone who loves corn bread (even without bacon). The Smoked Masa Harina (page 12) makes a great substitution, especially if you want to omit the bacon. Even without the smoking, masa harina's slightly nutty corn flavor gives the bread an extra flavor boost. We pour the corn bread batter over the cooked bacon in the skillet to bake, then unmold the bread onto a plate so the bacon is on top. It looks incredibly appetizing and you'll be swatting your family's fingers away to get it to the table in one piece.

If you happen to be one of those people who doesn't eat bacon, you can leave it out and substitute 2 ounces/56 grams melted butter. The bread will still be moist and full of corn flavor.

6 slices thick-cut bacon, cut into small, ½-inch-wide strips

Melted butter if needed

1 cup/160 grams corn flour

½ cup / 75 grams masa harina

½ cup / 65 grams Gluten-Free Flour Blend (What IiF Flour 3.0, page 29, Batch-3 Flour, page 30, or Aki's Low-Allergy Blend, page 31)

1 tablespoon / 12.5 grams sugar

2 teaspoons / 12 grams baking powder

1 teaspoon / 6 grams fine sea salt

½ teaspoon / 2.5 grams baking soda

2½ cups / 600 grams buttermilk, at room temperature

recipe continues

Preheat the oven to 450°F. (230°C.).

Put the bacon in a cold 10-inch cast-iron or other ovenproof skillet, set over medium-low heat, and cook, stirring occasionally, until the fat renders and the bacon crisps. Using a slotted spoon, transfer the bacon to a plate lined with paper towels.

Pour the bacon fat into a heatproof measuring cup. If there is less than ¼ cup, add melted butter to make up the difference. Do not clean out the skillet.

Put the corn flour, masa harina, flour, sugar, baking powder, salt, and baking soda in a large bowl and whisk to blend. Add the buttermilk and bacon fat and mix with a rubber spatula, stirring vigorously for about 30 seconds to blend well.

Scatter the cooked bacon over the bottom of the skillet and pour in the batter. Put the skillet in the oven and bake for 20 to 25 minutes, until the corn bread is golden brown. Let cool for 15 minutes, then invert the bread onto a wire rack to cool completely.

Crunchy bacon-topped corn bread, still warm and ready to indulge.

the lightest corn bread ever

makes 12 individual breads

Corn bread is normally somewhat dense and fine-textured because of the cornmeal. For this recipe, we played around with the idea of making corn bread into something airy and super-light. We use smoked masa harina to mimic the rich flavor of corn bread cooked in a skillet over a wood fire. We sweeten it with a little maple syrup to bring out the earthy notes in the corn. The powdered egg whites give structure to the bread without adding more liquid, as additional regular egg whites would. Then we aerate the batter in a whipped cream canister (found at Williams-Sonoma, specialty kitchen stores, and online), dispense it into paper cups, and cook it in the microwave.

There is a small amount of bourbon in this recipe. As of this writing, distilled alcohol is considered gluten-free as long as there are no other flavorings added after distilling. If you have found that you are sensitive to bourbon or other brown liquors, feel free to substitute rum or leave it out entirely. We like the complex flavor bourbon gives the bread, supplementing the natural corn flavor of the masa harina, but the bread will still be delicious without it.

½ cup / 130 grams whole milk

7 tablespoons / 105 grams pure maple syrup, preferably Grade B

4 large eggs

2 large egg whites

¼ cup / 50 grams sugar

1 tablespoon / 14 grams bourbon

6 tablespoons / 50 grams Gluten-Free Flour Blend (What IiF Flour 3.0, **page 29,** Batch-3 Flour, page 30, or Aki's Low-Allergy Blend, page 31)

5 tablespoons / 50 grams corn flour

2½ tablespoons / 25 grams Smoked Masa Harina (page 12)

½ cup / 35 grams powdered egg whites

½ teaspoon / 3 grams fine sea salt

⅛ teaspoon / 0.25 gram cayenne

6½ tablespoons / 3¼ ounces / 90 grams unsalted butter, melted

Special Equipment: *1-quart whipped cream dispenser; 12 unwaxed 10-ounce paper cups*

Put the milk, maple syrup, eggs, egg whites, sugar, and bourbon in a blender, turn it on to medium, and blend the mixture until it is smooth, about 15 seconds. Add the flour, corn flour, smoked masa harina, powdered egg whites, salt, and cayenne, increase the speed to high, and blend for 15 seconds, or until the mixture is smooth. Turn the speed down to medium-high, pour in the butter, and blend for 15 seconds.

Strain the batter through a fine-mesh sieve. (Straining is necessary to remove any large bits of masa harina or corn flour, which could clog the whipped cream canister.) Pour half the mixture into a 1-quart whipped cream dispenser and put the lid on. Charge the canister with two N_2O charges, shaking vigorously after adding each one to disperse the gas and allow it to be absorbed by the batter. The batter should feel and sound fluid in the canister.

Prepare 12 unwaxed 10-ounce paper cups for microwaving the bread: Turn the cups over and use a paring knife to make a ½-inch slit in the bottom and three ½-inch slits around the sides of each cup. Turn the cups back over.

Shake the whipped cream canister and fill one cup one-third full. (The batter will be thick enough that it won't spill out through the cuts in the cup.) Put the cup into the microwave and cook on high for 30 seconds. The batter will rise and solidify into a soft mass resembling a sea sponge. Immediately remove the bread from the microwave and invert the cup onto a cutting board or countertop. Let the corn bread cool upside down while you cook the remaining breads. Refill and recharge the canister when necessary.

When all of the breads are completely cool, run a paring knife around the inside of each cup to loosen the bread, invert the cup, and shake gently to remove the bread and serve. Alternatively, the corn bread can be refrigerated in the inverted cups overnight before being unmolded. The refrigerated corn bread will stay moist and tender and keep its light, airy texture and shape. Pull them out about 30 minutes before you want to serve them so they come to room temperature. You can eat them cold, but the texture and flavor are best at room temperature.

Tender, gooey, Sticky Maple Scones, pulled apart.

sticky maple scones

makes 8 or 9 scones (depending on the pan)

These scones are baked in a pool of maple syrup and butter. They steam a bit as they cook, so their insides stay moist and tender while the tops turn golden brown and the maple syrup bubbles and caramelizes around the scones. When they come out of the oven, you immediately turn them out onto a platter and they end up with sticky maple caramel tops. The scones are almost as soft as biscuits, tender and rich. We like them with thick-cut bacon or fennel sausage, a little protein to round out the meal.

maple syrup topping

1 cup / 240 grams pure maple syrup, preferably Grade B
4 tablespoons / 2 ounces / 56 grams unsalted butter, sliced
¼ teaspoon / 1.5 grams fine sea salt

scones

3 cups / 390 grams Gluten-Free Flour Blend (What IiF Flour 3.0, page 29, Batch-3 Flour, page 30, or Aki's Low-Allergy Blend, page 31), plus more for dusting
½ cup / 100 grams sugar
2 teaspoons / 12 grams baking powder
¾ teaspoon / 4.5 grams fine sea salt
½ teaspoon / 2.5 grams baking soda
8 tablespoons / 4 ounces / 113 grams cold unsalted butter, sliced
½ cup / 70 grams whole raw almonds
1¼ cups / 300 grams buttermilk

Preheat the oven to 400°F. (200°C.).

To make the topping, put the maple syrup and butter in a deep 8-inch square cake pan or a deep 9-inch cast-iron skillet and put in the oven for 5 minutes, or until the butter just melts. Remove from the oven and stir in the salt. Set aside on the stovetop so the butter stays liquid.

recipe continues

To make the scones, put the flour, sugar, baking powder, salt, and baking soda in a food processor and pulse to blend. Add the butter and almonds and pulse 4 or 5 times to blend and chop the nuts. Add the buttermilk and pulse just until the mixture comes together into a dough.

Turn the dough out onto a lightly floured countertop and knead a few times, until smooth. If the dough seems too wet, simply push it together and pat it into shape; it will be slightly less "short" in texture but still delicious. Shape into a 7-inch square or an 8-inch circle, depending on the pan you are using, and dust the top with flour. Cut the square into 9 equal pieces or the circle into 8 equal wedges and arrange them in the prepared pan, re-forming the square or circle in the pool of butter and maple syrup. The liquid will come up around each piece, bathing the scones in flavor.

Bake for 30 to 35 minutes, until the scones are golden brown on top. Remove from the oven, immediately run a butter knife around the perimeter of the pan, and turn the scones out onto a large plate or platter. (You must do this while everything is still bubbling hot, or the caramel will stick to the pan.) You may need to rap the pan a few times to help the scones break free. They will have baked together, but the individual pieces can be easily pulled apart. Let cool for at least 5 minutes and serve warm.

Sticky Maple Scones will float in their sticky topping in the baking dish.

Immediately run a knife around the perimeter of the pan when the scones come out of the oven and turn them out onto a large plate.

Unmolded hot Sticky Maple Scones, almost ready to be carefully broken apart.

lemon ginger scones

makes 1 dozen scones

We love the scent of these scones: it just seems to wake up all of our senses. They are especially nice in the wintertime, when citrus is in season and there is not much other fruit available. Lemons are known for their bright refreshing flavor and ginger for its warming and soothing qualities. Together they make a great combination to ease you into your day.

Meyer lemons have an intriguing floral flavor; substituting tangerine zest is fun way to change things up. You can buy diced candied ginger for this recipe, but we find that the sliced candied ginger that we get locally tends to be fresher and softer, so we buy that and simply dice it ourselves—or we make our own candied ginger (see page 25.) Good candied ginger has a wonderful chewy quality. It softens as it bakes and then firms up again as it cools, so that warm scones are chewier and cooled scones have a little bit of crunch.

3 cups / 390 grams Gluten-Free Flour Blend (What IiF Flour 3.0, page 29, Batch-3 Flour, page 30, or Aki's Low-Allergy Blend, page 31)

½ cup / 100 grams granulated sugar

1 tablespoon / 18 grams baking powder

¾ teaspoon / 4.5 grams fine sea salt

Grated zest of 1 lemon, preferably a Meyer lemon

8 tablespoons / 4 ounces / 113 grams cold unsalted butter, cut into large dice

1 cup / 240 grams heavy cream, plus extra for brushing

¼ cup / 46 grams diced candied ginger

¼ cup / 56 grams raw sugar

Preheat the oven to 400°F. (200°C.). Line a large baking sheet with parchment paper.

Put the flour, sugar, baking powder, salt, and lemon zest in a food processor and pulse to blend. Add the butter and pulse 2 or 3 times to blend; there should still be small chunks of butter in the mix. Add the heavy cream and pulse until the mixture comes together into a rough dough.

recipe continues

Turn the dough out onto a lightly floured surface and sprinkle the candied ginger over it. Use a bench scraper to fold the ginger into the dough until it is evenly distributed and the dough is smooth.

Divide the dough in half and roll each piece out into an 8-inch circle. Cut each circle into 6 equal wedges and arrange them on the prepared baking sheet. Brush with heavy cream and sprinkle the raw sugar over the tops.

Bake for 15 to 18 minutes, until the tops of the scones are a deep golden brown. Let cool for 10 minutes before serving warm, or let cool completely.

NOTE: *If you love ginger, we have a great trick for you. Buy or make extra candied ginger and put it in a Mason jar. Close the lid and put it on a rack set over 2 inches of water inside your pressure cooker. Cook at high pressure for 2 rounds of 90 minutes each (this is much easier with an electric pressure cooker, adding more water after the first round if necessary). The ginger will caramelize and soften and turn into some of the best natural candy you will ever taste.*

Use a bench scraper to cut Lemon Ginger Scones into triangles.

The raw sugar coating gives the scones a sweet and crunchy exterior.

Fragrant Lemon Ginger Scones cooling on a sheet pan.

Lemon Ginger Scones with salted butter.

yeasted and
sourdough breads

Slather the Chinese Steamed Buns with hoisin sauce and fill with Japanese Fried Chicken (page 18) and cucumbers.

chinese steamed buns

makes 12 buns

Chinese steamed buns are soft and slightly sweet, with a faintly nutty flavor from the sesame oil. We refrigerate the dough overnight to ensure hydration and give the yeast time to work. The steamed buns are traditionally stuffed with hoisin sauce, pickles or sliced vegetables, and roast duck or pork. You can serve these buns slathered with our Homemade Hoisin Sauce and stuffed with sautéed shrimp, roasted mushrooms, fried eggs, braised pork belly, or even Texas chili. Their sweet flavor and soft texture will go with almost anything your imagination can come up with. We sometimes serve them as dinner rolls, and they are the base for an infinite number of sandwiches. We often make extra dough just so we can have some fresh buns for the morning. We split them and griddle the insides, leaving the exterior soft, and stuff each one with ham, a soft-boiled egg, and a spoonful of hollandaise sauce.

3⅔ cups / 450 grams Gluten-Free Flour Blend (What IiF Flour 3.0, page 29, Batch-3 Flour, page 30, or Aki's Low-Allergy Blend, page 31)

1 tablespoon / 12.5 grams sugar

1 teaspoon / 3 grams instant yeast

½ teaspoon / 3 grams fine sea salt

1¾ cups + 1 tablespoon / 390 grams water

1 teaspoon / 4.5 grams baking powder

1 teaspoon / 3 grams Asian sesame oil

2 tablespoons / 20 grams olive oil

Homemade Hoisin Sauce (page 76) for serving

Put the flour, sugar, yeast, and salt into a large bowl and whisk together. Make a well in the center of the flour and pour in the water. Use your fingertips to start pulling the flour into the water and then begin to form a mass as you incorporate all of the flour. Keep squeezing and then kneading the mixture until it becomes a ball.

recipe continues

Turn the dough out onto a lightly floured surface and knead for 5 minutes, or until it is silky and smooth. Form the dough into a ball, put it into a bowl, and cover with plastic wrap. Let rise for 3 to 4 hours at room temperature, until it has doubled in size.

Transfer the dough to a countertop and flatten it with your hands. Sprinkle the baking powder over the dough, fold the dough over, and knead the dough for 5 to 7 minutes, until it is a silky, springy ball. Put the dough into a clean bowl, cover with plastic wrap, and refrigerate overnight.

The next day, remove the dough from the refrigerator and let it proof, still covered, at room temperature for 2 hours. The dough will have come to room temperature and risen slightly.

Turn the dough out onto a lightly floured surface. Use a bench scraper or a sharp knife to divide it into 12 even pieces. Roll each piece of dough into ball. Using a rolling pin, roll each ball into an oval approximately 3 inches in diameter.

Combine the sesame and olive oil in a small bowl. Brush the surface of each oval with the oil and then fold it in half (with the oil on the inside). Brush two plates that will fit inside your steamer with the oil blend and arrange 6 buns on each plate.

Pour 1 inch of water into a large pot, set a steaming rack inside and bring to a boil over high heat. Put the first plate of buns in the steamer, cover, and cook for 15 minutes. Turn off the heat, crack the lid, and let the buns rest for 1 minute. Remove the plate from the steamer, turn the heat back on and cook the second plate of buns in the same manner; add more water to the pot if needed. Serve immediately with hoisin sauce.

Let any leftover buns cool completely and wrap in plastic wrap. To reheat, steam for 10 to 15 minutes.

Just mixed Steamed Buns dough.

Steamed Buns dough dusted with flour and ready for kneading.

Kneaded dough shaped into a ball and ready to rise.

Risen dough dusted with baking powder.

Steamed Buns dough after the baking powder is kneaded in. It will become sticky.

Steamed Buns dough rising at room temperature after chilling overnight.

The combination of sesame and olive oils gives the buns a slightly nutty flavor.

Cooked Chinese Steamed Buns in a bamboo steamer.

homemade hoisin sauce

makes 4 cups

If you are making Chinese Steamed Buns (page 73), you need hoisin sauce. Have you ever read the label on a bottle of hoisin sauce? Let's just say it will make you want to put it back on the shelf. But once you've tasted soft steamed buns slathered with sweet, tangy hoisin sauce and stuffed with bits of leftover Japanese Fried Chicken (page 18) and thinly sliced jalapeños, or roasted mushrooms with fresh tarragon, or even just some spicy kimchi, you'll realize that hoisin does make everything better. Our solution? Make your own hoisin sauce. If you have this in your pantry, you'll never miss the stuff in a bottle.

10¼ ounces / 290 grams pitted prunes

1 medium onion, thinly sliced

2 cups / 450 grams apple cider

4½ tablespoons / 75 grams soy sauce

2½ teaspoons / 5 grams smoked paprika

2 teaspoons / 4.6 grams black peppercorns

1 piece star anise

Put the prunes, onion, apple cider, soy sauce, smoked paprika, peppercorns, and star anise in a pressure cooker and cook on high pressure for 20 minutes. Let the pressure release naturally.

Remove the lid, remove the star anise, and transfer and the mixture to a blender. Turn the blender on low, then gradually increase the speed to medium-high and puree for 30 seconds. Strain the puree through a fine-mesh strainer into a bowl and cool the sauce over an ice bath.

Hoisin sauce will keep in a covered container in the refrigerator for up to 3 months.

crumpets

makes 1 dozen crumpets

Crumpets and English muffins are classic British breads, but English muffins are much more common here in the States. They are generally split and toasted so that they are crispy, crunchy vehicles for butter and jam. Crumpets are softer and thinner and usually served whole, preserving their tender, slightly chewy interior. They have a wonderful soft, springy texture that makes them unique. Crumpets are classically served with tea, toasted and slathered with butter or honey or, if you're feeling decadent, with jam and clotted cream.

2 cups / 260 grams Gluten-Free Flour Blend (What IiF Flour 3.0, page 29, Batch-3 Flour, page 30, or Aki's Low-Allergy Blend, page 31)

1 tablespoon / 12.5 grams sugar

2 teaspoons / 6 grams instant yeast

1 cup / 240 grams buttermilk

1 cup / 225 grams water

3 large eggs

¾ teaspoon / 4.5 grams fine sea salt

¼ teaspoon / 1.25 grams baking soda

Special equipment: Six 3½-inch flan rings or ring molds

Put the flour, sugar, and yeast into a large bowl and use a whisk to blend them together.

Put the buttermilk, water, and eggs into a medium bowl and whisk together. Pour the buttermilk mixture over the flour mixture and whisk until you have a smooth batter. Cover the batter with plastic wrap and let it rise in a warm spot for 3 hours.

Preheat an electric griddle to 300°F. (150°C.) or set an cast-iron griddle or heavy pan over medium heat.

recipe continues

Remove the plastic wrap from the bowl. The batter will have risen and thickened, and bubbles will cover the surface. Sprinkle the salt and baking soda over the top and whisk them in. The batter will bubble and rise. Pour the batter into a large glass measuring cup or a bowl with a spout.

Put six flan rings on the hot griddle. Spray the rings and the griddle with nonstick cooking spray. Fill each ring just to the top with batter. Cook the crumpets for 12 to 15 minutes, until the tops are full of holes and appear dry and set. Use a spatula to flip the crumpets, still in their rings, and cook for another 5 minutes, or until firm to the touch. Transfer the crumpets to a rack and remove the rings with tongs. Repeat with the remaining batter.

Serve the crumpets warm, or cool and refrigerate until ready to use. Rewarm in a toaster or on a griddle in butter. (They can be stored in a zip-top bag in the refrigerator for up to a week.)

Griddled Crumpets cooling on a wire rack.

Slice the cooled Potato Bread for sandwiches or toast.

potato bread

This is our version of American sandwich bread. The recipe makes a slightly sweet loaf with a fine, moist crumb and a delicate yeasty flavor. The cooked potato adds its own flavor and contributes some fully hydrated starch to help bind the dough and hold on to moisture.

Note that the dough rises almost entirely before we put it in the oven. The lack of oven spring is one of those quirks of gluten-free baking and a good reminder that although some of these recipes might seem exactly the same as their wheat flour counterparts, they behave differently. It is important to read this recipe, especially the baking instructions, and follow it carefully.

10½ ounces / 300 grams russet potato (1 large or 2 medium), peeled, quartered, and thinly sliced

1½ cups / 337.5 grams water

1¼ teaspoons / 7.5 grams fine sea salt

1 cup / 260 grams whole milk

2 tablespoons / 6 grams instant yeast

1 tablespoon / 12.5 grams sugar

6 large eggs

4⅔ cups / 600 grams Gluten-Free Flour Blend (What IiF Flour 3.0, page 29, Batch-3 Flour, page 30, or Aki's Low-Allergy Blend, page 31)

Special Equipment: A 13-by-4-by-4-inch pain-de-mie or Pullman loaf pan

Put the potatoes, water, and ¼ teaspoon of the salt in a medium saucepan and bring to a simmer over medium heat, then turn the heat down and cook the potatoes until fork-tender, about 15 minutes. Transfer the potatoes and their liquid to a bowl and let cool.

Add the remaining 1 teaspoon salt, the milk, yeast, and sugar to the potatoes and stir to combine. Put the potato mixture and eggs in a blender. Turn the blender on low, gradually increase the speed to medium-high, and puree for 30 seconds, or until the mixture is smooth.

recipe continues

Transfer the potato mixture to the bowl of a stand mixer fitted with the paddle attachment (or use a hand mixer), add the flour, and mix on low until all of the potato mixture has been absorbed by the flour. Increase the speed to medium-high and beat for 30 seconds, or until the dough appears smooth and elastic.

Use a rubber spatula to scrape the dough into a clean bowl. Cover with plastic wrap and let it rise for 2½ hours, until not quite doubled.

Grease a 13-by-4-by-4-inch pain-de-mie or Pullman loaf pan and lid. Use a rubber spatula to stir the dough together and then transfer it to the prepared loaf pan. Cover loosely with plastic wrap and let rise for 2 hours, or until it reaches top of the pan.

Meanwhile, 1 hour before baking, preheat the oven to 400°F. (200°C.).

Remove the plastic wrap from the pan and slide the lid into place. Bake the bread for 45 minutes. Turn the heat down to 350°F. (180°C.) and bake for 30 minutes more.

Turn the heat down to 300°F. (150°C.). Remove the top of the pan and bake the bread uncovered for 20 minutes.

Remove the bread from the oven and invert it onto a rack set over a baking sheet. Lift off the pan and bake the bread for 10 more minutes. The internal temperature should be 210° to 212°F. (99° to 100°C.).

Turn off the oven, open the door, and let the bread cool on the rack for 30 minutes.

Remove the bread from the oven, transfer to a rack, and let cool to room temperature completely before cutting. Well-wrapped the bread will keep at cool room temperature for up to a week—if you don't finish it all before then.

Potato Bread dough,
first rise.

After the first rise, the
dough is transferred to a
loaf pan to rise again.

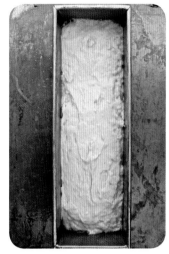

The dough is now fully
risen and ready to be baked.

Baked Potato Bread cooling
on a wire rack.

Warm Butter-Stuffed Dinner Rolls ready for the table.

butter-stuffed dinner rolls

makes 12 rolls

Dinner rolls tend to be special-occasion food, reserved for weekend or holiday dinners. When was the last time you made rolls? The beauty of these, besides being soft, crusty, and delicious, is that they freeze well, so you can keep the extras in your freezer and pull them out at a moment's notice. Ten to fifteen minutes in a hot oven, and any meal can be a special occasion.

While this recipe may resemble hundreds of other recipes for dinner rolls, aside from the gluten-free flour, one other ingredient stands out in the list: the egg white powder. We use it in many recipes because it contributes protein and structure to gluten-free baked goods without noticeably altering the flavor.

3¾ cups / 490 grams Gluten-Free Flour Blend (What IiF Flour 3.0, page 29, Batch-3 Flour, page 30, or Aki's Low-Allergy Blend, page 31)

¼ cup / 17 grams powdered egg whites

3 tablespoons / 37.5 grams sugar

1¾ teaspoons / 10.5 grams salt

1½ teaspoons / 4.5 grams instant yeast

1 cup + 2½ tablespoons / 300 grams whole milk, at room temperature, plus 2 tablespoons / 28 grams milk for the egg wash

⅔ cup / 150 grams buttermilk, at room temperature

2 large eggs, at room temperature

8 tablespoons / 4 ounces / 113 grams unsalted butter, melted, plus 2 ounces / 56 grams cold unsalted butter, cut into 12 pieces

1 large egg yolk

Put the flour, powdered egg whites, sugar, salt, and yeast into a large bowl and stir together with a whisk.

recipe continues

Put the milk, buttermilk, eggs, and melted butter into a medium bowl and whisk together. Pour the liquid mixture into the dry mixture and use a rubber spatula to fold the ingredients together until a dough forms. Let it stand for 10 minutes to hydrate the dry ingredients.

Turn the dough out and knead for 5 minutes, or until it is smooth and silky. Put the dough in a clean bowl, cover with plastic wrap, and let rise for 2 hours.

Gently loosen the dough from the bowl. Slide one hand under one side of the dough, fold that side of the dough over into the center, and press down gently so it adheres to itself. Give the bowl a quarter turn and repeat the folding process. Do this two more times. After the fourth fold, flip over the dough so the seams are on the bottom. Cover with plastic wrap and let rise for 2 hours.

Line a large baking sheet with plastic wrap. Knock the dough down and put it on the baking sheet. Cover the dough with another sheet of plastic wrap and refrigerate for at least 8 hours, or as long as overnight.

Spray a muffin tin with nonstick cooking spray. Remove the dough from the refrigerator and transfer to a work surface, still between the sheets of plastic wrap. Roll the dough out, between the sheets of plastic wrap, into a 10-by-13-inch rectangle. Cut the dough lengthwise in half. Brush the entire surface of the dough with some of the melted butter. Fold each piece of dough lengthwise in half. Brush with butter and then flip each piece over. Brush the bottom sides with butter.

Cut each strip of dough into 6 equal pieces. Roll each one into a ball and put into the muffin tin. Carefully press 1 piece of butter into the center of each ball. Cover the rolls gently with plastic wrap and let proof for 45 minutes, or until light and puffy; the tops should spring back when gently pressed with a finger.

Preheat the oven to 375°F. (190°C.).

Put the egg yolk and the 2 tablespoons milk into a small bowl and whisk together.

Remove the plastic from the rolls. Brush the tops of the rolls with the egg wash. Bake for 20 minutes. Rotate the tin and turn the oven up to 425°F. (220°C.). Bake for 15 more minutes, or until the rolls are a deep golden brown. Remove from the oven and cool on a rack for 10 minutes.

Serve the rolls warm.

Pats of butter are pressed into soft dough to create Butter-Stuffed Dinner Rolls.

Risen Dinner Roll dough, stuffed with butter, brushed with egg wash, and ready for the oven.

Invert the Dinner Rolls onto a rack and allow to cool before serving.

Moist, tender rolls that absorbed the butter from the center during baking.

Cooled and sliced Country Sourdough bread.

country sourdough

makes one 13-inch round loaf or one 13-by-4-inch loaf

This hearty loaf has a thick crust and a distinctive tang. The sourdough starter, made with sweet sorghum flour and golden flaxseed meal, adds its unique flavor created through the slow fermentation of wild yeasts. You also need to add a little commercial yeast, because the wild starter isn't enough to fully leaven the bread. We usually use instant yeast. It's the easiest to work with, because it doesn't require any proofing to activate it. You simply mix it into the dough and it does its thing.

We bake the dough in a seasoned cast-iron combo cooker from Lodge. We learned about in Chad Robertson's, Tartine Bread. His description whet our imaginations, so we bought one, tried baking country loaves in it, and never looked back (see Sources, page 351). It's a combination of a 3-quart deep skillet and a 10¼-inch shallow skillet that fit together so that the skillet can be used as a cover to create a Dutch oven. It's a handy piece of equipment that can be used for much more than baking bread. Although we like to use it for this bread, you can also bake the loaf in a pain-de-mie pan.

This bread is our favorite for fondue night because its deep flavor perfectly accents the floral, nutty Gruyère. Note that this dough is more liquid than most. It is important to let it rise to the top of the pan before baking in order to get the best texture. Your patience will be rewarded, because this is delicious bread.

1 cup + 3 tablespoons / 300 grams Gluten-Free Sourdough Starter (page 22)

1¼ cups / 280 grams water

1 tablespoon / 12.5 grams sugar

1¼ teaspoons / 7.5 grams fine sea salt

1 teaspoon / 3 grams instant yeast

6 large eggs

4⅔ cups / 600 grams Gluten-Free Flour Blend (What IiF Flour 3.0, page 29, Batch-3 Flour, page 30, or Aki's Low-Allergy Blend, page 31)

recipe continues

Special Equipment: Lodge 3-quart cast-iron combo cooker or a 13-by-4-by-4-inch pain-de-mie or Pullman loaf pan

Put the sourdough starter, water, sugar, salt, yeast, and eggs in a blender. Turn the blender on low, gradually increase the speed to medium-high, and blend for 30 seconds, or until the mixture is smooth.

Put the flour into the bowl of a stand mixer fitted with the paddle attachment (or use a hand mixer). Turn the mixer on low and pour in the sourdough mixture. Increase the speed to medium and beat until all the wet ingredients are incorporated, then increase the speed to medium-high and beat the dough for 30 seconds, or until it appears smooth and elastic.

Use a rubber spatula to scrape the dough into a clean bowl. Cover with plastic wrap and let rise for 3 hours.

Grease a 3-quart cast-iron combo cooker or a 13-by-4-by-4-inch pain-de-mie pan. Use a rubber spatula to stir the dough together, then pour it into the 3-quart deep skillet or the pain-de-mie pan. Cover with plastic wrap and let the dough rise for 2 hours, or until it reaches to the top of the pan.

Meanwhile, 1 hour before baking, preheat the oven to 400°F. (200°C.).

Remove the plastic wrap from the pan. Spray the lid of the combo cooker or loaf pan with nonstick cooking spray and put it in place.

Bake the bread for 45 minutes. Turn the heat down to 350°F. (180°C.), without opening the oven door and bake for 30 minutes.

Turn the heat down to 300°F. (150°C.). Remove the lid and bake the bread uncovered for 30 minutes. The internal temperature should be 210° to 212°F. (99° to 100°C.). Turn off the oven, open the door, and let the bread cool in the oven for 30 minutes.

Remove the bread from the oven, turn it out on to a rack, and let cool completely.

The bread can be wrapped in plastic wrap and kept at room temperature for up to a week.

Sorghum flour, flaxseed meal, and water mixed and ready to ferment into Sourdough Starter (page 22)

Using a scale to feed a happy Sourdough Starter.

Mixed Country Sourdough before the first rise.

Country Sourdough after the first rise, in the skillet ready to rise again before baking.

Country Sourdough risen almost to the top of the skillet and ready to be baked.

Skillet of freshly baked Country Sourdough bread, fresh from the oven.

microwave sourdough soft rolls

makes 16 rolls

Here's another delicious use for our sourdough starter. These rolls are a lighter, fluffier cousin of the Country Sourdough (page 89). This creates large bubbles in the dough that expand in the microwave as the dough sets around them, giving the finished cake a spongy appearance. We use a whipped cream canister to aerate the dough as we extrude it into paper cups. Each one cooks in 30 seconds, so we can make all 16 in the time it would take to heat up a conventional oven.

The sourdough give these rolls a fine crumb and a gentle tang that adds a nice accent to any meal. And their light, spongy texture makes them perfect for soaking up gravy. The optional toasted milk solids give them a nutty accent and a more rounded flavor.

2 cups / 480 grams Gluten-Free Sourdough Starter (page 22)

1 cup / 225 grams water

2 large eggs

½ cup / 65 grams Gluten-Free Flour Blend (What IiF Flour 3.0, page 29, Batch-3 Flour, page 30, or Aki's Low-Allergy Blend, page 31)

½ cup / 36 grams powdered egg whites

2 tablespoons / 25 grams sugar

¾ teaspoon / 4.5 grams fine sea salt

4 tablespoons / 2 ounces / 56 grams unsalted butter, melted

¼ cup / 16 grams Toasted Milk Powder (page 15; optional), plus more for dusting

Special Equipment: 1-quart whipped cream dispenser; 16 unwaxed 10-ounce paper cups

Put the sourdough starter, water, and eggs in a blender. Turn the blender on low, gradually increase the speed to medium-high, and blend until the mixture is fluid. Add the flour, powdered egg whites, sugar, salt, melted butter, and toasted milk powder, if using, and blend for 30 seconds, or until the dry ingredients are fully incorporated and the mixture is smooth.

Strain the mixture through a fine-mesh sieve, transfer to 1-quart whipped cream dispenser, and put the lid on. Charge the canister with two N_2O charges, shaking vigorously after adding each one to disperse the gas and allow it to be absorbed by the batter. The batter should feel and sound fluid in the canister.

Prepare 16 unwaxed 10-ounce paper cups for microwaving the rolls: Turn the cups over and use a paring knife to make a ½-inch slit in the bottom and three ½-inch slits around the sides of each cup. Turn the cups back over.

Shake the whipped cream canister and fill one cup one-third full. (The batter will be thick enough that it won't spill out through the cuts in the cup.) Put the cup into the microwave and cook on high for 30 seconds. The batter will rise and solidify into a soft mass resembling a sea sponge. Immediately remove from the microwave and invert the cup onto a cutting board or countertop. Let the roll cool upside down while you cook the remaining rolls.

Let the rolls cool until the cups are no longer hot to the touch. Run a small paring knife around the inside of each cup, invert the cup, and gently shake to remove the roll. Using a small strainer, dust toasted milk powder over the rolls, and serve immediately. Alternatively, the rolls can be refrigerated in the inverted cups overnight before being unmolded. The rolls will stay moist and tender and keep their light, airy texture and shape. Pull them from the refrigerator at least 30 minutes before serving so they come to room temperature. Dust with toasted milk powder before serving.

Straining the blended microwave sourdough batter before transferring to a whipped-cream canister, extruding, and "micro-baking."

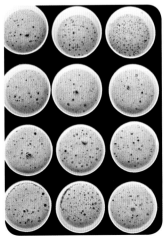

Finished Microwave Sourdough Soft Rolls, still in the cups after "baking."

buttermilk brioche

makes two 9-by-5-inch loaves

Brioche is one of our very favorite doughs. It has a rich, buttery flavor and endless versatility. Our no-knead version of the bread uses extra liquid and a long, slow hydration and fermentation period to develop texture and flavor. Here we've made it with buttermilk—that little bit of tang balances the richness of the butter. We also use this dough as a base for the Stollen (page 99) and Kouign Amann (page 97). While Brioche has a reputation for being finicky, this version requires a little extra time but not a lot of effort for perfect results.

7½ cups / 975 grams Gluten-Free Flour Blend (What IiF Flour 3.0, page 29,
    Batch-3 Flour, page 30, or Aki's Low-Allergy Blend, page 31)

1 tablespoon + ½ teaspoon / 21 grams fine sea salt

½ teaspoon / 1.5 grams instant yeast

½ cup / 100 grams sugar

8 large eggs, at room temperature

1 cup / 240 grams buttermilk, at room temperature

½ cup / 113 grams water, at room temperature

32 tablespoons (4 sticks) / 1 pound / 450 grams unsalted butter, melted and cooled

Milk or heavy cream for brushing the loaves

Put the flour, salt, yeast, and sugar in a large bowl and whisk to blend thoroughly.

Whisk together the eggs, buttermilk, and water in a medium bowl until well blended. Whisk in the butter. Pour the wet ingredients into the dry ingredients and stir with a rubber spatula or wooden spoon until the liquid is incorporated and there are no lumps; the mixture will resemble muffin batter. Cover the bowl with plastic wrap and let rest at room temperature for 3 to 4 hours. The dough will rise very slightly.

Using a rubber spatula, gently loosen the dough from the bowl. Dampen your hands with cool water. Slide one hand under one side of the dough, fold that side of the dough into the center, and press down gently so it adheres to itself. Give the bowl a quarter turn and repeat the folding process. Do this two more times. After the fourth fold, flip over the dough so the seams are on the bottom. (The dough will have a few air bubbles and feel elastic.) Cover the bowl with plastic wrap and let it rise at room temperature for at least 8 hours, or as long as overnight. The dough will have at least doubled and be light and crackly on the surface.

Line a baking sheet with plastic wrap. Repeat the folding procedure with the dough, then put it on the baking sheet and cover with another sheet of plastic wrap. Refrigerate the dough until it is firm, or for up to 3 days.

Grease two 9-by-5-inch loaf pans. Divide the dough in half. Place each half in one of the loaf pans. Let the dough proof for 1½ hours.

While the dough proofs, position a rack in the middle of the oven and preheat the oven to 375°F. (190°C.) if using a regular oven, or 350°F. (175°C.) if using convection.

Brush the loaves with milk. Bake for 1 hour, or until the loaves are a deep golden brown and sound hollow when you firmly tap the bottom of the pan with your finger; the internal temperature should be at least 208°F. (98°C.). Cool for 10 minutes in the pans on a rack, then turn the loaves out onto the rack and let cool completely.

Tightly wrapped in plastic wrap, the brioche will keep for up to a week at room temperature.

Buttermilk Brioche dough rising in a plastic container.

Fully risen dough, ready to be turned out of the container.

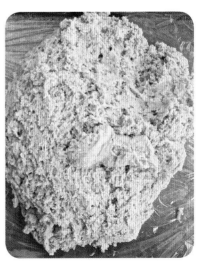

Turn the dough out onto a sheet pan lined with plastic wrap, so it's easy to cover, flatten, and chill.

Kouign Amann, gooey butter cakes with a caramelized sugar crust, cooling on a wire rack.

kouign amann

Kouign amann (queen a-mahn) *is a butter cake from Brittany. It is made with what is called a "laminated dough." Lamination is the technique of folding layers of butter into the dough, so that the finished bread or pastry has multiple flaky layers that rise high, created by the steam that evaporates out of the butter as the dough bakes. Picture the interior of a croissant, and you'll know exactly what we're talking about.*

A kouign amann takes things one step further by adding sugar to the butter between the layers so that as it bakes, the sugar caramelizes all around the outside, adding sweetness and crunch. By making individual pastries instead of one big cake, we can maximize the effect of those crusty, chewy bits of caramel. These are pure indulgence.

2 cups / 240 grams powdered sugar, sifted

½ batch, approximately 2 pounds 10 ounces / 1200 grams Buttermilk Brioche dough (page 94), chilled

4 tablespoons / 2 ounces / 56 grams unsalted butter, melted

¼ cup / 50 grams granulated sugar

Softened butter and granulated sugar for the molds

Special Equipment: Twelve 8-ounce soufflé cups (or a jumbo muffin tin)

Lay two 22-inch-long pieces of plastic wrap on your countertop, overlapping them to form a 14-by-22-inch rectangle. Dust the plastic wrap with some of the powdered sugar and put the cold brioche dough in the center. Liberally dust the top of the dough with powdered sugar and cover with two pieces of overlapping plastic wrap. Roll the dough into a rough 10-by-18-inch rectangle. Remove the top layer of plastic wrap and dust the surface of the dough with powdered sugar. Turn the dough so a long side is toward you. Fold the left third of the dough over the middle third of the dough. Dust the newly exposed surface with powdered sugar. Fold the right third of the dough over the top to create a smaller rectangle of

recipe continues

dough resembling a folded letter. Dust the newly exposed surface with powdered sugar. Flip the dough over and rotate it 90 degrees so the folds are now positioned horizontally. Dust the top with powdered sugar so that all sides have a light, even coating. Be sure to use half of the powdered sugar.

Cover the dough with the two pieces of plastic wrap and roll it into a 10-by-18-inch rectangle again. Repeat the dusting and folding process again. Wrap the dough in plastic wrap and refrigerate it for at least 30 minutes.

Butter and sugar twelve 8-ounce soufflé cups. (If you don't have soufflé cups, you can use a jumbo muffin tin.) Line two baking sheets with parchment paper. (Or put the muffin tin on a lined baking sheet.)

Remove the dough from the refrigerator. Repeat the dusting and folding process once again. Then roll the dough out into a 10-by-18-inch rectangle.

Cut the dough lengthwise in half, then cut each half into 6 equal pieces. Brush the top of the dough with some of the melted butter. Carefully lift a piece of dough and slide it into a soufflé cup, buttered side up, pushing the center down into the cup and letting the corners fold inward naturally. Repeat with the remaining 11 pieces of dough. Brush the tops again with melted butter.

Arrange six cups on each lined baking sheet. Cover with plastic wrap and let the dough proof for 1½ hours, or until the pastries have risen and look puffy.

While the dough proofs, position the racks in the upper and lower thirds of the oven (or put one rack in the center if using a muffin tin) and preheat the oven to 375°F. (190°C.) if using a regular oven, or 350°F. (175°C.) if using convection.

Sprinkle the top of each pastry with 1 teaspoon / 4 grams of the granulated sugar. Bake the kouign amann for 20 minutes. Rotate the pans top to bottom and front to back and bake for 20 more minutes, or until the kouign amann is caramel in color. Remove the pans from the oven and let cool for 15 minutes.

Remove the pastries from the soufflé cups and enjoy immediately, or let them cool on a rack.

marcona almond marzipan–enriched stollen

makes four 12-inch-long loaves

When Alex was growing up, his father worked for a German investment firm, and every Christmas, he would bring home a stollen as his Christmas bonus. It was something that Alex looked forward to every holiday season. Fast-forward a few decades, and Christmas stollen is still a special treat. Now Alex makes his own and it tastes even better than his memories.

Classic stollen is a rich yeast bread studded with citron and other dried fruits, often baked with a vein of marzipan running through it. In a nod to Jamaican fruit cake, we soak the dried fruits in dark rum to give them more flavor. We make our own marzipan, and as a final flourish, we brush each cooked loaf with brown butter and coat it with powdered sugar. This both adds flavor and helps seal the outside of the loaves, so they keep longer.

NOTE: *After you make the brioche dough, put the dried fruit and rum in a bowl and let soak while the dough rises.*

1 cup / 112 grams dried cranberries

1 cup / 80 grams golden raisins

½ cup / 78 grams dried blueberries

½ cup / 113 grams dark rum

Buttermilk Brioche dough (page 94), taken through the first rise

1 cup / 140 grams Marcona almonds

28 ounces / 800 grams Marcona Almond Marzipan (page 102) or store-bought marzipan

2 large eggs, at room temperature

1 teaspoon / 4 grams vanilla paste or pure vanilla extract

½ cup / 120 grams heavy cream for brushing the stollen

8 tablespoons / 4 ounces / 113 grams unsalted butter, sliced

1 cup / 200 grams granulated sugar

Powdered sugar for dusting

recipe continues

Put the cranberries, golden raisins, dried blueberries, and rum in a bowl. Stir the dried fruit and cover the bowl. Let the fruit absorb the rum for at least 4 hours and preferably 24 hours.

After the brioche has risen, drain the dried fruits. (You can reserve the rum for another fruit soaking.) Scatter the almonds and soaked fruits over the dough and use a rubber spatula to fold the nuts and fruits into the dough. Line a baking sheet with plastic wrap and scrape the dough onto the baking sheet. Cover the dough with another sheet of plastic wrap and press the dough into a rough rectangle. Refrigerate for at least 4 hours and up to 2 days.

Meanwhile put the marzipan into the bowl of a stand mixer fitted with the paddle attachment (or use a hand mixer). Add the eggs and vanilla paste, turn the mixer on low, and gradually increase the speed to medium-high, mixing until a thick paste resembling peanut butter comes together. Turn the marzipan out and wrap in plastic wrap. Refrigerate until you are ready to make the stollen.

To assemble the stollen, line two baking sheets with parchment paper. Remove the marzipan and dough from the refrigerator. Divide the marzipan into 4 equal pieces. Roll each piece of marzipan between two pieces of plastic wrap into a 4-by-12-inch rectangle.

Divide the dough into 4 equal pieces. One at a time, roll each piece between two pieces of plastic wrap into an 8-by-12-inch rectangle. Put a piece of marzipan on one side of the dough and roll the dough up into a tube, enclosing the marzipan. Put the tube the seam side down on one of the prepared baking sheets and repeat with the remaining dough and marzipan, putting 2 loaves on each sheet. Cover with plastic wrap and let proof for 1½ hours until the dough rises and looks puffy.

Preheat the oven to 350°F. (175°C.). Brush the stollen with the heavy cream. Bake for 55 minutes or until the stollen are golden brown and slightly cracked looking; the internal temperature should register at least 208°F. (90°C.).

While the stollen is baking, put the butter into a medium saucepan and cook over medium heat until it melts, then stir until the milk solids turn golden brown, about 7 minutes. Remove the pan from the heat and place it in a warm spot to keep the brown butter liquid.

When the stollen is baked, transfer the breads to two racks set over two baking sheets. Let cool for 15 minutes.

Brush each loaf with about 2 tablespoons of the brown butter and sprinkle with ¼ cup of the granulated sugar. Let the loaves cool completely then dust them with powdered sugar. Well-wrapped, the stollen can be stored at cool room temperature for up to 1 month.

Turn the dough out onto a sheet pan lined with plastic wrap, so it's easy to cover, flatten, and chill.

Soaked fruits sprinkled on brioche dough, ready to be folded in for Stollen.

Use a rubber spatula to fold the soaked fruits into the brioche dough.

Fully mixed Stollen dough, ready to be chilled.

Chilled Stollen dough ready to be rolled into loaves.

Rolling Stollen, step one: ¼ of the Stollen dough rolled out and covered with enriched marzipan.

Step two: Roll the dough and marzipan into a log.

Step three: The finished log, tightly rolled and ready to proof.

Proof the Stollen logs, lightly covered with plastic wrap, on a baking sheet lined with parchment paper.

Brush the proofed logs with cream just before baking.

Brush the baked logs with brown butter and sprinkle with granulated sugar.

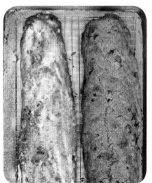

Dust the Stollen with a final layer of powdered sugar to finish.

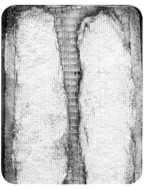

marcona almond marzipan

28 ounces | 800 grams marzipan

Marzipan is a sweet paste made out of ground almonds and sugar or honey, occasionally with the addition of egg whites. Homemade marzipan has a flavor you just can't get from a tube. We asked ourselves if there was a way to make it even better. The answer was sitting in our freezer—a bag of Marcona almonds. Marconas are large Spanish almonds, always sold without their skins. They are softer than California almonds, with a sweeter flavor.

The food processor makes this a very easy recipe, and after you taste it, you will want to use it in everything.

1¼ pounds (4 cups) / 560 grams Marcona almonds

⅓ cup / 100 grams light corn syrup

½ cup / 100 grams granulated sugar

½ cup / 56 grams powdered sugar

½ teaspoon / 3 grams fine sea salt

Put the almonds, corn syrup, granulated sugar, powdered sugar, and salt into a food processor and pulse 15 times to begin breaking the nuts down and grinding them into a meal. Use a rubber spatula to scrape down the sides of the processor. Turn the processor back on the grind the mixture for 1 minute. Turn the food processor off. Squeeze the mixture in your hand: it should be very fine-grained and come together like pie dough. Process for another minute or so if necessary.

Transfer the mixture to a large bowl and knead it together for 3 to 5 minutes. It will form into a large ball.

Put the paste into a zip-top bag, push out all the air, seal the bag, and use a rolling pin to roll the marzipan out flat. This final step will press the paste together. The marzipan can be refrigerated for up to 2 months.

Marcona Almond Marzipan beaten with eggs and vanilla to become more flavorful and pliable for Stollen (page 99).

Roll out the sheets of enriched marzipan into 4-by-12-inch rectangles so they fit within the Stollen.

variation: *stollen doughnuts*

Once the marzipan-stuffed dough has been formed into loaves, you can roll them out into rectangles approximately 3/8 inch thick, and then follow the procedure on pages 106–7 to cut and fry the dough into doughnuts (*see photograph on page 109*). Stollen doughnuts are best eaten warm. They can be heated in the microwave for 8 to 10 seconds or in a 350°F. (175°C.) oven for 10 minutes.

*Marcona Almond Marzipan–Enriched Stollen (page 99),
cooled, sliced, and ready to serve.*

doughnuts

makes 2 dozen doughnuts

We often use brioche dough to make doughnuts. The problem with many yeasted doughnuts is that they are tender when warm but become leaden and dry as they cool. To fix this, we swapped out half the butter in our Buttermilk Brioche recipe for peanut oil. (If anyone has a peanut allergy, use your favorite neutral vegetable oil.) As with our cake recipes, our theory was that since oil is liquid at room temperature, the finished doughnuts would remain moister. The result was pretty amazing doughnuts. They fry up crisp on the outside with a soft, tender interior. We've included a recipe for lemon buttermilk glaze, but these are equally good rolled in powdered sugar or dipped in Chocolate Glaze (page 197).

7½ cups / 975 grams Gluten-Free Flour Blend (What IiF Flour 3.0, page 29, Batch-3 Flour, page 30, or Aki's Low-Allergy Blend, page 31)

(1 tablespoon + ½ teaspoon / 21 grams fine sea salt

½ teaspoon / 1.5 grams instant yeast

½ cup / 100 grams sugar

8 large eggs, at room temperature

1 cup / 225 grams water, at room temperature

1 cup / 240 grams buttermilk, at room temperature

16 tablespoons (2 sticks) / 8 ounces / 225 grams unsalted butter, melted and cooled

1 cup / 225 grams peanut or vegetable oil

Rice bran oil or peanut oil for deep-frying

lemon-buttermilk glaze

2 cups / 240 grams powdered sugar

¼ cup / 60 grams buttermilk

4 teaspoons / 20 grams fresh lemon juice, preferably from a Meyer lemon

⅛ teaspoon / 0.75 gram fine sea salt

2 lemons

recipe continues

Special Equipment: A 3-inch doughnut cutter (or a 3-inch round cutter and a smaller cutter for the doughnut holes)

Put the flour, salt, yeast, and sugar in a large bowl and whisk to blend thoroughly. Whisk together the eggs, water, and buttermilk in a medium bowl until well blended. Whisk in the butter and oil. Pour the wet ingredients into the dry ingredients and stir with a rubber spatula or wooden spoon until the liquid is incorporated and there are no lumps; the mixture will resemble muffin batter. Cover the bowl with plastic wrap, and let rest at room temperature for 3 to 4 hours. The dough will rise slightly but not double.

Using a rubber spatula, gently loosen the dough from the bowl. Dampen your hands with cool water. Slide one hand under one side of the dough, fold that side of the dough into the center, and press down gently so it adheres to itself. Give the bowl a quarter turn and repeat the folding process. Do this two more times. After the fourth fold, flip over the dough so the seams are on the bottom. Cover with plastic wrap and let rise at room temperature for at least 8 hours, or as long as overnight. The dough will have more than doubled and be light and crackly on the surface.

Repeat the folding procedure with the dough, then put on it a baking sheet, press it out to fit the pan, and cover with a sheet of plastic wrap. Refrigerate the dough until it is firm, or for up to 3 days.

Line two large baking sheets with parchment paper and lightly dust with flour.

Remove the chilled dough from the refrigerator. Dust your countertop lightly and evenly with flour. Turn the dough out onto the floured countertop and dust it with flour. Use a rolling pin to roll the dough out to a thickness of 3/8 inch, adding a little extra flour if it begins to stick. Use a 3-inch doughnut cutter to cut the donuts (or use 3-inch round cutter to cut out the doughnut and a smaller round cutter to cut a the holes) and put them on the prepared baking sheets, leaving about 1 inch space between them; separate the holes from the doughnuts so they can be fried on their own. Cover the pans loosely with plastic wrap and let the doughnuts proof for 1 hour. Gently ball up the dough trimmings, put into a bowl, cover, and refrigerate to firm up for at least 1 hour, then reroll to make more doughnuts.

Fill a large pot with 2 inches of oil and heat over medium-high heat until it reaches 350°F. (176°C.). Set a wire rack over a baking sheet and have a slotted spoon or spider ready for turning the doughnuts.

Add 4 or 5 doughnuts to the hot oil and cook for 1 minute on the first side, then use slotted spoon to flip the doughnuts over and cook for 1 minute on the other side. Flip them one more time and cook for 1 more minute, or until deep golden brown on both sides. Use the slotted spoon to transfer the doughnuts to the rack to cool. Cook the remaining doughnuts in batches. To cook the holes, put 12 into the oil at a time and cook for 45 seconds, then turn them over and cook for 45 seconds more. Some of the holes may not flip—use the slotted spoon to stir them in the oil so they cook evenly. Remove the holes from the oil and transfer to the rack. Let cool for at least 5 minutes.

To make the glaze, put the powdered sugar in a bowl and add the buttermilk, lemon juice, and salt. Use a whisk to stir the mixture together until it forms a smooth glaze. Whisk again until smooth right before using.

Line two baking sheets with parchment paper and butter the paper very lightly. Place a wire rack over another baking sheet. Dip the doughnuts one at a time into the bowl of glaze, turning them to be sure to coat them thoroughly, and transfer to the prepared pans. Use a Microplane (rasp) grater to grate some lemon zest over the doughnuts. Once all the doughnuts are glazed, put the holes into the bowl with the glaze and grate some lemon zest into the bowl. Use a spoon to stir the holes in the glaze until evenly coated. Transfer the holes to the rack and grate more zest over the tops. Allow the glaze to set before serving.

See process photographs on the following page

Doughnut dough after the first rise.

Chilled dough, ready to be rolled out.

Proof doughnuts and holes on a sheet pan lined with parchment paper.

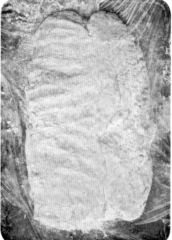

Proofed doughnuts, ready to be fried.

Fried and glazed doughnuts, warm, sweet, tender, and ready to eat.

A variation on Stollen (page 99): Fried and sugared Stollen Doughnuts (page 103).

flatbreads
and crackers

Use scissors to cleanly cut the finished pizza.

pizza dough

This is our no-knead gluten-free pizza dough recipe. We like to add a little bit of smoked masa puree to give it extra elasticity and some smoky flavor, but if you don't have masa on hand it's still a great dough without it. We're not going to tell you what to top it with, though we will give you our basic pizza sauce to try. Beyond that, the toppings and the style of cooking are up to you. We have cooked this dough in a home oven, on a grill, and in a wood-burning oven, and the results have always been applauded.

7 cups / 900 grams Gluten-Free Flour Blend (What IiF Flour 3.0, page 29,
Batch-3 Flour, page 30, or Aki's Low-Allergy Blend, page 31)

3 tablespoons / 18 grams fine sea salt

1 tablespoon / 12.5 grams sugar

½ teaspoon / 1.5 grams instant yeast

3 cups / 675 grams water

2 tablespoons / 28 grams olive oil

1 cup / 230 grams Masa Harina Puree (page 13; optional)

White rice flour for dusting the peel

Sauce and toppings of your choice (our Uncooked Tomato Sauce recipe follows)

Olive oil for drizzling

Combine the flour, salt, sugar, and yeast in a large bowl and whisk together to thoroughly blend the yeast into the flour. Pour in the water and olive oil, add the masa puree if using, and stir with a rubber spatula until the water is absorbed and there are no lumps of flour or masa. Cover the bowl with plastic wrap and leave it at room temperature for 6 hours.

Using a rubber spatula, gently loosen the dough from the bowl and stir it together. Cover the bowl with plastic wrap and let it rise at room temperature for 18 hours. The dough should rise to at least twice its size.

Use a rubber spatula to fold the dough over upon itself. Cover the dough and refrigerate for at least 4 hours and up to 2 days.

recipe continues

Preheat the oven with pizza stone to 500°F. (260°C.). Remove the dough from the refrigerator and turn out onto a clean countertop. Divide into seven 9.2 ounces/260-gram portions. Lay two overlapping pieces of plastic wrap on the counter and put a ball of dough in the center. Cover with another two sheets of plastic wrap. Use a rolling pin to roll the dough into a 12-inch circle. If you have a pizza pan, put the dough on the pan and use the bottom of a 1-cup dry measuring cup to shape the edges of the dough, then lay the shaped dough on the counter. Repeat with the other 6 balls of dough; stacking the rounds between sheets of plastic wrap if necessary to save space. If baking that day, let the dough proof on the counter, covered with plastic wrap, for 3 hours.

Lightly and evenly dust a pizza peel or the back of a baking sheet with white rice flour. Flip one piece of the dough over, still in the plastic wrap, and remove the bottom layer of plastic. Use the plastic wrap to move the dough onto the dusted peel. Gently remove the plastic wrap. Top the pizza with a light layer of sauce and toppings of your choice. Drizzle olive oil over the top.

Slide the pizza onto the hot baking stone and bake for 5 to 7 minutes, until the cheese is melted and the bottom and edges are golden brown. (Time and temperature will vary if baking in a wood fired pizza oven or on a grill.) Cut into slices and serve hot. Unbaked rounds of dough can be frozen for up to 1 month. Lay on baking sheets and put in your freezer; thaw at room temperature. If your freezer isn't large enough, wrap individual balls of dough in plastic wrap and freeze. Remove and let thaw at room temperature for 1 hour or thaw overnight in the refrigerator. Then proceed with shaping and proofing the dough.

uncooked tomato sauce for pizza

makes 3½ cups sauce

This is our favorite pizza sauce. It cooks on the pizza and its fresh flavor lets the dough and toppings come together as a harmonious whole. Some people prefer a cooked sauce, and that's easy enough to make or buy, but our favorite wood-burning pizza joints use uncooked sauce, and now you can too.

One 28-ounce / 794-gram can San Marzano whole peeled tomatoes

1 teaspoon / 6 grams fine sea salt

Open the can of tomatoes and pour everything into a bowl. Add the salt and crush the tomatoes with your hands, mixing in the salt, until there are only small pieces of tomato in the sauce. Use immediately, or cover and refrigerate for up to a week.

The dough will rise to about twice its original volume.

Pizza Dough, fully risen and ready to chill.

Chilled Pizza Dough, ready to portion.

Shape Pizza Dough into circles for a final rising before baking.

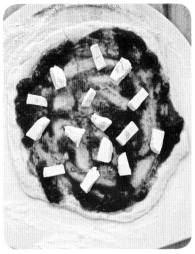

Remember to dust the peel with rice flour before baking.

Grilled Garlic and Onion Flatbread is great for cradling grilled lamb, marinated cucumbers, and a little yogurt and hot sauce.

grilled garlic and *onion flatbread*

makes 8 flatbreads

The flavors of this easy flatbread marry well with a variety of cuisines. The garlic and onion are pureed in the blender, turning them into a liquid that is easily dispersed throughout the dough. We include a combination of cumin, soy sauce, and Bragg Liquid Amino (a seasoning liquid fermented from non-GMO soybeans and water) to round out the flavor and add a hint of umami.

The little bit of yeast in the recipe adds more flavor than leavening, as the dough slowly ferments during its resting period. The majority of what happens on the grill is steam leavening, the liquid inside the dough expanding to make the flatbreads light and puffy, though still sturdy enough to stand up to a grilled sausage—or grilled kebabs, chops, or fish. We like these in the summertime, when we're cooking outdoors. We grill the proteins, then the vegetables, and finally the breads. We do grilled chicken with guacamole and pico de gallo. Or grilled lamb with marinated cucumbers, yogurt, and hot sauce. Sometimes we like sliced flank steak with grilled corn, the kernels sliced off the cob and tossed with diced ripe tomatoes and fresh basil. Grilled shrimp and summer squash tossed with fresh pesto also work well, or even grilled marinated portabellos with ginger coleslaw.

1 garlic clove

1 medium onion, sliced

1½ teaspoons / 9 grams herb salt or fine sea salt

½ teaspoon / 3 grams soy sauce

½ teaspoon / 3 grams Bragg Liquid Aminos (optional)

½ teaspoon / 1 gram ground cumin

3⅓ cups / 430 grams Gluten-Free Flour Blend (What IiF Flour 3.0, page 29, Batch-3 Flour, page 30, or Aki's Low-Allergy Blend, page 31)

½ teaspoon / 1.5 grams instant yeast

recipe continues

Put the garlic, onion, salt, soy sauce, liquid aminos, if using, and cumin in a blender and puree until smooth.

Add enough water, using the measurement on the side of the blender, to make 16 ounces of liquid.

Put the flour and yeast in a medium bowl and whisk to blend. Pour the liquid into the flour and mix with a rubber spatula until a dough comes together. Turn the dough out onto a clean countertop and knead it a few times until smooth.

Put the dough in a clean bowl, cover with plastic wrap, and let sit at room temperature for at least 1 hour, and up to 6 hours. You want to make sure that the flour is fully hydrated. (You can also wrap the dough in plastic wrap and refrigerate it for up to 24 hours. Let it come to room temperature for at least 30 minutes before rolling out.)

Preheat a grill to medium-high.

Divide the dough into 8 equal pieces about 3 ounces / 85 grams each. On a clean counter-top, roll each one out into a round approximately ¼ inch thick. The rounds can be stacked on a plate as you make them, with parchment or plastic wrap between them.

Lay the flatbreads on the grill and cook for 2 minutes. Give them a quarter turn and cook for 1 to 2 minutes more, until they rise and there are nice grill marks on the bottoms. Flip the flatbreads and cook for 2 minutes. Give them all a quarter turn and cook for another 1 to 2 minutes, until they are well marked on the second side and cooked through. Transfer to a basket or large bowl lined with a cloth napkin and serve immediately.

Kneaded Garlic and Onion Flatbread dough, ready for steam leavening on the grill.

focaccia de recco

serves 8 to 12 as a starter or side dish

This stuffed cheese bread originated in Recco, a little town in Liguria, Italy. It is fun to serve for a crowd. For our nontraditional version, we use a combination of sharp cheddar cheese and creamy Fontina. As the cheese melts inside the dough, it creates steam that makes the bread puff dramatically in the oven as it turns a deep golden brown. It collapses as it cools, the scent of warm cheese streaming through the kitchen, and then you cut it into bite-sized pieces.

The slightly salty cheese squeaks between your teeth, having morphed into something chewier and more intense than it was before cooking. The bread is thin and almost cracker-like, providing a contrasting crunch—which brings to mind cheese and crackers, presented in a whole new way.

1⅓ cups / 200 grams Gluten-Free Flour Blend (What IiF Flour 3.0, page 29, Batch-3 Flour, page 30, or Aki's Low-Allergy Blend, page 31)

¼ teaspoon / 1.5 grams fine sea salt

¼ teaspoon / 1.5 grams instant yeast

3 tablespoons / 42 grams olive oil, plus additional for brushing the breads

½ cup / 115 grams warm water

1½ cups / 5¼ ounces / 150 grams grated sharp cheddar cheese

1½ cups / 5¼ ounces / 150 grams grated Fontina cheese

Coarse sea salt

Freshly ground black pepper

Mix the flour, salt, and yeast together in a large bowl. Stir in the olive oil and use your fingertips to mix it evenly into the flour. The flour will take on the appearance of coarse sand. Stir in the warm water and knead the mass into a soft, sticky dough.

Dust some flour onto your work surface turn the dough out, and knead for 5 minutes, or until it is smooth and silky. Invert a clean bowl over the top of the dough and let it rest for 15 minutes.

recipe continues

Uncover the dough and knead it for another 5 minutes. Lightly flour the inside of the bowl and put the dough inside. Cover the bowl with plastic wrap and let the dough rise in a warm spot for 3 hours, or until it roughly doubles in volume.

Turn the dough out, flatten, and fold it from the top down to the middle, then rotate a quarter turn. Do this fold 3 more times, then put the dough back in the bowl, seam side down, cover, and let it rise for another 3 hours.

Preheat the oven to 500°F. (260°C.). Line a 13-by-18-inch baking sheet with a silicone mat or parchment paper.

Line the counter top with two 20-inch-long sheets of overlapping plastic wrap. Divide the dough into 2 equal pieces and roll each one into a ball. Put one ball on the plastic wrap and cover it with two more overlapping sheets. Roll the dough out into a thin sheet about the size of the baking sheet. Remove the top layer of plastic and invert the dough into the prepared baking pan; remove the remaining plastic wrap. Cover the dough with the cheese, leaving a ½-inch border of dough uncovered.

Roll the second ball of dough out into an equal-sized rectangle and lay it over the cheese-covered dough. Fold the edges of the bottom dough up over the top dough, pinching the edges together all around. Brush the top with olive oil, sprinkle with coarse salt, and grind black pepper over the top.

Bake the bread for 15 minutes, or until the dough is bubbly, golden, and crispy. Remove from the oven and allow the bread to rest for 5 minutes.

Slide the bread onto a cutting board and cut it lengthwise in half, then cut each half into 6 slices. Serve warm.

Roll out the bottom layer of Focaccia de Recco dough.

Cover the bottom layer of the dough with cheese.

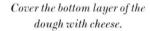

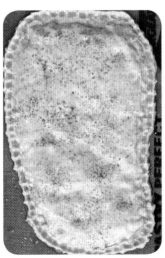

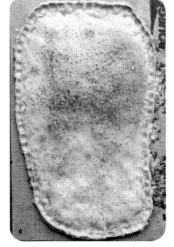

Pinch the layers together by folding the bottom layer over the top, then season with olive oil, salt, and pepper.

Piping hot Focaccia de Recco straight from the oven, golden brown and crispy on top.

Crunchy, cheesy Focaccia de Recco (page 119), ready to serve.

water crackers

makes about 2 dozen crackers

These crackers are light and crisp, with a faintly fruity flavor from the olive oil. The baking powder gives the dough a bit of extra lift so the crackers have small air bubbles throughout. The dough comes together easily and can be rolled out very thin. We like to keep these plain for versatility, but you could sprinkle them with sesame or poppy seeds if you prefer. They are perfect alongside the Baked Brie (page 173) or with a cheese platter.

1¾ cups / 230 grams Gluten-Free Flour Blend (What IiF Flour 3.0, page 29, Batch-3 Flour, page 30, or Aki's Low-Allergy Blend, page 31)

½ teaspoon / 3 grams baking powder

½ teaspoon / 3 grams fine sea salt

½ cup + 2 tablespoons / 150 grams water

2 tablespoons / 28 grams extra virgin olive oil

Position the racks in the upper and lower thirds of the oven and preheat the oven to 400°F. (200°C.). Line two 13-by-18-inch baking sheets with parchment paper.

Put the flour, baking powder, and salt in the bowl of a stand mixer fitted with the paddle attachment (or use a hand mixer) and mix on low to blend. Increase the speed to medium and pour in the water. The flour will form little balls and the mixture will look like a rough streusel. Pour in the olive oil and increase the speed to medium-high. The dough will come together into a rough mass.

Turn the dough out onto a clean countertop and knead until smooth, about 5 minutes.

Divide the dough into 2 pieces. Lay two 24-inch-long pieces of plastic wrap on the countertop, overlapping them slightly. Put one piece of dough in the center of the plastic wrap and cover it with two more overlapping pieces of plastic. Use a rolling pin to roll the dough into a rough rectangle about 12 by 16 inches and ⅛ inch thick. Remove the top layer of plastic wrap and use a 2-inch round cutter to cut out crackers. Use a fork or dough docker to poke holes across the surface of the dough. This will prevent the crackers from rising too much.

recipe continues

Use an offset spatula to transfer the crackers to one of the prepared baking sheets, leaving at least 2 inches of space between them. Combine the scraps of dough with the second dough ball and roll out as you did the first one. Cut out crackers and arrange on the second baking sheet. (The scraps can be pressed together, rolled out, and baked separately to use for cracker crumbs.)

Bake the crackers for 6 minutes, then rotate the pans, top to bottom and front to back, and bake for 6 more minutes. The crackers will puff slightly and should be light brown and dry. If they are still moist, bake them for an additional 3 minutes or so, until dry. Remove the crackers from the baking pan and transfer to a rack to cool.

The crackers can be kept in an airtight container at room temperature for up to a week.

Light, crisp Water Crackers.

cheddar cheese coins with sesame seeds

makes about 2½ dozen crackers

We love these flaky little crackers. They taste like the essence of cheddar cheese and are so much better than those little fish crackers the kids eat. We added some sesame seeds for a background nuttiness and crunch. Add a pinch of cayenne or jalapeño powder if your taste runs that way, but we like these just as they are, super-cheesy—and Amaya, our daughter approved them too.

1⅓ cups / 170 grams Gluten-Free Flour Blend (What IiF Flour 3.0, page 29,
   Batch-3 Flour, page 30, or Aki's Low-Allergy Blend, page 31), plus more for dusting

4 ounces / 113 grams extra sharp cheddar cheese, shredded

1 teaspoon / 6 grams fine sea salt

8 tablespoons / 4 ounces / 113 grams cold unsalted butter, diced

1 large egg yolk

2 tablespoons / 28 grams cold water

¼ cup / 36 grams sesame seeds

Put the flour, cheddar cheese, and salt in a food processor and pulse 3 or 4 times to blend. Add the butter and pulse 3 or 4 times, or until the mixture resembles coarse meal. Add the egg yolk and water and pulse 2 or 3 times. Add the sesame seeds and pulse 1 or 2 more times. The dough should resemble small pebbles and hold together when you squeeze a bit in your hand.

Turn the dough out onto a floured countertop in a pile. Sprinkle the top lightly with flour. Starting at one end, use the heel of your hand to smear a small amount of the dough at a time against the counter. Do this quickly, being sure not to work any sections of dough more than once. (This technique, known as *fraisage*, forms flaky layers of fat and flour.) Once all of the dough has been layered, pull it together and knead it 1 or 2 times, then form it into a rough log.

Put the dough on a large piece of plastic wrap and use it to roll the log to a length of about 15 inches (or make two 7½-inch logs it that seems more manageable). Wrap in the plastic wrap and chill for at least 3 hours, or as long as overnight.

Position the racks in the upper and lower thirds of the oven and preheat the oven to 375°F. (190°C.). Line two baking sheets with parchment paper.

Unwrap the log of dough and slice into ½-inch-thick rounds. Arrange them on the prepared pans, about 1 inch apart.

Bake for 15 to 18 minutes, until the crackers are set. Let them cool for 5 minutes on the pans then transfer to wire racks to cool completely.

The cheese coins will keep in an airtight container at room temperature for up to a week.

brown-butter crackers

makes about 3 dozen crackers

Modeled after the classic Ritz cracker, these rich, buttery crackers are slightly sweet with a haunting nuttiness from the brown butter. The flavor of the brown butter is amplified by the toasted milk solids. The caramelized milk solids add richness to the crackers through flavor, not fat.

16 tablespoons (2 sticks) / 8 ounces / 225 grams unsalted butter

2¼ cups / 295 grams Gluten-Free Flour Blend (What IiF Flour 3.0, page 29, Batch-3 Flour, page 30, or Aki's Low-Allergy Blend, page 31)

1 tablespoon / 12.5 grams sugar

1 teaspoon / 6 grams fine sea salt

1 teaspoon / 5 grams baking powder

3 tablespoons / 15 grams sifted Toasted Milk Powder (page 15)

1 large egg

½ cup / 120 grams buttermilk

Maldon salt for sprinkling the crackers

Position the racks in the upper and lower thirds of the oven and preheat the oven to 375°F. (190°C.). Line two large baking sheets with parchment paper.

Put 6 ounces of the butter in a medium saucepan and melt over medium heat, whisking constantly as it sizzles and pops. When the butter stops sputtering, continue to whisk, scraping the bottom of the pan so the milk solids do not stick and scorch, until the milk solids turn light brown and the butter is fragrant and nutty. Remove from the heat and let the butter cool to room temperature.

Put the flour, sugar, salt, baking powder, and toasted milk solids in the bowl of a stand mixer fitted with the paddle attachment (or use a hand mixer) and mix on low to blend. With the mixer on low slowly drizzle in the brown butter, with the brown butter solids. The dough will become crumbly.

Whisk the egg with the milk and pour into the mixer, increase the speed to medium-high, and mix until the dough comes together into a ball. Remove the dough from the mixer and knead it for a minute or so on your countertop, just to bring everything together in a smooth mass.

Divide the dough into 2 pieces. Lay out two 24-inch-long pieces of plastic wrap on the countertop, overlapping them slightly. Put one piece of dough in the center of the plastic wrap and cover with two more overlapping pieces of plastic. Use a rolling pin to roll the dough to a thickness of about ⅛ inch. Remove the top layer of plastic wrap and use a 2-inch round cutter to cut out crackers. Use a fork or dough docker to poke holes across the surface of the dough; this will prevent the crackers from rising too much. Use an offset spatula to transfer the crackers to one of the prepared baking sheets, leaving at least 2 inches of space between them. Combine the scraps of dough with the second dough ball and roll out as you did the first one. Cut out crackers and arrange on the second baking sheet. (The scraps can be pressed together, rolled out, and baked separately to use for cracker crumbs.)

Put the pans of crackers in the oven and bake for 8 minutes. Rotate the pans top to bottom and front to back and bake for 4 minutes longer.

Meanwhile, melt the remaining 2 ounces butter in a small saucepan over medium heat, whisking constantly as it sizzles and pops, and cook to brown butter as above. Remove from the heat, and let the butter cool to room temperature.

Remove the crackers from the oven, brush them with the brown butter, and sprinkle lightly with sea salt. Put them back in the oven and bake them for 4 more minutes, or until just set and golden brown around the edges. Remove the pans from the oven and let the crackers cool completely on the pans.

Store the crackers in a zip-top bag or airtight container for up to a week.

Brown-Butter Crackers, docked, laid out on a sheet pan, and ready to be baked.

Baked, lightly salted, flaky Brown-Butter Crackers cooling on a sheet pan.

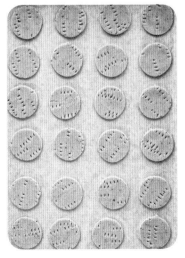

pasta and
dumplings

A plateful of fettuccine Egg Noodles with Pepperoni Bolognese.

egg noodles

serves 4 as a side dish

These egg noodles bring homemade pasta back to the gluten-free table. The dough comes together in a matter of minutes and the noodles boil up quickly. They have a tender, elastic texture and a light eggy flavor. You could use the dough to make long noodles like fettuccine and serve them with the Pepperoni Bolognese (page 135), or shorter wide noodles to serve buttered alongside braised beef or Stroganoff. Or make linguine and toss it with fresh vegetables and tomato sauce. The possibilities are endless.

1¾ cups / 230 grams Gluten-Free Flour Blend (What IiF Flour 3.0, page 29, Batch-3 Flour, page 30, or Aki's Low-Allergy Blend, page 31)

2 large eggs

2 tablespoons / 32.5 grams whole milk

Put the flour in a large bowl and make a well in the center of it. Whisk the eggs and milk in a small bowl and pour into the center of the flour. Use your fingers or a fork to mix the liquid into the flour and bring the dough together.

Turn the dough out onto the counter and knead, without adding any additional flour, until it becomes smooth and silky, about 5 minutes. Wrap in plastic wrap and let it rest at room temperature for at least 30 minutes before rolling it out.

Roll out the dough and cut into noodles following the directions for your pasta machine. Or roll the dough out by hand as thin as you can and cut into noodles.

Freshly rolled fettuccine noodles.

Seamless Ravioli, cooked and served in a pool of Pepperoni Bolognese.

seamless ravioli with pepperoni bolognese

serves 4

This is an incredibly simple technique that makes extraordinary "seamless" ravioli (sometimes called ravioli gnudi*). We make a seasoned cheese filling and drop small scoops of it into a bowl of flour. The moisture in the cheese attracts the flour, which coats the surface and then hydrates. Since this outer layer forms naturally around the cheese filling, there are no seams to burst when you cook the ravioli. When you drop the flour-coated balls into gently boiling water, the flour gelatinizes, forming a skin around the filling.*

The rich floral notes of the lemon zest in the ravioli help highlight the sweet, fruity nature of the tomatoes in the Pepperoni Bolognese and balance the rich flavors of the pepperoni and cheeses. The sauce recipe makes a double batch, so you can freeze half for a rainy day.

seamless ravioli (makes about 50)

2 cups / 500 grams whole-milk ricotta

1 large egg

1 ounce / 30 grams Parmigiano-Reggiano cheese, grated

¼ teaspoon / 1.5 grams fine sea salt

¼ teaspoon / 0.55 gram freshly ground black pepper

Grated zest of 1 lemon, preferably a Meyer lemon

4 cups / 520 grams Gluten-Free Flour Blend (What IiF Flour 3.0, page 29, Batch-3 Flour, page 30, or Aki's Low-Allergy Blend, page 31)

pepperoni bolognese

1¼ pounds / 575 grams pepperoni, casing removed

2 large onions, sliced

¼ cup / 56 grams olive oil

2 cups / 450 grams full-bodied red wine

Two 28-ounce / 794-gram cans whole peeled San Marzano tomatoes

Freshly grated Parmigiano Reggiano for serving

recipe continues

To make the ravioli, put the ricotta, egg, cheese, salt, pepper and lemon zest into a medium bowl and use a rubber spatula to stir the ingredients together. Put half of the flour on a baking sheet, in a large baking dish, on a tray, forming a thick bed. Put the remaining flour into a medium bowl. Use a teaspoon to form a ball of the ricotta mixture, drop into the bowl of flour, and gently cover the ball with flour, then use your hand to scoop up the ball and put it on the bed of flour. Continue to scoop and cover all of the ricotta in flour, then dust the tops and fill in the spaces between the balls with the remaining flour from the bowl. Invert a second baking sheet (or dish or tray) over the ricotta balls and refrigerate overnight.

The following morning, remove the sheet from the refrigerator and flip over the ricotta balls. They will have absorbed the flour and be firm to the touch. Cover and refrigerate until ready to use, or for up to 3 days. Flip the ravioli daily so they to absorb flour evenly around their circumference.

To make the sauce, put the pepperoni and onions in a food processor and pulse the machine 4 or 5 times, then use a rubber spatula to scrape the sides of the bowl. Process for 15 seconds more, or until the pepperoni and onions are roughly minced.

Set a 4-quart pot over medium-high heat. When the pot is hot, add the olive oil, then add the pepperoni and onion mixture and stir to coat with oil. Turn the heat down to medium, cover the pot, leaving the lid slightly askew to let out a small trickle of steam, and simmer the pepperoni mixture for 30 minutes, stirring occasionally to make sure it does not stick. It will darken in color and fat will rise to the surface.

Pour the wine into the pot, stir, and mostly cover the pot. Cook the wine down until reduced by half, about 20 minutes.

Open the cans of tomatoes and pour them into a large bowl. Use your hands to crush the tomatoes into medium pieces. Remove the lid from the pot and stir in the tomatoes, then turn the heat down to low, mostly cover the pot, and cook the sauce for 1 hour, or until it has thickened and darkened in color. It will be rich and spicy, with a slight tang from the wine and pepperoni. Remove from the heat and let cool for 30 minutes.

Put the sauce into a large bowl set over an ice bath to cool completely. You only need half the sauce for the ravioli, so divide it between two containers. The sauce can be stored an airtight container in the refrigerator for up to a week or frozen for 2 months.

When ready to serve, transfer the ravioli to a clean tray. Bring a large pot of water to a boil and salt the water generously. Reheat the sauce in a medium pot.

Add the ravioli to the boiling water and cook for 3 minutes.

Transfer the ravioli to the pot of sauce and cook for another minute or so, so they cook through and absorb some of the sauce. Serve immediately, with grated Parmigiano-Reggiano.

NOTE: "Boiling salted water" is such an abstract term, but it's hard to specify the exact amount of salt for every recipe because we all use different pots. Instead, we'll give you a ratio: For cooking pasta, we use 2 percent salt by weight for the boiling water. So for every liter of water, that's 20 grams of salt, or in U.S. terms, for every quart of water, 1 tablespoon of fine sea salt.

See process photographs on the following page

Scoop balls of Seamless Ravioli filling (page 135) one at a time into a bowl of flour and transfer to a tray of flour to be buried.

The filling will absorb the flour and form a seamless outer shell of hydrated flour.

After a day in the fridge, turn the Seamless Ravioli in their bed of flour to ensure an even coating.

Finished Seamless Ravioli, with a pasta skin encasing the filling, ready to cook.

Cook and cut through a few Seamless Ravioli to test the skin.

Mince pepperoni and onions for Bolognese sauce in a food processor.

potato gnocchi

Alex learned to make gnocchi at the restaurant Clio in Boston. He made them almost every day for months, and his were some of the best. Good gnocchi are light and tender, like little pillows. They have a rich potato flavor and are equally at home swimming in meat sauce or drenched in melted butter. There's a lot of talk about tough, rubbery dumplings as a result of overworking the potatoes, but as long as you move quickly and have a light touch, your gnocchi should be perfect. The fact that there's no gluten in the flour blend only helps the cause.

2½ pounds / 1.15 kilograms russet potatoes, peeled

1½ teaspoons / 9 grams fine sea salt

2 large egg yolks

1¼ cups / 160 grams Gluten-Free Flour Blend (What IiF Flour 3.0, page 29, Batch-3 Flour, page 30, or Aki's Low-Allergy Blend, page 31)

2 ounces / 60 grams Parmigiano-Reggiano cheese, grated

Put the potatoes in a heatproof bowl that fits inside a pressure cooker. Season the potatoes with the salt. Put 1 inch of water in the bottom of the pressure cooker and put the bowl inside. Cook the potatoes on high pressure for 20 minutes. Let the pressure release naturally.

Remove the potatoes from the pressure cooker and press them through a food mill or potato ricer into a bowl. Use a bench scraper to chop the egg yolks into the warm potatoes, moving quickly so the yolks don't cook before they are incorporated. Sprinkle the flour over the potatoes and use the bench scraper to fold it in. Sprinkle the cheese over the potato mixture and fold it. Knead the dough just until smooth.

Turn the dough out and cut into 4 pieces of approximately equal size. Roll each piece into cylinder approximately ½ inch thick. Cut the cylinders into 1-inch pieces. Roll the pieces of dough on a gnocchi board if you have one, or use a fork to give them the characteristic ridges. Lay out the gnocchi on a parchment-paper-lined baking sheet and refrigerate until cold, at least 30 minutes.

recipe continues

Bring a large pot of water to a boil. Add the gnocchi and cook for 3 to 4 minutes. Cut one open to be sure they are cooked through: it should be fully hydrated and a uniform color throughout. Undercooked gnocchi have a slightly darker, dense center.

Transfer the gnocchi to a pot of sauce and cook for an additional 2 to 3 minutes, then serve.

Shaped Potato Gnocchi, ready to be cooked.

kimchi cavatelli with bulgogi sauce

serves 6 as a main course

Korean food is one of our favorite cuisines. We love its big, bold flavors, accented with sweetness and spice. Bulgogi is a classic dish made with grilled marinated beef, and we've taken those traditional flavors and turned them into a braised beef sauce. The kick comes from the cavatelli, which is infused with spicy kimchi. It's a sensational combination and one we especially enjoy as the weather turns cold.

bulgogi sauce

4½ cups / 1 kilo Asian pear or apple cider

2 cups / 470 grams kimchi

2 large onions, sliced

½ cup + 1 tablespoon + 1 teaspoon / 150 grams soy sauce

3 ounces / 85 grams fresh ginger, peeled and sliced

4 teaspoons / 10 grams smoked paprika

One 5-pound / 2250 gram boneless first-cut chuck shoulder roast

Fine sea salt

½ cup / 113 grams peanut or vegetable oil

2 large onions

5 medium carrots, peeled

4 large Asian or ripe Bosc pears, peeled and cored

6 scallions, white and green parts

6 garlic cloves

kimchi cavatelli

1½ cups / 397.5 grams kimchi

1 cup / 225 grams whole-milk ricotta cheese

1 large egg

3½ cups / 455 grams Gluten-Free Flour Blend (What IiF Flour 3.0, page 29,
   Batch-3 Flour, page 30, or Aki's Low-Allergy Blend, page 31), or as needed

6 scallions, white and green parts, finely sliced, for garnish

Preheat the oven to 250°F. (120°C.).

To make the braising liquid, put the cider, kimchi, sliced onions, soy sauce, ginger, and smoked paprika into a blender. Turn the blender on low, gradually increase the speed to high, and puree the mixture for 30 seconds, or until smooth. Strain the marinade through a fine-mesh strainer into a large bowl.

Put the chuck roast on a cutting board. Use a sharp knife to cut a crosshatch pattern, making the cut ½ inch deep ½ inch apart, over the entire surface of the meat. Sprinkle salt generously all over the shoulder.

Heat a heavy-bottomed skillet over medium-high heat. Add the peanut oil. When the oil shimmers, carefully put the beef shoulder into the pan and brown the shoulder for 3 minutes on the first side, about 3 minutes. Use a meat fork and a large kitchen spoon to lift the meat and flip it over. Brown the second side of the meat, about 3 minutes. Brown the meat on all sides, using the fork and spoon to help balance the shoulder in the pan. Then sear the top and bottom of the shoulder again if they are not deeply browned and caramelized. Transfer the shoulder to the bowl with the braising liquid.

Put the onions, carrots, pears, scallions, and garlic into a food processor and pulse 10 times to roughly mince the vegetables.

Put the vegetables, beef shoulder, and braising liquid into a large (12-quart) ovenproof pot set over medium heat. When the liquid comes to a simmer, cover the pot, put it in the oven, and cook the beef for 6 hours. The meat should be almost covered with liquid but browned on top, look as if it's starting to fall apart, and be fork-tender. Let the meat cool, uncovered in the sauce for 30 minutes.

Transfer the meat to a cutting board. Pour the sauce into a large bowl. Use a fork and spoon to shred the meat, discarding the chunks of fat and connective tissue, and put it back into the sauce. Cool the bulgogi sauce over an ice bath. Once it's completely cold, cover and refrigerate overnight.

To make the pasta, put the kimchi, ricotta, and egg in a blender. Turn the blender on low, gradually increase the speed to medium-high, and puree until smooth, about 30 seconds. Strain the mixture through a fine-mesh strainer.

Put the flour in the bowl of a food processor. Add the kimchi mixture and process until a soft, firm dough forms. Turn the dough out onto a lightly floured countertop and knead until smooth and silky. Depending upon the consistency of the kimchi and the ricotta, you may

recipe continues

pasta and dumplings   *143*

need to add a few more tablespoons of flour to the dough. Shape the dough into a ball, wrap in plastic wrap, and let rest for at least 30 minutes.

Flour a large baking sheet. Using a rolling pin, roll the dough out on a clean work surface to a thickness of about ¼ inch. Cut into ½-inch-wide strips.

Work with one strip at a time, keeping the remaining strips covered with a damp towel so they don't dry out. Cut each strip into ½-inch squares, using a butter knife or bench scraper. Turn each square diagonally and drag the butter knife or bench scraper at a 45-degree angle across the square from left to right: the pasta will curl along the blade of your implement, leaving you with a beautifully shaped cavatelli. It may take a few tries to master the technique, but once you develop a rhythm, things move quickly. Alternatively, for ridged cavatelli, roll each square of dough over the tines of a fork, folding and rolling the dough over itself and creating ridged pasta, or use a gnocchi board. Lay the finished pasta out on the floured baking sheet. Cook the cavatelli immediately or freeze. Freeze on the baking sheet until frozen hard, then transfer to a zip-top bag and freeze for up to 1 month; cook directly from their frozen state.

To serve, put the bulgogi sauce in a large pot and bring to a simmer over low heat, stirring occasionally. Meanwhile, bring a large pot of salted water to a boil over medium-high heat.

Cook the cavatelli in the boiling water for 5 minutes, or until just cooked through but with a little bit of chew to them. Use a skimmer to transfer the cavatelli to the sauce and cook for 2 to 3 minutes longer. Serve in warm bowls, topped with the thinly sliced scallions.

3 ways to shape Kimchi Cavatelli: Use a knife, a fork, or a gnocchi board.

Kimchi Cavatelli glazed with Bulgogi Sauce and topped with thinly sliced scallions.

masa malloredus

serves 8 as a side dish or starter

Malloredus, also known as Sardinian gnocchi, and cavatelli are the same shape (you can use a gnocchi board to form malloredus). The difference is in the texture. Traditional malloredus are made entirely with semolina flour and have a bit more bite and chew than cavatelli. For this gluten-free version, we made the dough with masa harina, to create that same strong texture. The malloredus have a nutty corn flavor that makes them a wonderful accompaniment to a rich chili, or serve them simply glazed with butter and Parmesan or blue cheese. They keep well in the freezer, so you can make a big batch and have some on hand for your next craving.

1⅔ cups / 250 grams instant masa
250 grams Masa Harina Puree (page 13)
½ cup / 113 grams water

Put the masa flour into a bowl. Add the masa puree and use your fingertips to break it up and mix it with the flour. Sprinkle in the water and knead the dough until it is smooth and elastic.

Wrap the dough in plastic wrap and refrigerate for 30 minutes.

Flour a large baking sheet.

Remove the dough from the refrigerator. Using a rolling pin, roll the dough out ½ inch thick. Cut the dough into ½-inch squares. Roll each square along a gnocchi board with your thumb so that it folds over itself, and transfer to the baking sheet.

Refrigerate the malloredus if cooking the same day. Or freeze them on the baking sheet until frozen hard, then transfer to a zip-top bag and freeze for up to a month; cook directly from frozen.

To serve, cook the malloredus in a large pot of boiling salted water until just tender, but with a nice chew to them. Fold into a warm sauce or ragout and serve immediately.

Finished Masa Harina Puree in a food processor.

Shape the Masa Malloredus by cutting the dough into small squares, rolling each into a ball, and molding against a fork.

Boiled Masa Malloredus, glazed with butter and cheese for a test bite.

agnolotti

serves 6 to 8 as a starter or side dish

Agnolotti is a small, filled Italian pasta traditionally made in a half moon or three-pointed triangular shape, said to resemble a priest's hat (the name means "priests' caps.") Here in the United States, thanks to Thomas Keller and his iconic French Laundry Cookbook, *agnolotti are more often a stuffed pasta with three scalloped edges. That's the model we used for inspiration. We filled these light and tender agnolotti with creamy cheddar cheese sauce to create inside-out macaroni and cheese. We use a bit of sodium citrate (also known as sour salt) to emulsify and stabilize the cheese sauce. It helps keep the fats in the cheese in suspension as the agnolotti cook. Once cooked, they need nothing more than some brown butter and a handful of chopped chives to finish them. Eat these as a starter, along with a salad, or serve them as a side dish with roasted chicken, fish, or mushrooms.*

dough

1¾ cups / 227.5 grams Gluten-Free Flour Blend (What IiF Flour 3.0, page 29, Batch-3 Flour, page 30, or Aki's Low-Allergy Blend, page 31), or as needed

½ cup / 35 grams powdered egg whites

1 large egg

5 large egg yolks

2 tablespoons / 30 grams whole milk

1 tablespoon / 14 grams olive oil

cheddar cheese filling

1 cup / 260 grams whole milk

1 tablespoon / 15 grams sodium citrate (see Sources, page 351)

¼ teaspoon / 0.5 gram cayenne

1 pound 2 ounces / 500 grams sharp cheddar cheese, grated

Cornmeal for dusting

To mix the dough by hand, put the flour and powdered egg whites in a large bowl and whisk to blend. Form a well in the center of the flour.

Put the egg, yolks, milk, and olive oil in a small bowl and whisk together, then pour into the well. Use your fingers or a fork to begin stirring from the center outward, gradually incorporating the flour until the mixture forms a soft dough.

Turn the entire contents of the bowl out onto your countertop and knead with your hands, pulling in more flour as needed, until you have a smooth, silky dough. Cover with plastic wrap and let rest for 30 minutes.

To make the dough with a food processor, put the flour and powdered egg whites in the processor bowl and pulse to blend. Add the egg, egg yolks, milk, and olive oil and pulse 5 times, or until the mixture comes together into a rough dough.

Turn the dough out onto a lightly floured surface and knead, adding additional flour as needed, until it becomes smooth and silky. Cover with plastic wrap and let rest for 30 minutes.

To make the filling, put the milk, sodium citrate, and cayenne into a medium saucepan and bring to a simmer over medium heat, stirring with a silicone spatula. Slowly stir in handfuls of the cheese, allowing each one to mostly melt before the next addition. Turn the heat down to low and cook, stirring, for 30 seconds longer to make sure all the cheese is melted. Transfer the cheese mixture to a bowl and set over an ice bath to cool, stirring occasionally. The filling will thicken as it cools.

When the cheese mixture is cold, put it into a piping bag fitted with a ½-inch plain tip. Refrigerate until you are ready to make the agnolotti.

To shape the agnolotti, divide the dough into thirds. Work with one piece at a time and keep the rest wrapped in plastic wrap. Set the rollers of a pasta machine at the widest setting and roll the dough through the machine at least three times, folding the dough between runs so that it is of uniform thickness with smooth edges. Dust with flour if the dough is sticky or feels tacky, but do this judiciously, because too much flour will prevent the dough from adhering to itself when it is folded over. Set the machine to the next setting and roll the dough through it twice. Continue in this manner with each consecutively lower setting until the dough is thin enough that you can see your hand through it, but not as fragile as tissue paper.

recipe continues

Lay the sheet of dough out horizontally on a lightly floured work surface. Take the pastry bag from the refrigerator and pipe a uniform log of the filling down the center of the strip of dough, leaving a ½-inch border at each end. Fold the dough over, encasing the tube of filling. Using your thumb and the pad of your hand, press the dough over onto itself and around the tube of filling, aligning the edges of dough and pressing out any air pockets, so that the filling is completely and uniformly encased in dough.

Hold both your hands above the dough, with your thumbs and forefingers in a pinching position, and, starting at the left end of the dough, and keeping ¾-inch-between your hands, pinch the pasta and the filling together so that a pillow of dough and filling is formed. The pinching action will create a flat spacer, about ¾ inch wide, on either side of the filling. Move your hands to the right so that your left hand will repinch the space initially formed by your right hand while you use your right hand to help create a second pasta pillow. Continue moving along the entire length of the pasta. Then double-check the spacing making sure the spaces in between are completely flat and the filling has been forced into plump pillows on either side of each space.

Using a fluted pasta cutter, trim the long open edge of the dough ¾ inch from the bottom of the pasta pillows; discard the trim. Then, starting at the folded edge, roll the cutter between the pillows of pasta to separate the agnolotti; use one continuous motion per cut. The cutting will fold the edges of the pasta dough in on themselves, sealing the edges. Place the agnolotti on a cornmeal-dusted baking sheet and cover loosely with a tea towel.

Repeat the process with the remaining dough and filling.

Refrigerate the pasta if you will be cooking it the same day, or freeze it. Freeze the agnolotti on the baking sheet until frozen hard, then transfer to a zip-top bag and freeze for up to 4 weeks. Cook directly from the frozen state.

Cook the agnolotti in a large pot of boiling salted water until tender, 2 to 3 minutes for fresh pasta, 5 to 6 minutes for frozen. Taste the pasta to check the texture before draining it. Toss with sauce and serve immediately.

NOTE: *Sodium citrate, also known as sour salt, is used in the agnolotti filling to make it smooth and creamy. It has a salty and slightly tart flavor, hence the name. It is an emulsifier and in this case binds the fat into the cheese mixture to keep it from separating out of the sauce and becoming greasy.*

A plate of assorted steamed and fried Asian Dumplings (page 152) and dipping sauce.

asian dumplings

*makes about 2 dozen Chinese-style dumplings or
3 dozen Japanese-style dumplings*

*These are a family favorite. There could be some quibbling about whether they
are Japanese gyoza or Chinese jiaozi. In our minds, it comes down mainly to
the size of the dumplings and the thickness of the dough. In restaurants, Chinese dumplings tend to be bigger, with a thicker skin, and Japanese dumplings
are smaller, with a thin skin. You can roll these out however you please. Cooked
properly, they will have slightly chewy skins and a crisp bottom. We are giving
you our favorite pork filling, but you could substitute an equal amount of
chopped sautéed mushrooms for the meat to make them vegetarian.*

dough

2⅓ cups / 300 grams Gluten-Free Flour Blend (What IiF Flour 3.0, page 29,
    Batch-3 Flour, page 30, or Aki's Low-Allergy Blend, page 31)

¾ cup / 170 grams water

pork filling

1 pound / 455 grams ground pork

2 cups / 200 grams Napa cabbage, finely shredded, and then finely chopped

4 scallions, white and green parts, finely sliced

2 garlic cloves, minced

1 tablespoon / 6.25 grams minced peeled fresh ginger

¼ cup / 56 grams water

2 tablespoons / 33 grams soy sauce, preferably tamari

1 tablespoon / 14 grams Asian sesame oil

1 tablespoon / 15 grams finely chopped pickled ginger

¼ teaspoon / 1.5 grams fine sea salt

dipping sauce

½ cup / 130 grams soy sauce, preferably tamari

¼ cup / 56 grams rice vinegar

1 tablespoon / 14 grams Asian sesame or chile oil

3 scallions, white and green parts, thinly sliced

Peanut or vegetable oil, for cooking

To make the dough, put the flour in a medium bowl. Put the water in a microwave-safe measuring cup and microwave for 1 minute. It should be hot but not quite boiling. Pour the water into the flour, stirring with a fork. Once the dough begins to come together, switch to your hands, scraping any dough from the fork into the bowl. The dough will be very warm; wait a minute or two if it is too hot to handle, then press and knead it until it comes together in a rough ball.

Turn the dough out onto the countertop and knead it until it becomes smooth and silky, 3 to 5 minutes. Wrap the dough in plastic wrap and let it rest at room temperature for at least 30 minutes, and up to 3 hours before using. It will soften as it rests. (The dough can also be refrigerated for up to 2 days. Let it come to room temperature for at least 30 minutes before rolling it out.)

Meanwhile, make the filling: Put the ground pork, Napa cabbage, scallions, garlic, fresh ginger, water, soy sauce, sesame oil, pickled ginger, and salt in a medium bowl and mix well, so that everything is evenly distributed. Cover and refrigerate.

To assemble the dumplings, line a baking sheet with parchment paper and dust it with flour. Divide the dough in half. It may be sticky—if so, sprinkle it with flour. Cover one half of the dough with plastic wrap. Roll the other half out into a log approximately 1 inch in diameter. Cut the log into pieces 1 to 1½ inches thick, depending on whether you want larger or smaller dumplings. Using a rolling pin, roll each piece out into a circle, getting the dough as thin as you can without tearing it. Put 1 to 2 teaspoons of filling in the center of each circle, depending on the size of your dumplings, leaving a ½ inch border all around the filling. (If the dough is dry, you can wet the edges with your finger.) Lift up a dumpling and, beginning on one side, press and pleat the edges together, moving along the circumference of the dumpling, pleating one side only as you press it against the flat back side of the dough, until the dumpling is sealed. The first dumpling is something of a tester, as it will give you a feel for the amount of filling that works comfortably and the technique of pleating the dough; each successive dumpling will be easier. Lay the finished dumpling on the prepared baking sheet. Repeat until all of the dumplings are made.

recipe continues

Cover the dumplings loosely with plastic wrap and refrigerate until ready to cook, or up to 6 hours, or freeze them. Freeze on the baking sheet until frozen hard, then transfer to an airtight container and freeze for up to 1 month. Cook directly from the frozen state.

When you're ready to cook the dumplings, make the dipping sauce: Put the soy sauce, rice vinegar, sesame oil, and scallions in a small bowl and mix to blend. Set aside.

Set a large skillet over medium-high heat and add 2 tablespoons of peanut oil. Once the oil begins to shimmer, put about a dozen dumplings in the pan. They can be close together, but make sure that the bottoms are flat on the bottom of the pan. Once they brown on the bottom, about 2 minutes, pour in ½ cup water, or enough to coat the entire bottom of the pan, and put the lid on the pan. Let the dumplings steam for 2 to 3 minutes, until the water is gone, then take off the lid. Cook for 1 to 2 minutes longer, until the bottoms are dry and crisp. Use a spatula to remove the dumplings from the pan, putting them crispy bottom facing up on a serving plate or platter. Wipe out the pan, add more oil, and cook the remaining dumplings in batches. Serve immediately, with the dipping sauce alongside.

Logs of dumpling dough are cut into pieces, rolled out, stuffed with a scoop of filling, and pinched into finished dumplings. Then they are laid out on a tray and covered with a towel so they don't dry out while the rest are being made.

Dumplings cooking on a tray lined with parchment paper, in a stainless steel steamer.

Pan-frying Asian Dumplings.

manicotti with scallion crepes

Manicotti can be humdrum or delicious. Many restaurants simply serve tubes of pasta filled with cheese in a pool of tomato sauce. But some make their own delicate crepes, and the difference is something special. Maybe it's because you know someone took the time to make the crepes by hand. Truth be told, even with that step, these manicotti are not difficult to prepare. You can also assemble the whole casserole in advance, cover, and refrigerate until ready to bake, which makes this the perfect weeknight dinner for busy families on the go.

For the sauce, we use a combination of bacon and prosciutto ends. Our local markets sell both of these at a discount, and since we're going to grind them into the sauce, we don't need beautiful slices (if you don't have a grinder, you can use a food processor; see below). Ask around and you may find that your local supermarket will discount them for you, if not, you can use sliced. We cook them down with white wine and fire-roasted canned tomatoes to make a chunky sauce that is full of flavor.

sauce

8 ounces / 225 grams bacon ends (from high-quality, smoky bacon; see headnote)

8 ounces / 225 grams prosciutto ends (see headnote)

2 large onions

1⅓ cups / 300 grams dry white wine

One 28-ounce / 785 gram can crushed fire-roasted tomatoes

recipe continues

scallion crepes

6 scallions, white and green parts, trimmed

2 large eggs

¾ cup / 195 grams whole milk

¼ cup / 56 grams water

1 cup / 130 grams Gluten-Free Flour Blend (What IiF Flour 3.0, page 29,
   Batch-3 Flour, page 30, or Aki's Low-Allergy Blend, page 31)

3 tablespoons / 1½ ounces / 40 grams unsalted butter, melted

½ teaspoon / 3 grams fine sea salt

ricotta filling

1 pound / 450 grams ricotta cheese

5½ ounces / 155 grams fresh mozzarella, cut into small dice

1 large egg, lightly beaten

¼ cup / 25 grams grated Parmigiano-Reggiano cheese

Small handful flat-leaf parsley leaves, chopped

¼ teaspoon / 1.5 grams fine sea salt

To make the sauce, cut the bacon ends, prosciutto ends, and onions into large dice. Put them through a meat grinder fitted with a ¼-inch die. (You can chop the meat and onions in a food processor, but be careful not to over process them; you want some texture.)

Transfer the mixture to a medium pot, set it over medium-low heat, cover, and sweat the meat and onions for about 20 minutes, until soft.

Remove the lid and add the white wine. Turn the heat up to medium and cook, stirring occasionally, until the mixture is almost dry.

Lightly crush the tomatoes and add them, along with all their liquid, to the pot. Bring the mixture to a simmer and cook for about 20 minutes, until the sauce thickens and the flavors come together. The sauce can be used now, but it will benefit from resting in the refrigerator overnight. (The cooled sauce can be refrigerated up to 3 days.)

To make the crepes, if you have a butane torch, put the scallions on a rack set over a baking sheet and use the torch to char them on all sides. This is an optional step, but it really deepens the flavor of the allium. Let cool.

Thinly slice the scallions and put them in a blender, along with the eggs, milk, water, flour, butter, and salt. Turn the blender on low, slowly increase the speed to medium, and blend for 10 seconds, or until you have a smooth puree. Let the batter rest for 20 minutes before using.

Set a rack over a baking sheet. Set an 8-inch nonstick crepe or sauté pan over medium-low heat. Once it gets hot, add 2 tablespoons of batter to the pan, swirling it so that it coats the bottom, and cook for about 20 seconds, until just set. Flip the crepe and cook for another 10 seconds, or until just set, then transfer to the rack to cool. Repeat until all of the batter is used up. Once the crepes are cool, they can be stacked on a small plate. (Makes approximately 18 crepes.)

Preheat the oven to 350°F. (175°C.).

To assemble the manicotti, put the ricotta cheese, mozzarella, egg, half of the Parmigiano-Reggiano, the parsley, and salt in a medium bowl and mix gently with a rubber spatula to combine. Transfer to a pastry bag fitted with a ½-inch plain tip (or use a large zip-top bag; snip off one bottom corner).

Spread approximately one-third of the sauce in an even layer in the bottom of a 12-by-15-inch roasting pan. Lay one crepe on a work surface and pipe 2 lines of cheese across the bottom third of it, about 1 inch from the bottom edge. Lift the bottom of the crepe up and over the cheese, and roll it into a cylinder. Lay the crepe seam side down in the roasting pan. Repeat with the remaining crepes, nestling them together in the pan. Spoon the remaining sauce over the top. Sprinkle with the remaining Parmigiano-Reggiano.

Cover with foil and bake for 20 minutes. Remove the foil and bake for 20 minutes more, or until the cheese is golden brown and the casserole is bubbling and heated through. Serve immediately.

pastries

pâte à choux | gougères

makes about 2 dozen puffs

Pâte à choux is an easy and versatile dough. If you have Sourdough Starter in the pantry, you can even make sourdough puffs for a wonderfully tangy variation. Our favorite thing to make with the dough is gougères. Served hot from the oven, they are addictive little clouds of cheesy goodness. You could also make plain puffs and stuff them with whipped cream cheese and minced lox, beet tartare, pimento cheese, or deviled ham for hors d'oeuvres. Or use the vanilla pudding and ganache from the Boston Cream Pie (page 267) to fill and frost cream puffs or éclairs. Or put scoops of ice cream in the puffs and drizzle them with Chocolate Glaze (page 197) or Bourbon Caramel Sauce (page 244).

pâte à choux paste

1 cup / 225 grams water

8 tablespoons / 4 ounces / 113 grams unsalted butter

½ teaspoon / 3 grams fine sea salt

1 cup / 130 grams Gluten-Free Flour Blend (What IiF Flour 3.0, page 29,
    Batch-3 Flour, page 30, or Aki's Low-Allergy Blend, page 31)

4 large eggs

¼ cup / 60 grams Gluten-Free Sourdough Starter (page 22; optional)

gougères (optional)

1 cup / 3½ ounces / 100 grams shredded Gruyère cheese

¼ teaspoon / 0.5 gram freshly ground black pepper

¼ teaspoon / 0.75 gram grated nutmeg

Put the water, butter, and salt in a medium saucepan and bring to a boil over medium-high heat. Reduce the heat to medium and quickly stir in the flour with a silicone spatula. Once the flour is absorbed, cook, stirring constantly, until the mixture forms a ball, 3 to 5 minutes; there will be a light coating of flour mixture on the bottom of the pan.

Transfer the dough to the bowl of a stand mixer fitted with the paddle attachment (or use a hand mixer) and mix on medium-low for 1 to 2 minutes to cool it down. Beat in the eggs one at a time, making sure each egg is completely incorporated before adding the next; do not rush this process. The dough may look curdled or lumpy as you beat in the eggs, but it will come together in the end. Once all of the eggs have been absorbed, you will have shiny, sticky dough. If using the sourdough starter, add it and mix until fully blended.

If making gougères, add the cheese and black pepper and nutmeg to taste and mix for about a minute, until incorporated. Set the mixing bowl in an ice bath and let the dough cool completely, stirring occasionally. (At this point the dough can be covered and kept in the refrigerator for up to 2 days.) Let the batter rest at room temperature for 6 hours so the sourdough starter has a chance to ferment. The dough will loosen up a bit and you will see a few bubbles rising to the surface.

Preheat the oven to 425°F. (220°C.). Line two baking sheets with parchment paper.

Transfer the dough to a pastry bag fitted with a large plain tip. Being careful to hold the pastry bag straight up, pipe small mounds of dough, about 1 tablespoon each, onto the prepared baking sheets, leaving 2 inches of space between them. (As an alternative, you can spoon the pâte à choux into greased mini muffin tins, filling them three-quarters full.)

Bake for 10 minutes. Lower the oven temperature to 350°F. (180°C.), without opening the oven door, and bake for 10 to 15 more minutes, until the puffs rise, turn a deep golden brown, and are soft and custardy but set on the inside. If the puffs are not fully cooked, they will deflate as they cool; the easiest way to check is to pick one up—undercooked puffs will feel heavy in your hand.

Let the gougères cool for 5 minutes on the warm stovetop and serve warm. Small plain puffs should be cooled completely before splitting them open and stuffing them with the filling of your choice.

See process photographs and éclairs variation on the following page

Sourdough Pâte à Choux base, mixed and ready for rising.

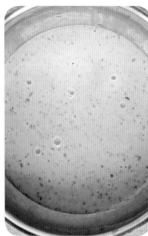
Risen Sourdough Pâte à Choux, ready to be transferred into a piping bag.

Sourdough Pâte à Choux in a mini-muffin pan, ready for the oven.

Baked Sourdough Pâte à Choux in a mini-muffin tin.

variation: *éclairs*

Pipe straight lines of dough approximately 3½ inches long and 1 inch wide. Wet the tines of a fork and run them gently down the tops; making straight lines; this will help the dough rise evenly. Bake for 15 minutes at 425°F. (220°C.) and then 15 to 20 minutes at 350°F. (180°C.). Let cool completely.

Use the Vanilla Pudding on page 267 to fill them and the Chocolate Ganache from the Boston Cream Pie (page 268) or the Chocolate Glaze on page 197 for icing the tops. Put the custard in a piping bag fitted with a large plain tip. Split the éclairs and pipe the custard into the bottom halves. Replace the tops and then carefully dip the tops into the ganache or glaze. Put the éclairs on a rack set over a baking sheet and chill for 1 hour before serving.

Golden brown, crisp, gooey Gruyère Pâte à Choux.

Pass-Around Stromboli Wheels on a plate, ready to be served.

pass-around stromboli wheels

makes 2 dozen wheels

This yogurt dough is something special. It is a rich pastry dough that you can use to make tarts or hand pies or small turnovers. It's more tender and elastic than pie dough; unsweetened, allowing for sweet or savory fillings; and end- lessly versatile. It is pliable and can be rolled out very thin. And the yogurt adds a lactic tang that keeps it from being too rich.

Classic stromboli are large turnovers made with pizza dough and stuffed with various Italian meats and cheeses; here we've made savory stromboli wheels that are full-flavored, slightly salty, and great for large gatherings. Alterna- tively, you could fill these rolls with grated cheddar cheese and diced apples, sautéed mushrooms and shredded Gruyère, or feta cheese and minced fresh herbs. For a sweet version, spread the dough with jelly or caramel sauce, layer it with thin slices of fruit or berries, or stuff it with nuts or chocolate chips.

yogurt pastry dough

2 cups / 260 grams Gluten-Free Flour Blend (What IiF Flour 3.0, page 29, Batch-3 Flour, page 30, or Aki's Low-Allergy Blend, page 31)

½ teaspoon / 2.5 grams baking soda

¼ teaspoon / 1.5 grams fine sea salt

6 tablespoons / 3 ounces / 85 grams unsalted butter, melted

½ cup / 120 grams Greek yogurt

1 large egg

filling

15 slices provolone cheese (¼ to ⅓ pound / 113 to 150 grams)

15 slices Genoa salami (¼ to ⅓ pound / 113 to 150 grams)

12 slices mozzarella cheese (¼ to ⅓ pound / 113 to 150 grams)

12 slices prosciutto (¼ to ⅓ pound / 113 to 150 grams)

2 tablespoons / 28 grams extra virgin olive oil

½ cup / 50 grams grated Parmigiano-Reggiano cheese

recipe continues

To make the dough, put the flour, baking soda, and salt into a bowl and whisk together. Put the melted butter, yogurt, and egg into another bowl and whisk together until smooth. Use a fork to stir the yogurt mixture into the flour. As the dough forms, use your fingertips to bring it together. Then turn it out onto a clean countertop and briefly knead into a smooth ball. The dough can be used immediately or wrapped in plastic wrap and refrigerated until needed.

Lay out two 18-inch-long sheets of plastic wrap on the counter, overlapping them to form a 13-by-18-inch rectangle. Put the dough in the center of the plastic wrap and cover with two more overlapping pieces of plastic wrap. Roll the dough into a 12-by-16-inch rectangle. Remove the top layer of plastic wrap.

Lay the provolone over the dough, leaving a ¼-inch border all around. Cover the provolone with the salami, cover the salami with the mozzarella slices, and cover the mozzarella with the prosciutto. Using the plastic wrap, roll the dough up around the filling as if you were making a jelly roll. Brush the dough all over with the olive oil and sprinkle the Parmesan over the dough. Wrap in plastic wrap and refrigerate for at least 1 hour.

Preheat the oven to 400°F. (200°C.). Line two baking sheets with parchment paper.

Unwrap the roll on a cutting board and turn seam side down. Cut it into 24 slices, about ½ inch thick. Arrange the slices about 1 inch apart on the parchment-lined baking sheets.

Bake for 20 minutes, or until the dough is golden brown. Remove from the oven and let the stromboli cool briefly on the pans, then serve warm.

Sliced Stromboli Wheels,
ready to bake.

Baked Stromboli Wheels,
cooling on a sheet pan.

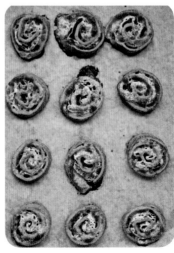

yeasted puff pastry

makes about 3¼ pounds

It's easy to find regular puff pastry in the freezer section of your supermarket, but not so much the gluten-free version. Luckily, it's quite easy to make and absolutely delicious. Puff pastry is another yeasted laminated dough (see Kouign Amann, page 97). It does take a little bit of time to fold and roll the butter layers into the dough, but the results are worth it. The pastry bakes up into golden brown layers of light, buttery goodness.

We've followed this recipe with two of our favorite recipes made with puff pastry, Bacon and Onion Tart (page 171) and Baked Brie (page 173). You could also use it for a tarte Tatin, beef Wellington, fruit turnovers, or anything else your heart desires. This recipe makes a big batch, so you can use half and store the other half in the freezer until inspiration hits.

first dough

1½ cups / 195 grams Gluten-Free Flour Blend (What IiF Flour 3.0, page 29, Batch-3 Flour, page 30, or Aki's Low-Allergy Blend, page 31)

24 tablespoons (3 sticks) / 12 ounces / 337.5 grams unsalted butter, at room temperature

¾ teaspoon / 4.5 grams fine sea salt

1 cup / 225 grams cold water

second dough

3½ cups / 455 grams Gluten-Free Flour Blend, plus extra for dusting

1 tablespoon / 12.5 grams sugar

½ teaspoon / 1.5 grams instant yeast

16 tablespoons (2 sticks) / 8 ounces / 225 grams frozen unsalted butter, coarsely chopped

recipe continues

To make the first dough, put the flour, butter, and salt in the bowl of a stand mixer fitted with the paddle attachment (or use a hand mixer). Turn the machine on low, gradually increase the speed to medium-high, and mix for 15 seconds, or until the butter and flour come together into a paste. Add the water and turn the mixer on low. Once the water is absorbed, turn off the mixer. Don't worry, the dough is supposed to look like a shaggy mess at this point.

To make the second dough, put the flour, sugar, yeast, and frozen butter in a food processor and pulse 10 times to cut the butter into the flour. It should look like very coarse meal.

Add the mixture to the dough in the bowl of the stand mixer. Turn the mixer on low, gradually increase the speed to medium, and mix for 10 seconds, or until a rough dough forms; it will be butter specked and shaggy. Transfer to a clean bowl and cover with plastic wrap. Let the dough rise in a warm place for 3 to 4 hours, until it rises slightly and develops a rich yeasty aroma.

Lay two 22-inch-long sheets of plastic wrap on the countertop, overlapping them to form a 14-by-22-inch rectangle. Put the dough in the center of the plastic wrap and cover with two more pieces of plastic wrap. Use a rolling pin to gently roll the soft dough into a 13-by-18-inch rectangle. Put the dough, still covered, on a baking sheet and refrigerate until firm, about 2 hours.

Remove the dough from the refrigerator. Lay two 22-inch-long sheets of plastic wrap on the countertop, overlapping them to form a 14-by-22-inch rectangle, with a long side toward you. Unwrap the dough and put it in the center of the plastic wrap. Fold the right third of the dough over the middle. Fold the left third dough over the center, as you would tri-fold a letter, forming a 3-layer block of dough. Rotate the dough 90 degrees so the seams are parallel to the edge of the counter. Lightly dust the top and bottom of the dough with flour. Cover the dough with two 20-inch-long sheets of overlapping plastic wrap and roll the dough into a 13-by-18-inch rectangle again. Take off the top layer of plastic wrap and fold the dough into thirds as before, using the bottom layer of plastic to help lift the dough. Dust the dough with flour, rotate it 90 degrees, and flip it over. Dust the top with flour. Cover the dough with the sheets of plastic wrap again and roll into a 13-by-18-inch rectangle. Remove the top layer of plastic wrap and fold the dough into thirds again. Wrap the dough in plastic wrap and refrigerate for 2 hours, or until it is firm.

Remove the dough from the refrigerator and give it two more "turns": Roll it out again into a 13-by-18-inch rectangle, and fold it into thirds; repeat. Wrap the dough in plastic wrap and refrigerate for 2 hours, or until it is firm.

The pastry is now ready to use, or it can be frozen, well wrapped, for up to 4 weeks.

Shaggy just-mixed Puff Pastry dough, ready to be removed from the mixing bowl for the first rise.

Shaggy Puff Pastry dough after rising for 3 to 4 hours. It is now ready to be rolled out.

Notice the streaks of butter as the dough is first rolled out.

Puff Pastry dough, first fold.

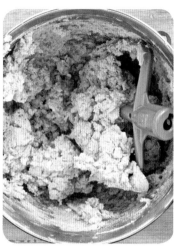

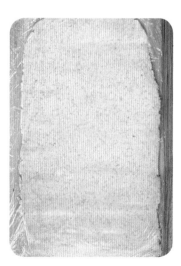

Puff Pastry dough, second fold.

Ready to use for pastries.

Yeasted Puff Pastry dough, rolled out between layers of plastic wrap, ready for filling.

Bacon and Onion Tart, sliced and ready to eat.

bacon and onion tart

serves 8 to 12 as a starter or side dish

This is a twist on the Alsatian flatbread tarte flambé or Flammekuchen. Puff pastry dough is rolled thin and layered with sour cream, thinly sliced onion, and bacon, then baked in a hot oven. You could use sautéed mushrooms instead of or on top of the onions, or substitute thin slices of your favorite salumi for the bacon. Either one crisps up like a charm. We've been known to tuck crab-meat under the onions or even add some freshly shucked clams during the last 10 minutes of baking time. It's a very versatile preparation that you can use to delight your guests.

½ batch Yeasted Puff Pastry (page 167)

½ cup / 120 grams sour cream

¼ teaspoon / 1.5 grams fine sea salt

1 medium onion, thinly sliced

4 ounces / 113 grams bacon, cut into matchstick pieces

recipe continues

Bacon and Onion Tart, crispy and hot out of the oven.

Preheat the oven to 400°F. (205°C.). Line a 13-by-18-inch baking sheet with parchment paper.

Lay two 22-inch-long sheets of plastic wrap on the countertop, overlapping them to form a 14-by-22-inch rectangle. Unwrap the dough and put it in the center of the plastic wrap. Lightly dust the top and bottom of the dough with flour. Cover the dough with two more sheets of overlapping plastic wrap. Roll the dough out into a 13-by-18-inch rectangle. Take off the top layer of plastic wrap. Use the bottom layer of plastic to help lift the dough onto the prepared baking pan, then pull out the plastic wrap from underneath.

Put the sour cream in a bowl and mix in the salt. Spread the sour cream over the surface of the puff pastry. Spread the sliced onions over the sour cream. Sprinkle the bacon over the onions.

Bake the tart for 20 minutes. Rotate the tart pan and bake for 20 more minutes, until golden brown and crisp. Remove the pan from the oven and let the tart rest for 5 minutes, then cut slices and serve hot.

baked brie

serves 12 to 15 as a starter

Baked Brie is a staple at our holiday gatherings. We put it out when everyone is arriving, and it's the perfect snack to get people mingling and chatting. Having to take turns scooping out the cheese and watching other guests enjoy the gooey goodness turns new acquaintances into friends. If you wanted to gild the lily, you could spread a layer of preserves over the top of the cheese before wrapping it in the puff pastry. Fig jam, blackberry preserves, and orange marmalade have all met with great success. Alex has even been known to slide a layer of sliced pepperoni in there, just because he loves it so much.

½ batch Yeasted Puff Pastry (page 167)

1 large wheel (2.2 pounds / 1 kilogram) Brie

1 egg yolk

2 tablespoons / 30 grams heavy cream

Preheat the oven to 400°F. (205°C.).

Lay two 22-inch-long sheets of plastic wrap on the countertop overlapping them to form a 22-inch square. Unwrap the dough and put it in the center of the plastic wrap. Lightly dust the top and bottom of the dough with flour. Cover the dough with two more sheets of plastic wrap. Roll the dough into a square about an ⅛ inch thick. Remove the top layer of plastic.

Use a spoon to scrape the thin layer of white mold off the outside of the Brie, leaving the rind intact. Put the Brie in the center of the puff pastry square. Use the bottom sheets of plastic to help fold the pastry around the Brie, covering the sides and most of the top; the puff pastry will not cover the cheese entirely. Flip the pastry-wrapped cheese over and put it in a 3-quart cast-iron Tarte tatin pan or 10-inch deep-dish pie pan, so when you cut into it the oozing cheese stays with pastry until ready to bake. You can bake this immediately or cover it with plastic wrap and refrigerate it until you are ready to bake, up to 36 hours.

recipe continues

Put the egg yolk and heavy cream in a small bowl and use a pastry brush to mix them together. Brush the puff pastry all over with the egg wash.

Put the Brie on a baking sheet and bake for 45 minutes, or until the top is brown and crusty and the cheese is molten underneath. Remove from the oven and let rest for 5 minutes.

Put the Tarte Tatin pan on a trivet and serve with crackers and slices of Honeycrisp or another juicy apple.

These just-fried Apple Fritters (page 176) should be dusted with powdered sugar and served warm.

apple fritters

makes about 2 dozen fritters

There's nothing like a warm fritter on a chilly fall afternoon. These apple fritters are crisp on the outside, tender in the inside, and full of fruit. They are leavened with whipped egg whites instead of baking powder, avoiding any potential bitterness or chemical aftertaste. As with many of the recipes in this book, we love this one for its versatility. Apple fritters may be our favorite, but you can use any fruit you like. The apple cider can be changed out for any other fruit juice or even bourbon, eau-de-vie, or a flavorful liqueur, if you like to walk on the wild side. These are wonderful for a special breakfast but can really be served at any time of day. The dusting of powdered sugar ensures that these small bites are finger-licking good.

Rice bran oil or peanut oil for deep-frying

1 cup + 2 tablespoons / 150 grams Gluten-Free Flour Blend (What IiF Flour 3.0, page 29, Batch-3 Flour, page 30, or Aki's Low-Allergy Blend, page 31)

¼ cup / 50 grams granulated sugar

½ teaspoon / 3 grams fine sea salt

½ cup / 113 grams water

3 tablespoons / 42 grams apple cider

2 large eggs, separated

½ teaspoon / 2 grams vanilla paste or pure vanilla extract

2 cups / 455 grams finely diced peeled apples

¼ teaspoon / 0.5 gram ground cinnamon

1 cup / 112 grams powdered sugar

Fill a deep fryer or large heavy pot with oil and heat to 375°F. (190°C.).

Meanwhile, put the flour, sugar, and salt in a medium bowl and whisk to blend.

Put the water, apple cider, egg yolks, and vanilla in a measuring cup and whisk to blend. Pour the liquid into the flour mixture and mix until just blended.

Put the diced apples in a bowl, add the cinnamon, and toss to coat. Fold the apples into the fritter batter and let it rest as the oil heats up. Put the powdered sugar in a small strainer set over a bowl.

When the oil is ready, whip the egg whites to soft peaks and fold into the batter. Use a ¾-ounce scoop to drop fritters into the hot oil, without crowding, and fry, flipping them once, until a deep brown on both sides, about 5 to 6 minutes. Transfer to a bowl lined with paper towels or a rack. Liberally dust both sides of the fritters with powdered sugar while they are still warm. Continue to fry until you've used up all of the batter, and serve warm.

single-layer cakes
and bundt cakes

A close up of the fine, tender crumb of the Moist Corn Pound Cake.

moist corn pound cake

makes one 9-by-5-inch loaf cake

This buttery pound cake is bursting with corn flavor. It has a fine texture, with a very delicate crunch, and a nicely browned crust. It's so simple and yet the flavor is complex. You could add a splash of rum or bourbon to the batter along with the vanilla if your tastes run that way, but this kid-friendly version is darned near perfection.

1½ cups / 210 grams corn flour

1½ cups / 195 grams Gluten-Free Flour Blend (What IiF Flour 3.0, page 29, Batch-3 Flour, page 30, or Aki's Low-Allergy Blend, page 31)

20 tablespoons (2½ sticks) / 10 ounces / 285 grams unsalted butter, diced, at room temperature

1 cup / 200 grams sugar

1 teaspoon / 6 grams baking powder

½ teaspoon / 3 grams fine sea salt

1 cup (packed) / 205 grams dark brown sugar

5 large eggs, at room temperature

1½ cups / 360 grams buttermilk, at room temperature

1 teaspoon / 4 grams pure vanilla extract

Preheat the oven to 350°F. (180°C.). Butter a 9-by-5-by-3-inch loaf pan and dust with corn flour.

Put the corn flour and flour in a medium bowl and whisk together.

Put the butter, sugar, baking powder, and salt in the bowl of a stand mixer fitted with the paddle attachment (or use a hand mixer) and beat on low until creamy and light. With the mixer running, add the brown sugar ¼ cup at a time, mixing until all of the sugar has been incorporated and the mixture is creamy. With the mixer still on low, add the eggs one at a time, mixing until each egg is fully incorporated before adding the next; the mixture should be light and fluffy.

recipe continues

Put the buttermilk and vanilla in a small measuring cup and stir them together. Add one-third of the flour mixture to the butter mixture and mix on low until the flour is fully absorbed. Add half the buttermilk and mix until it is absorbed, then beat in half of the remaining flour. Beat in the remaining buttermilk, followed by the remaining flour mixture.

Use a rubber spatula to scrape the batter into the loaf pan, spreading it evenly, and smooth the top. (It will have the texture of stiffly whipped cream.) Bake for 80 to 90 minutes, until a cake tester inserted in the center comes out clean; the internal temperature should be 208° to 210°F. (98° to 99°C.). Cool for 15 minutes in the pan on a rack, then invert onto a rack to cool completely.

You can serve this plain or gild the lily with whipped cream and fruit. Well-wrapped, the cake will keep for 5 days at room temperature—though ours is always a distant memory by then.

Golden-brown Moist Corn Pound Cake, cooled and ready to be sliced.

oatmeal cherry cake with coconut pecan topping

makes one 8-inch square cake

Oatmeal cake may seem like a strange idea, but one bite of this tender, sweetly spiced cake, and you will be hooked. It reminds us of granola because of all of the different flavors and textures, starting with the nutty oats. We added dried cherries, much as we would to a bowl of oatmeal, giving the cake a sweet tang. Broiling the topping lightly toasts the coconut and pecans while caramelizing the frosting.

oatmeal cake

1½ cups / 360 grams buttermilk

1 cup / 100 grams rolled oats

16 tablespoons (2 sticks) / 8 ounces / 225 grams unsalted butter, at room temperature

1½ cups (packed) / 320 grams light brown sugar

1 teaspoon / 6 grams baking powder

¾ teaspoon / 4.5 grams fine sea salt

½ teaspoon / 2.5 grams baking soda

½ teaspoon / 1 gram ground cinnamon

1 teaspoon / 4 grams vanilla paste or pure vanilla extract

2 large eggs, at room temperature

1⅓ cups / 175 grams Gluten-Free Flour Blend (What IiF Flour 3.0, page 29, Batch-3 Flour, page 30, or Aki's Low-Allergy Blend, page 31)

½ cup / 65 grams dried sweet cherries

coconut pecan topping

1½ cups (packed) / 320 grams light brown sugar

6 tablespoons / 3 ounces / 85 grams unsalted butter

1 cup / 56 grams unsweetened flaked dried coconut

1 cup / 110 grams chopped pecans

½ cup / 120 grams heavy cream

¼ teaspoon / 1.5 grams fine sea salt

recipe continues

Mix together the buttermilk and rolled oats in a bowl. Cover and set aside for at least 30 minutes to hydrate. (This can be done the day before; leave out overnight.)

Preheat the oven to 325°F. (165°C.). Butter and lightly flour a 9-by-13 inch cake pan.

To make the cake, put the butter, brown sugar, baking powder, salt, baking soda, cinnamon, and vanilla in the bowl of a stand mixer fitted with the paddle attachment (or use hand mixer) and beat on medium-low until light and creamy, 2 to 3 minutes. Add the eggs one at a time, mixing until each one is fully incorporated before adding the next. Add the oat mixture and beat until incorporated. Add the flour and beat until the batter is smooth and silky, about 2 minutes. Fold in the dried cherries.

Pour the batter into the prepared baking pan, using an offset spatula to spread it evenly, and smooth the top. Bake for 30 to 35 minutes, or until the cake springs back when gently pressed with a finger; it should be just beginning to pull back from the sides of the pan; the internal temperature should be 190 to 195°F. (88° to 91°C.).

Meanwhile, make the topping. Put the brown sugar, butter, coconut, pecans, cream, and salt in a small bowl and mix vigorously with a rubber spatula until soft and spreadable.

When the cake is done, remove it from the oven and turn on the broiler.

Spread the topping evenly over the cake (still in its pan) and broil on the top rack for 3 to 4 minutes, until the topping bubbles and the coconut is golden brown. Remove from oven and let cool for at least 15 minutes before serving.

Getting the first piece out can be a little tricky; a pie trowel or offset spatula is helpful here, then the rest are easy.

Oatmeal Cherry Cake, hot out of the oven, with a broiled, caramelized coconut pecan topping.

Slice the moist, tender Oatmeal Cherry Cake with a serrated knife to easily cut through the crust and transfer the slices.

A luscious slice of Caramel Cake with soft salted caramel.

easy one-bowl caramel cake

makes one 8-inch square cake

Every parent should have a recipe like this in his or her repertoire. It's easy, comes together quickly, and has infinite variations. This makes a beautiful white cake with a light texture and a moist crumb, which is drenched in a caramel glaze. We also include a variation for a blueberry streusel cake. It's a great starter cake for young cooks, because it's all made in one bowl. We usually make this in a stand mixer, but it turns out just as well with a hand mixer. The only caveat is that all of the ingredients have to be at room temperature for the batter to come together. If you forget to plan ahead, the eggs can be warmed in a bowl of warm water; diced butter will come to room temperature in your mixing bowl in 10 to 15 minutes (about the time it takes to preheat the oven); and cold milk can be warmed in the microwave for about 30 seconds.

The caramel glaze is moist without being too sticky. We add a touch of butter and vanilla to amplify the flavor of the caramelized sugar. Cut into squares, this makes a great dessert cake, reminiscent of those little snack cakes with caramel frosting, only better.

vanilla cake

2 cups / 260 grams Gluten-Free Flour Blend (What IiF Flour 3.0, page 29, Batch-3 Flour, page 30, or Aki's Low-Allergy Blend, page 31)

1½ cups / 300 grams sugar

1 tablespoon / 18 grams baking powder

1 teaspoon / 6 grams fine sea salt

1 cup / 260 grams whole milk, at room temperature

3 large eggs, at room temperature

16 tablespoons (2 sticks) / 8 ounces / 225 grams unsalted butter, diced, at room temperature

1 teaspoon / 4 grams vanilla paste or pure vanilla extract

recipe continues

caramel glaze

2¼ cups (packed) / 480 grams light brown sugar

1 cup / 240 grams heavy cream

¼ teaspoon / 1.5 grams fine sea salt

2 tablespoons / 1 ounce / 28 grams unsalted butter

1 teaspoon / 4 grams pure vanilla extract

fleur de sel, for garnish (optional)

Preheat the oven to 350°F. (180°C.). Butter and flour a 9-by-13-inch baking pan.

To make the cake, put the flour, sugar, baking powder, and salt in the bowl of a stand mixer fitted with the paddle attachment (or use a hand mixer) and mix on low until blended. Add the milk, eggs, butter, and vanilla, mixing on low, then slowly increase the speed to medium. Once the batter is smooth, mix for 2 minutes.

Pour the batter into the prepared pan and spread it evenly, with a small spatula, then smooth the top. Bake for 30 minutes, or until the cake just begins to pull away from the sides of the pan; the internal temperature should be 190° to 195°F. (88° to 91°C.). Remove from the oven and let cool completely in the pan on a rack.

To make the caramel glaze, put the brown sugar, cream, and salt in a small pot and stir just until the sugar has dissolved. Set over medium-high heat and cook until the mixture reaches 235°F. (113°C.).

Remove from the heat and carefully stir in the butter and vanilla; it will steam and bubble vigorously. Set the pot in a bowl of ice water and stir constantly for 5 minutes, or until the caramel thickens but is still pourable.

Pour half of the caramel over the top of the cake, tilting the pan as needed to spread it evenly over the top. Don't let it seep down the sides, or the cake will stick to the pan. Then set the pan down and pour the rest of the glaze over the top. After 5 minutes, lightly sprinkle fleur de sel over the top, if using. Let cool completely before serving.

Getting the first piece out can be a little tricky—a pie trowel or offset spatula is helpful here.

Light, silky "one-bowl batter" for Caramel Cake or Blueberry Streusel Cake.

Pour the caramel glaze over the golden-brown sponge cake after baking and cooling. Sprinkle with fleur de sel.

variation: *blueberry streusel cake*

This blueberry streusel cake is almost like a crumble. The cooked blueberries are juicy and tender, barely contained by the tender cake layer, and the crunchy almond streusel on top adds a contrasting nutty flavor and bit of texture to keep things interesting.

recipe continues

almond streusel

½ cup (packed) / 106 grams light brown sugar

½ cup / 70 grams unblanched whole almonds

½ cup / 50 grams rolled oats

6 tablespoons / 50 grams Gluten-Free Flour Blend (What IiF Flour 3.0, page 29,
    Batch-3 Flour, page 30, or Aki's Low-Allergy Blend, page 31)

1 teaspoon / 2 grams ground cinnamon

¼ teaspoon / 1.5 grams fine sea salt

6 tablespoons / 3 ounces / 85 grams cold unsalted butter, diced

blueberry cake

2 cups / 340 grams blueberries

Batter for vanilla cake (above)

Preheat the oven to 350°F. (180 C.). Butter and flour a 9-by-13-inch baking pan.

To make the streusel, put the brown sugar, almonds, oats, flour, cinnamon, and salt in a food processor and pulse 3 or 4 times, until well mixed. Add the butter and pulse 3 or 4 times, until the mixture looks clumpy. Turn the mixture out into a bowl and squeeze it with your fingers a few times to form bigger clumps. Cover and refrigerate while you make the vanilla cake batter.

Scatter the blueberries evenly over the bottom of the prepared baking pan. Pour the batter over the blueberries pan and spread it evenly with a small offset spatula, then smooth the top. Sprinkle the streusel over the top.

Bake as directed, and let cool in the pan.

Blueberries layered into a buttered baking dish for Blueberry Streusel Cake.

Slowly pour batter over the berries and use a small offset spatula to gently cover them completely.

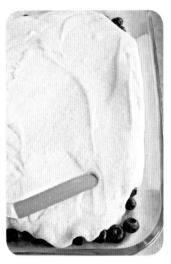

Sprinkle almond streusel over the cake batter.

A layer of streusel tops the cake batter before baking.

Golden-brown Blueberry Streusel Cake, hot from the oven.

A platter of sliced Blueberry Streusel Cake (page 189) for breakfast, layers of fruit and cake with a sandy topping.

jenny's chocolate bundt cake

makes 1 small Bundt cake

We created this for Jenny, a family member and good friend. She was diagnosed with celiac disease a few years ago and was worried that she'd never enjoy our cakes and cookies again. This cake is one of the first things we made for her, and it quickly became a favorite. It's moist and chocolaty, with a tender crumb. Aki likes just a dusting of powdered sugar instead of icing, but if you prefer something a little sweeter you can make one of the glazes on pages 195–97 or the Caramel Glaze on page 188.

2 cups / 260 grams Gluten-Free Flour Blend (What IiF Flour 3.0, page 29, Batch-3 Flour, page 30, or Aki's Low-Allergy Blend, page 31)

1 cup / 85 grams high-quality natural cocoa powder

16 tablespoons (2 sticks) / 8 ounces / 225 grams unsalted butter, at room temperature

2 cups / 400 grams granulated sugar

1 teaspoon / 6 grams fine sea salt

1 teaspoon / 5 grams baking soda

½ teaspoon / 3 grams baking powder

4 large eggs, at room temperature

1 cup / 225 grams buttermilk, at room temperature

¼ cup / 30 grams powdered sugar for dusting

Preheat the oven to 350°F. (180°C.). Butter a 7½-inch (6-cup) Bundt pan and dust with flour.

Whisk together the flour and cocoa in a medium bowl. Set aside.

Put the butter, granulated sugar, salt, baking soda, and baking powder in the bowl of a stand mixer fitted with the paddle attachment (or use hand mixer) and beat on low until light and fluffy. Add the eggs one at a time, mixing until each one is fully incorporated before adding the next. Add one-third of the flour mixture and mix until just blended. Add half the buttermilk and mix until just blended. Repeat with half of the remaining flour mixture, followed by the remaining buttermilk, and then the last of the flour mixture.

recipe continues

Scrape the batter into the prepared cake pan. Bake for 55 to 65 minutes, until the cake springs back when lightly touched and a cake tester inserted in the center comes out clean; the internal temperature should be 203° to 208°F. (95° to 98°C.). Let cool in the pan on a rack for 15 minutes, then turn out onto a rack to cool completely.

Just before serving, dust the top of the cake with the powdered sugar. The cake will keep in an airtight container for up to a week.

glazes for cakes large and small

We love Bundt cakes for their handsome shape and versatility. It's easy to simply dust one with powdered sugar, but sometimes you want something a little fancier. We've included recipes for a few of our favorite glazes here. Most call for powdered sugar rather than granulated because the small amount of cornstarch in the sugar helps the glaze set to a firm finish. When you make one of these glazes, if it seems too thick for your taste, add a little more milk or water or other liquid to thin it out, or just heat it very gently. Then set the cooled Bundt or other cake on a rack set on a baking sheet and slowly pour the glaze over the top.

Cupcakes can just be dunked in the bowl of liquid glaze to coat the tops, or you can spoon some glaze over the top. If you want to add sprinkles, sugar, chopped nuts, or fruit, simply sprinkle them on before the glaze sets.

Each of the following recipes makes enough glaze to coat a small (6-cup) Bundt cake or to drizzle nicely over a large (12-cup) Bundt. To fully coat a larger Bundt cake or frost at least a dozen cupcakes, double the recipes.

vanilla glaze

makes about 1 cup

2 cups / 240 grams powdered sugar

3 tablespoons / 48.75 grams whole milk

½ teaspoon / 2 grams vanilla paste or pure vanilla extract

Put the powdered sugar, milk, and vanilla in a small bowl and stir until smooth. Use immediately.

recipe continues

lime glaze

makes about 1 cup

2 cups / 240 grams powdered sugar

¼ cup / 56 grams fresh lime juice

⅛ teaspoon / 0.75 gram fine sea salt

Grated zest of 1 lemon

Put the powdered sugar, lime juice, salt, and lemon zest in a small bowl and stir until smooth. Use immediately.

maple glaze

makes about 1¼ cups

2 tablespoons / 1 ounce / 28 grams unsalted butter

¼ cup / 60 grams pure maple syrup, preferably Grade B

⅛ teaspoon / 0.75 gram fine sea salt

2 cups / 240 grams powdered sugar

Put the butter, maple syrup, and salt in a small saucepan and stir over medium heat until the butter has fully melted; remove from the heat.

Put the powdered sugar in a small bowl, add the butter mixture, and stir until smooth. Use immediately.

honey lemon glaze

makes just over a cup

2 cups / 240 grams powdered sugar

3 tablespoons / 50 grams honey

2 tablespoons / 28 grams fresh lemon juice

⅛ teaspoon/ 0.75 gram fine sea salt

Put the powdered sugar, honey, lemon juice, and salt in a small bowl and stir until smooth. Use immediately.

bourbon chocolate glaze

makes about 1 cup

2 cups / 240 grams powdered sugar

⅛ teaspoon / 0.75 gram fine sea salt

¼ cup / 65 grams Bourbon Chocolate Syrup (page 248), or your favorite chocolate syrup

Put the powdered sugar and salt in a small bowl, add the chocolate syrup, stir until smooth. Use immediately.

cocoa glaze

makes about 1¼ cups

2 cups / 240 grams powdered sugar

¼ cup / 30 grams natural cocoa powder

4 tablespoons / 2 ounces / 56 grams unsalted butter, at room temperature

2 tablespoons / 32.5 grams whole milk

⅛ teaspoon/ 0.75 gram fine sea salt

Put the powdered sugar and cocoa in a medium bowl and whisk to blend. Whisk in the butter. Add the milk and salt and whisk until smooth. Use immediately.

chocolate glaze

makes about 1½ cups

6 ounces / 170 grams bittersweet chocolate, finely chopped

1 cup / 240 grams heavy cream

1 teaspoon / 6 grams light corn syrup

¼ teaspoon / 1.5 grams fine sea salt

Put the chocolate in a heatproof bowl.

Put the heavy cream, corn syrup, and salt in a small saucepan and bring to a simmer over medium-high heat. Immediately pour over the chocolate and whisk until smooth. Use immediately.

Allow Deep, Dark Yeasted Chocolate Bundt Cake to cool completely before slicing.

deep, dark yeasted chocolate bundt cake

makes 1 large Bundt cake

Alex became obsessed with yeasted cakes when developing this recipe: There are few other recipes for yeasted cakes around, fine-tuning this one required numerous trials. The obstacle was determining how much moisture and hydration was needed for the long-fermented cake. Alex loves the complexity and tang that fermentation adds to the batter. This cake is moist and rich, and a small slice goes a long way.

2⅔ cups / 350 grams Gluten-Free Flour Blend (What IiF Flour 3.0, page 29, Batch-3 Flour, page 30, or Aki's Low-Allergy Blend, page 31)

¾ cup + 1 tablespoon + 1 teaspoon / 100 grams natural cocoa powder

½ cup + 2 tablespoons / 50 grams nonfat milk powder

2 cups (packed) / 400 grams light brown sugar

1 teaspoon / 3 grams instant yeast

1 teaspoon / 6 grams fine sea salt

4 large eggs, at room temperature

1 cup + 2½ tablespoons / 300 grams whole milk

3 tablespoons + 1 teaspoon / 40 grams vanilla paste or pure vanilla extract

32 tablespoons (4 sticks) / 1 pound / 450 grams unsalted butter, melted and cooled

Put the flour, cocoa, milk powder, sugar, yeast, and salt in a large bowl and whisk together.

Put the eggs, milk, vanilla paste, and melted butter in a medium bowl and whisk together until fully blended. Pour the wet mixture into the dry and whisk until a smooth batter is formed. Cover the bowl with plastic wrap or transfer the batter to a 6-quart container with a lid. Leave the batter at room temperature for 4 hours.

Use a rubber spatula to stir the batter together again. It may have risen a bit and have some bubbles, but will look essentially the same. Cover the batter again and let sit at room temperature for 18 hours. It will nearly double in volume and be thick, with a slightly glossy sheen and bubbles from the yeast throughout.

recipe continues

Butter a 10-inch (12-cup) Bundt pan.

Use a rubber spatula to gently stir the batter until smooth, then pour it into the Bundt pan. Cover the pan loosely with plastic wrap and let the batter rise again for 30 minutes. It will continue to bubble and rise slightly.

Preheat the oven to 325°F. (165°C.).

Discard the plastic wrap and bake the cake for 1¼ hours, or until a cake tester inserted in the center comes out clean; the internal temperature should be 208° to 210°F. (98° to 99°C.). Cool the cake in the pan on a rack for 15 minutes.

Invert the cake onto the rack and remove the pan. Let the cake cool completely before serving.

yeasted vanilla bundt cake

makes 1 large Bundt cake

While it is similar to the chocolate cake, this vanilla cake deserves a spot of its own. We love Nielsen-Massey's vanilla paste, and we always use it when vanilla extract is called for. It's thicker, slightly sweet, and loaded with flecks of real vanilla bean. It has a much more complex flavor than extract. The vanilla flavor is the star in this cake, so we urge you to use the best vanilla you can get your hands on. Scraping the seeds from a fresh pod into the batter will bump the vanilla up a notch; in that case, use 1 bean and 2 tablespoons paste or extract. A great way to store vanilla beans is in a large Mason jar with a couple of inches of dark rum or vodka in the bottom of the jar. The liquid will help keep the beans moist and the alcohol will absorb the vanilla flavor. Once you've used the beans, you can the use the rum or vodka to make drinks or flavor cakes. This cake can be glazed (see page 195) or dusted with powdered sugar if you like. Or toast slices and serve with butter and maple syrup. No matter how you serve it, it will be a cake to remember.

3½ cups / 455 grams Gluten-Free Flour Blend (What IiF Flour 3.0, page 29, Batch-3 Flour, page 30, or Aki's Low-Allergy Blend, page 31)

½ cup + 2 tablespoons / 50 grams nonfat milk powder

2 cups / 400 grams sugar

1 teaspoon / 3 grams instant yeast

1 teaspoon / 6 grams fine sea salt

4 large eggs

1 cup + 2½ tablespoons / 300 grams whole milk

3 tablespoons + 1 teaspoon / 40 grams vanilla paste or pure vanilla extract

32 tablespoons (4 sticks) / 1 pound / 450 grams unsalted butter, melted and cooled

recipe continues

Put the flour, milk powder, sugar, yeast, and salt in a large bowl and whisk to blend together.

Put the eggs, milk, vanilla paste, and melted butter in a medium bowl and whisk together until fully blended. Pour the wet mixture into the dry and whisk until a smooth batter is formed. Cover the bowl with plastic wrap or transfer the batter to a 6-quart container with a lid. Leave the batter at room temperature for 4 hours.

Use a rubber spatula to stir the batter together again. It may have risen a bit and have some bubbles, but it will look essentially the same. Cover the batter again and let sit at room temperature for 18 hours. It will nearly double in volume and be thick, with a slightly glossy sheen and bubbles from the yeast throughout.

Butter 10-inch (12-cup) Bundt pan.

Use a rubber spatula to gently stir the batter until smooth, then pour it into the Bundt pan. Cover the pan loosely with plastic wrap and let the batter rise for 30 minutes. It will continue to bubble and rise slightly.

Preheat the oven to 350°F. (175°C.).

Discard the plastic wrap and bake the cake for about 65 minutes, until a cake tester inserted in the center comes out clean; the internal temperature should be 208° to 210°F. (98° to 99°C.). Cool the cake in the pan on a cooling rack for 15 minutes.

Invert the cake onto the rack and remove the pan. Let the cake cool completely before serving.

Allow Yeasted Vanilla Bundt Cake to cool completely before slicing.

A moist, tender slice of Triple-Ginger Cake.

triple-ginger cake

makes one 9-inch cake

This cake is moist and slightly sticky, with big, deep flavors. A springform cake pan with a removable bottom is a great choice for baking this cake; it makes it easy to lift the cake out of the pan and we like the straight sides. We've used a combination of fresh and dried ginger to capture as much of its floral essence as possible, and then we make the glaze with spicy (nonalcoholic) ginger beer to really ratchet up the flavor. Real ginger beer is fermented with fresh ginger, rather than carbonated water flavored with ginger, giving it both a more intense flavor and less carbonation. Among our favorites are Regatta, Reed's, Fentimans, and Fever-Tree.

ginger cake

1 cup / 225 grams water

2 teaspoons / 10 grams baking soda

1 cup / 340 grams molasses

3 ounces / 85 grams fresh ginger, peeled and sliced

1 cup / 200 grams sugar

1 teaspoon / 2 grams ground cinnamon

¾ teaspoon / 4.5 grams fine sea salt

¼ teaspoon / 0.5 gram ground ginger

¼ teaspoon / 0.5 gram ground mace

2 large eggs, at room temperature

16 tablespoons (2 sticks) / 8 ounces / 225 grams unsalted butter, melted

2½ cups / 325 grams Gluten-Free Flour Blend (What IiF Flour 3.0, page 29, Batch-3 Flour, page 30, or Aki's Low-Allergy Blend, page 31)

ginger glaze

3¾ cups / 450 grams powdered sugar

¼ cup / 56 grams spicy ginger beer

recipe continues

Preheat the oven to 350°F. (175°C.).

Butter a 9-inch springform pan; wrap the bottom of the pan with foil in case of leaks. Put the pan on a baking sheet lined with a silicone mat or a sheet of parchment paper.

To make the cake, put the water in a large glass measuring cup and microwave for 1 minute. Add the baking soda and stir to dissolve. Add the molasses and stir well to blend. Set aside.

Put the fresh ginger, sugar, cinnamon, salt, ground ginger, and mace in a food processor and pulse until the fresh ginger is finely ground. Add the eggs to the food processor one at a time, pulsing to blend after each addition. Turn the processor on and stream in the melted butter. Add all of the flour, pulsing to blend. Turn the processor on and stream in the water/molasses mixture, stopping the machine once it has been incorporated. The batter will be thin, and you may need to scrape down the sides and pulse a few times to mix completely.

Pour the batter into the prepared cake pan. Bake for about 1 hour and 10 minutes, until a skewer inserted in the center comes out clean; the internal temperature should be 190° to 195°F. (88° to 90°C.). Let the cake cool completely in the pan on a rack.

Remove the cake from the pan and put it on a rack set over a baking sheet.

To make the glaze, put the powdered sugar in a large glass measuring cup or a bowl with a spout and slowly whisk in the ginger beer until the mixture is smooth and pourable. Spoon the glaze over the top of the cake. Let it stand, uncovered, for at least 2 hours so the glaze can set.

Triple-Ginger Cake, freshly baked and cooling in the pan.

Triple-Ginger Cake glazed with a sweet and spicy ginger glaze.

japanese cheesecake

makes one 10-inch cake

Japanese cheesecakes, known for their fluffy, feather-light texture and delicate flavor, are incredibly popular in Japan. If you search them out here in the States, you may find them in Japanese and other Asian bakeries. Traditionally they are baked in a water bath for gentle, even cooking. We use a muffin tin filled with water to create a moist environment in the oven, which circumvents the problem of how to get the cake out of the hot water bath when it's done. The cake briefly cooling in the turned-off oven helps keep it from falling while preserving its soft texture. This is a cake for all cheesecake lovers.

1½ pounds / 775 grams cream cheese, at room temperature

6 large eggs, separated

2½ cups / 600 grams sour cream

1 cup / 130 grams Gluten-Free Flour Blend (What IiF Flour 3.0, page 29, Batch-3 Flour, page 30, or Aki's Low-Allergy Blend, page 31)

¾ cup / 150 grams granulated sugar

1 teaspoon / 6 grams fine sea salt

1⅔ cups / 200 grams powdered sugar, sifted

Position the racks in the middle and lower third of the oven and preheat the oven to 300°F. (150°C.). Fill the cups of a 12-cup muffin tin (or use a baking pan) with water three-quarters full and put the tin on the bottom oven rack.

Spray a 10-inch springform pan with nonstick cooking spray and use a paper towel to wipe it evenly over the inside. Cut a 6-by-32-inch strip of parchment paper and insert it in the pan to create a collar; press it against the sides of the pan—it should adhere to the spray and stay in place without tape.

Put the cream cheese, egg yolks, sour cream, flour, granulated sugar, and salt in a blender. Turn the speed on to low, gradually increase to high, and blend for 30 seconds, or until the mixture is homogenous. Use a rubber spatula to scrape down the sides. Turn the blender on low, gradually increase the speed to medium-high, and blend for 5 to 10 seconds more to ensure that the mixture is smooth.

recipe continues

Put the egg whites in the bowl of a stand mixer fitted with the whisk attachment (or use a hand mixer) and mix on low until they are broken up. Add a tablespoon of the powdered sugar and whip until egg whites absorb the sugar and become foamy. Still on low speed, continue adding the sugar 2 tablespoons at a time. Once all the sugar has been added, increase the speed to high and whip the whites to shiny, almost stiff peaks, about 5 minutes.

Using a rubber spatula, fold the cream cheese mixture into the beaten whites in 3 additions, until well combined. Pour the batter into the prepared springform pan.

Bake the cheesecake for 75 minutes, or until it is just starting to brown and is set but still jiggles slightly like Jell-O when the pan is shaken gently. Turn the oven off, open the door, and let the cheesecake cool for 15 minutes in the oven.

Remove the cake from the oven and cool for at least an hour at room temperature then refrigerate for at least 6 hours, or, ideally, overnight, before serving.

Whip egg whites with powdered sugar into shiny, almost stiff peaks. It will take about 5 minutes.

Line the springform pan with a parchment-paper collar before filling with cheesecake batter. Let the pan rest on a moist kitchen towel to keep the bottom insulated.

Baked cheesecake, after an initial cooling period in the oven, slowly coming to room temperature.

Light, creamy Japanese Cheesecake unmolded and transferred to a serving plate.

First slice of the rich, delicate Japanese Cheesecake.

Sliced Lemon Yogurt Cannoli Cake lifts easily out of the baking dish no matter where you slice it.

lemon yogurt cannoli cake

makes one 9-by-13-inch cake

This moist cake has all the flavors of our favorite cannoli, from Nick's Pizza in Forest Hills, NY. Theirs is a delicate cookie shell wrapped around sweetened mascarpone cheese, garnished with toasted pistachios. We add a hint of lemon zest to the cake batter and use the juice in the frosting. Boyajian makes a wonderful lemon oil that we use to bump up the lemon flavor in the cake (see Sources, page 351; you can substitute lemon extract if necessary). In season, we take advantage of aromatic Meyer lemons, but this is almost as good with a regular lemon. Then we slather the cake with a lightly sweetened mascarpone cheese frosting and top it with roasted pistachios.

The trick with mascarpone frosting is to use a simple syrup made with milk. That allows us to thin and sweeten the rich cheese without diluting its flavor and it avoids the chance of it curdling from being overbeaten. The flavors are bright, and the cake is moist, with a creamy, crunchy frosting.

lemon yogurt cake

1¾ cups / 225 grams Gluten-Free Flour Blend (What IiF Flour 3.0, page 29, Batch-3 Flour, page 30, or Aki's Low-Allergy Blend, page 31)

1 cup / 200 grams sugar

2 teaspoons / 12 grams baking powder

½ teaspoon / 3 grams fine sea salt

¼ teaspoon / 0.5 gram grated nutmeg

¼ teaspoon / 0.5 gram ground cinnamon

1½ cups / 340 grams plain yogurt, room temperature

½ cup / 112.5 grams peanut oil

2 large eggs, at room temperature

Grated zest of 1 lemon, preferably a Meyer lemon

¼ teaspoon / 1 gram lemon oil or extract

recipe continues

mascarpone frosting

½ cup / 120 grams whole milk

½ cup / 100 grams sugar

¼ teaspoon / 1.5 grams fine sea salt

1 teaspoon / 4 grams vanilla paste or pure vanilla extract

2 cups / 450 grams mascarpone

Juice of 1 lemon, preferably a Meyer lemon

1 cup / 130 grams salted roasted pistachios

Preheat the oven to 350°F. (180°C.). Spray a 9-by-13-inch baking pan with nonstick cooking spray.

To make the cake, whisk together the flour, sugar, baking powder, salt, nutmeg, and cinnamon in a medium bowl.

Put the yogurt, peanut oil, eggs, lemon zest, and lemon oil in another medium bowl and whisk together. Pour the wet mixture into the flour and stir until just combined.

Pour the batter into the prepared pan and tap it on the counter a few times to spread the batter evenly. Bake for 25 minutes, or until a cake tester inserted in the center comes out clean and the cake is just beginning to pull away from the sides of the pan; the internal temperature should be 190° to 195°F. (88° to 91°C.). Let the cake cool completely in the pan on a rack.

To make the frosting, put the milk, sugar, salt, and vanilla paste into a medium saucepan, bring to a simmer over medium heat, whisking to dissolve the sugar, and cook for 1 minute. Remove from the heat, pour the milk into a bowl set over and ice bath and stir occasionally until cold.

When the milk is cold, put the mascarpone in a medium bowl and whisk in the milk mixture until smooth. Stir in the lemon juice.

Spread the frosting evenly over the top of the cooled cake. Put the pistachios into a food processor and pulse them 15 times to roughly chop them, then sprinkle the pistachios evenly over the cake.

To serve, slice into 24 rectangles. Getting the first piece out can be a little tricky; a pie trowel or offset spatula is helpful here, then the rest are easy.

This simple syrup, made with milk, is the perfect base for the mascarpone frosting, sweetening the cheese and preventing the frosting from breaking.

Lemon yogurt cake batter just poured into the baking dish and ready for the oven.

Baked lemon yogurt cake fresh from the oven, flecked with lemon zest and pulling away from the sides of the pan.

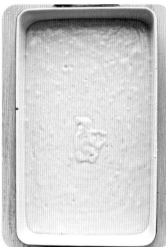
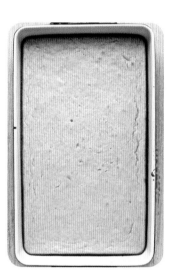

Lemon yogurt cake smothered in mascarpone frosting.

Lemon Yogurt Cannoli Cake finished with crunchy chopped roasted pistachios.

small cakes
and bars

A full tray of light, fluffy Microwave Sweet Rice Cakes.

microwave sweet rice cakes

makes 12 small cakes

Mochi are classic Japanese treat, enjoyed by Japanese people everywhere and always served to celebrate the New Year. It's considered good luck to eat mochi at the first meal on New Year's Day. Traditional mochi are chewy rice cakes that can be sweet or savory. They are made of steamed glutinous rice that is pounded into soft, sticky mass and wrapped around various fillings. Somehow their texture never really appealed to Alex, and as we started working with glutinous rice flour, he wanted to make a nontraditional alternative. These sweet rice cakes are light and airy, totally different from mochi. They emphasize the delicate flavor of the sweet rice accented by the brown butter, and are undeniably fun to eat.

Like their counterparts, they can be served with sweet or savory accompaniments depending on your taste. We like these with grilled shrimp and Homemade Hoisin Sauce (page 76) or, as dessert, with fresh berries and Sweet-and-Spicy Ginger Cream Ice Cream (page 25).

8 tablespoons / 4 ounces / 113 grams unsalted butter

1 large egg

½ cup + 3 tablespoons / 175 grams whole milk

½ cup / 100 grams sugar

50 grams glutinous rice flour (sweet rice flour)

¼ cup + ¾ teaspoon / 18 grams powdered egg whites

½ teaspoon / 1.5 grams fine sea salt

Special Equipment: 1-quart whipped cream dispenser; 12 unwaxed 10-ounce paper cups

Melt the butter in a small saucepan over medium heat, then continue to cook until the butter stops bubbling and popping, stirring it to prevent the milk solids from sticking and burning. When the milk solids are a light golden brown, remove the pan from the heat and let the butter cool.

recipe continues

Put the egg, milk, and sugar in a blender, turn the blender on low, and gradually increase the speed to medium-high. When the mixture is smooth and fluid, sprinkle in the rice flour, powdered egg whites, and salt and blend for 30 seconds, or until the egg whites and rice flour are fully incorporated and the mixture is smooth again. Reduce speed to low, pour in the warm brown butter and the milk solids, and blend for 30 seconds, or until the butter is absorbed.

Pour half the mixture into a 1-quart whipped cream dispenser and put the lid on. Charge the canister with two N_2O charges, shaking vigorously after each one to disperse the gas and allow it to be absorbed by the batter. The batter should feel and sound fluid in the canister.

Prepare 12 unwaxed 10-ounce paper cups for microwaving the cakes: Turn the cups over and use a paring knife to make a ½-inch slit in the bottom and three ½-inch slits around the sides of each cup. Turn the cups back over.

Shake the whipped cream canister and fill one cup one-third full. (The batter it will be thick enough that it won't spill out through the cuts in the cup.) Put the cup into the microwave and cook on high for 30 seconds. The batter will rise and solidify into a soft mass resembling a sea sponge. Immediately remove the cake from the microwave and invert the cup onto a cutting board or countertop. Let the cake cool upside down while you cook the remaining cakes. Refill and recharge the canister as necessary.

When the cakes are completely cool, run a paring knife around the inside of each cup to loosen the cake, invert the cup, gently shake to remove the cake from the cup, and serve. Alternatively, the cakes can be refrigerated in the inverted cups overnight before being unmolded. The refrigerated cakes will stay moist and tender and keep their light, airy texture and shape. Pull them out about 30 minutes before you want to serve them so they come to room temperature; you can eat them cold, but the texture and flavor are best at room temperature.

Microwave Sweet Rice Cake, extra batter in blender, first batch charged in a whipped-cream canister, dispensed into one cup, and "micro-baked" into a light sponge cake.

Fill the paper cups with aerated batter for Microwave Sweet Rice Cakes.

Microwave the batter-filled cups for 30 seconds.

Immediately remove and invert the cups.

Allow the cakes to cool while still inverted, then run a paring knife around the edge and gently shake each cake out of its cup.

microwave chocolate sponge cakes

makes 9 small cakes

"Daddy, are you making sweet cakes?" This is the question our daughter Amaya asks when she sees Alex pull out the whipped cream canister. She adores these light, airy cakes. He's even taken the show on the road and made the cakes with her preschool class. The kids helped mix everything together and then each made his or her own cake. A good time was had by all. When the kids aren't around we add a splash of bourbon. These delicate chocolate cakes are the opposite of the Triple-Chocolate Cake (page 247). Their flavor is chocolate at its most ethereal, dancing across your palate and melting on your tongue. Using a whipped cream canister and the microwave in harmony, with the powdered egg whites in the batter, allows us to steam these cakes instantly—the egg whites add structure, the nitrous oxide incorporates bubbles into the batter, and the microwave uses quick heat to set the cakes.

7 ounces / 200 grams bittersweet chocolate, chopped

8 tablespoons / 4 ounces / 113 grams unsalted butter, sliced

¾ cup / 195 grams whole milk

3 large eggs

½ cup (packed) / 106 grams dark brown sugar

2 tablespoons / 28 grams bourbon or dark rum (optional)

¾ teaspoon / 3 grams vanilla paste or pure vanilla extract

½ cup + 1 tablespoon / 75 grams Gluten-Free Flour Blend (What IiF Flour 3.0, page 29, Batch-3 Flour, page 30, or Aki's Low-Allergy Blend, page 31)

¼ cup / 30 grams natural cocoa powder

5½ tablespoons / 24 grams powdered egg whites

½ teaspoon / 3 grams fine sea salt

Special Equipment: 1-quart whipped cream dispenser; 9 unwaxed 10-ounce paper cups

Put the chocolate and butter in a microwave-safe bowl and microwave for 30 seconds. Stir them together and microwave for 30 seconds more. Continue to microwave and stir until the chocolate and butter are melted and smooth, about 2 minutes total.

Put the milk, eggs, brown sugar, bourbon, if using, and vanilla paste in a blender, turn it turn on to medium speed, and blend until the mixture is smooth, about 15 seconds. Add the flour, cocoa, powdered egg whites, and salt, increase the speed to high, and blend for 15 seconds, or until the mixture is smooth. Turn the speed down to medium-high, pour in the chocolate mixture, and blend for 15 seconds.

Pour half of the batter into a 1-quart whipped cream dispenser and put the lid on. Charge the canister with two N_2O charges, shaking vigorously after adding each one to disperse the gas and allow it to be absorbed by the batter. The batter should feel and sound fluid in the canister.

Prepare 9 unwaxed 10-ounce paper cups for microwaving the cakes: Turn the cups over and use a paring knife to put a ½-inch slit in the bottom and three ½-inch slits around the sides of each cup. Turn the cups back over.

Shake the whipped cream canister and fill one cup one-third full. (The batter will be thick enough that it won't spill out through the cuts in the cup.) Put the cup into the microwave and cook on high for 30 seconds. The batter will rise and solidify into a soft mass resembling a sea sponge. Immediately remove the cake from the microwave and invert the cup onto a cutting board or countertop. Let the cake cool upside down while you cook the remaining cakes. Refill and recharge the canister as necessary.

When the chocolate cakes are completely cool, run a paring knife around the inside of each cup to loosen the cake, invert the cup, gently shake to remove the cake from the cup, and serve. Alternatively, the cakes can be refrigerated in the inverted cups overnight before being unmolded. The refrigerated cakes will stay moist and tender and keep their light, airy shape and texture. Pull them out about 30 minutes before you want to serve them so they come to room temperature; you can eat them cold, but the texture and flavor are best at room temperature.

individual gingerbread cakes

makes 12 small cakes

A great gingerbread is normally a damp cake destined to be eaten with knife and fork. It is moist and rich and warmly spiced, much like our Triple-Ginger Cake (page 205). By aerating the batter and lightening the cake, we found that the individual flavors of the spices come through more clearly. The cakes can be unmolded and eaten out of hand, hand torn like cotton candy. They have all the flavor and moisture of the original without any need for plates.

½ cup / 130 grams whole milk

5 tablespoons / 106 grams dark molasses

½ cup / 100 grams sugar

4 large eggs

2 large egg whites

1 tablespoon / 14 grams dark rum

¾ teaspoon / 3 grams vanilla paste or pure vanilla extract

¾ cup / 100 grams Gluten-Free Flour Blend (What IiF Flour 3.0, page 29, Batch-3 Flour, page 30, or Aki's Low-Allergy Blend, page 31)

½ cup / 35 grams powdered egg whites

¼ cup / 30 grams natural cocoa powder

2½ teaspoons / 5 grams ground ginger

½ teaspoon / 3 grams fine sea salt

⅛ teaspoon / 0.25 gram cayenne

⅛ teaspoon / 0.25 gram ground cinnamon

⅛ teaspoon / 0.25 gram ground cloves

⅛ teaspoon / 0.25 gram ground cardamom

⅛ teaspoon / 0.25 gram grated nutmeg

6½ tablespoons / 3¼ ounces / 90 grams unsalted butter, melted

Special Equipment: 1-quart whipped cream dispenser; 12 unwaxed 10-ounce paper cups

Put the milk, molasses, sugar, eggs, egg whites, rum, and vanilla paste in a blender, turn it on to medium, and blend the mixture until smooth, about 15 seconds. Add the flour, powdered egg whites, cocoa powder, ginger, salt, cayenne, cinnamon, cloves, cardamom, and nutmeg, increase the speed to high, and blend for 15 seconds, or until the mixture is smooth. Turn the speed down to low and pour in the melted butter, then blend for 15 seconds.

Pour half the mixture into a 1-quart whipped cream dispenser and put the lid on. Charge the canister with two N_2O charges, shaking vigorously after each one to disperse the gas and allow it to be absorbed by the batter. The batter should feel and sound fluid in the canister.

Prepare 12 unwaxed 10-ounce paper cups for microwaving the cakes: Turn the cups over and use a paring knife to make a ½-inch slit in the bottom and three ½-inch slits around the sides of each cup. Turn the cups back over. Shake the whipped cream canister and fill one cup one-third full. (The batter will be thick enough that it won't spill out through the cuts in the cup.) Put the cup into the microwave and cook on high for 30 seconds. The batter will rise and solidify into a soft mass resembling a sea sponge. Immediately remove the ginger-bread from the microwave and invert the cup onto a cutting board or countertop. Let it cool upside down while you cook the remaining gingerbread. Refill and recharge the canister as necessary.

When all of the cakes are completely cool, run a paring knife around the inside of each cup to loosen the cake, invert the cup, gently shake to remove the cake from the cup, and serve. Alternatively, the gingerbread can be refrigerated in the inverted cups overnight before being unmolded. The refrigerated gingerbread will stay moist and tender and keep its light, airy texture and shape. Pull the cakes out about 30 minutes before you want to serve them so they come to room temperature; you can eat them cold, but the texture and flavor are best at room temperature.

A look inside the moist Coconut Cannelés.

coconut cannelés

makes 10 to 12 cannelés

Cannelés are small French cakes that originated in Bordeaux. They are baked in special copper molds that are brushed with beeswax and they have a crisp, almost chewy exterior that gives way to a soft, custardy interior. We're not afraid to mess with tradition, and we've used toasted coconut and coconut milk to flavor the cannelés to create something just as delicious as the original but with a twist. There's nothing else quite like these.

The batter is similar to a crepe batter and the preparation hinges on a few key steps. One is a gentle mixing process so that the batter isn't aerated. The second is letting the batter rest for at least 24 hours so that the flour is completely hydrated before baking. That's what creates the moist, tender interior. This has the added benefit of giving you a batter that can be baked to order whenever you want to make a batch, so you can serve the cannelés at their peak. If you are entertaining you can have the batter and molds ready to go and bake them once your guests arrive.

The final defining step is coating the molds with a very thin layer of beeswax and butter. If the layer is too thick, it will stick to your teeth and leave a lingering aftertaste that will undermine the delicate flavor of the cake. For this reason we use old-fashioned individual cannelé molds, as opposed to modern silicone pans, because you can empty them quickly when coating them, ensuring a perfectly thin layer. The trick is making sure that both the beeswax mixture and your molds are hot when you bring them together. Tongs are very helpful, as they make it much easier to handle the hot molds.

Don't let the number of steps here intimidate you. Cannelés are not that hard to make and the finished cakes are well worth the relatively small amount of effort you put into them.

recipe continues

small cakes and bars   225

cannelés

1¾ cups / 100 grams unsweetened coconut flakes

1⅔ cups / 400 grams coconut milk

½ cup / 130 grams whole milk, or as needed

½ cup / 130 grams maple syrup

2 tablespoons / 1 ounce / 28 grams unsalted butter

2 large eggs

2 large egg yolks

¾ cup / 100 grams Gluten-Free Flour Blend (What IiF Flour 3.0, page 29,
   Batch-3 Flour, page 30, or Aki's Low-Allergy Blend, page 31)

¼ cup / 50 grams sugar

½ teaspoon / 3 grams fine sea salt

¼ cup / 60 grams orange juice

8 tablespoons / 4 ounces / 113 grams food-grade beeswax

4 ounces / 113 grams unsalted butter

Special Equipment: *12 cannelé molds*

Preheat the oven to 250°F. (120°C.).

Spread the coconut flakes out on a baking sheet and bake for 30 minutes, or until they turn a deep golden brown. Remove from the oven and transfer to a medium saucepan.

Add the coconut milk and whole milk and bring to a simmer over medium heat. Remove from the heat, cover, and let steep for 30 minutes.

Strain the milk through a fine-mesh sieve; discard the solids. Measure out 2 cups/500 grams of the strained milk. Add a little more whole milk if there is not quite enough. Put the strained milk, syrup, and butter in a medium saucepan and bring to a simmer over medium heat. Remove from the heat and transfer to a blender.

Turn the blender on low and add the eggs and egg yolks. Blend until smooth. Stop the blender and add the flour, sugar, and salt. Turn the blender back on low and blend until smooth. Stop the blender and add the orange juice. Blend on low until fully combined. Transfer the batter to a container and refrigerate, uncovered, until completely cool, about an hour.

Cover the container of batter and refrigerate for at least 24 hours and up to 3 days, so the batter can hydrate and the flavors have time to develop.

Preheat the oven to 250°F. (121°C.). Line a baking sheet with parchment paper and put the cannelé molds on the pan. Put the pan in the oven.

Put the beeswax and butter in a quart-sized mason jar or heatproof bowl in a medium saucepan with 2 inches of water in the bottom set over low heat and stir occasionally until the beeswax and butter have melted and come together. (The beeswax is extremely hard and rather than trying to chop it, we put it in the pot as a chunk and melt it slowly.) Pull the pan with the molds out of the oven and set it on the stovetop beside the saucepan. Use a 1-ounce ladle to spoon the beeswax mixture into the molds: Pick up one mold with tongs, fill it to the top, and then immediately turn it over and dump the excess wax back into the pan; shake the mold gently and let as much wax run out as possible—you want just a very thin coat of beeswax lining the mold—and then invert the mold onto the parchment paper–lined pan. Repeat with the remaining molds. Put the molds in the refrigerator to chill for at least 1 hour before baking. (Coated molds can be covered and kept in the refrigerator for up to a week.) Put the pan with the extra beeswax in the freezer. Once the wax is cold you can peel it off the paper and store it in an airtight container to use again.

Position a rack in the lower third of the oven and preheat the oven to 475°F. (245°C.). Line a baking sheet with a silicone liner or parchment paper.

Take the cannelé batter out of the refrigerator. It will have separated—use a small rubber spatula to stir it a few times to bring it back into a smooth batter. Pour the batter into the prepared molds, filling them three-quarters of the way to the top. Put them on the lined baking sheet, leaving about 2 inches of space between them. Put them on the lower oven rack, turn the temperature down to 400°F. (200°C.), and bake for 45 minutes. Rotate the pan and bake for an additional 45 minutes, or until the cannelés are a deep, dark golden brown. Use tongs to immediately invert each mold and unmold the cake, then gently transfer them to a rack to cool. Cannelés are best eaten the day they are made.

See process photographs on the following page

The fully blended Coconut
Cannelé batter (page 225),
ready to hydrate overnight.

Coating the inside of the
cannelé molds with the molten
beeswax and butter mixture.

The frozen beeswax and
butter–lined cannelé molds,
ready to be filled with batter.

Fully baked Coconut Cannelés,
ready to be unmolded.

Caramelized Coconut
Cannelés cooling on a rack.

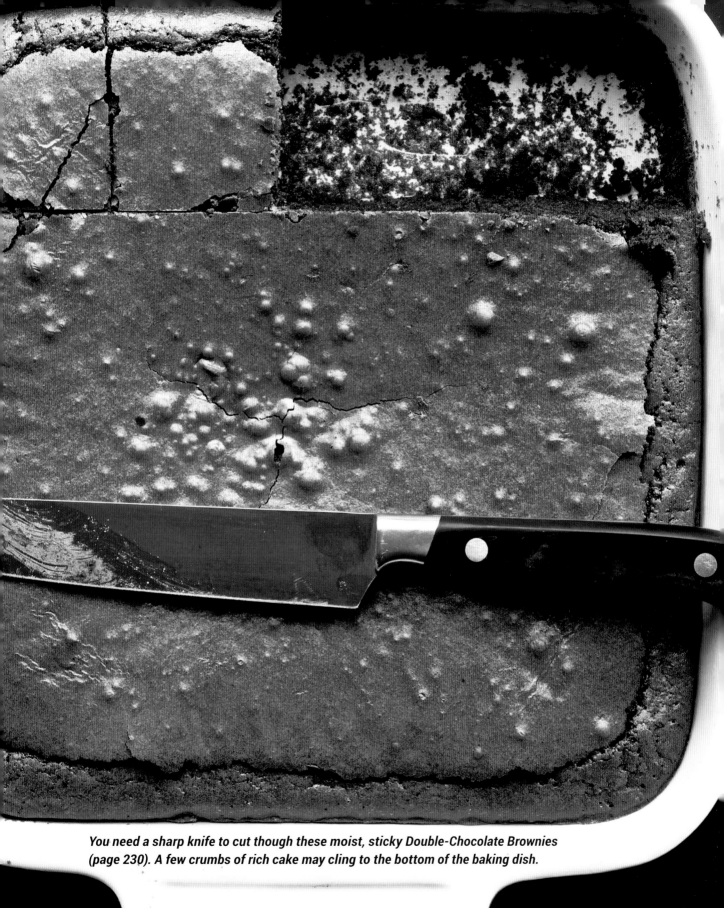

You need a sharp knife to cut though these moist, sticky Double-Chocolate Brownies (page 230). A few crumbs of rich cake may cling to the bottom of the baking dish.

double-chocolate brownies

makes 9 to 16 brownies

These moist, chewy brownies use a blend of cocoa and chocolate to get their deep chocolate flavor. As with most brownie recipes, this is quickly pulled together. We love oat flour for brownies because it adds a great chewy texture. You can eat these straight from the pan, or you can chill them for a slightly fudgier texture. Either way, they will satisfy any chocolate cravings you may encounter.

6 ounces / 170 grams bittersweet chocolate, chopped

12 tablespoons / 6 ounces / 170 grams unsalted butter, sliced

1 cup / 130 grams oat flour

2 cups / 400 grams sugar

½ cup / 60 grams natural cocoa powder

1 teaspoon / 6 grams fine sea salt

6 large eggs (cold)

Preheat the oven to 350°F. (175°C.). Butter an 8-inch square baking pan.

Put the chocolate and butter in a microwave-safe bowl and microwave for 30 seconds. Stir and microwave for 30 seconds more. Continue to microwave and stir until melted and smooth, about 2 minutes total. Let cool.

Put the oat flour, sugar, cocoa powder, and salt in a medium bowl and whisk to blend. Add the melted chocolate and butter and whisk to blend. Add the eggs one at a time, stirring each one in well with a rubber spatula. Once all of the eggs have been incorporated, give the batter another 20 to 25 strokes to be sure that everything is well blended.

Pour the batter into the prepared pan and use a small offset spatula to spread it evenly. Bake for 40 to 45 minutes, until the brownies are just set in the center; they should feel firm when gently pressed with a finger and there will be no jiggle if you shake the pan. Let cool completely in the pan on a rack before cutting.

Double-Chocolate Brownie topped with vanilla ice cream.

Once cooled, chewy Peanut Butter Blondies slice cleanly and are easily lifted from the pan.

peanut butter blondies

makes 9 to 16 blondies

"Did you put chocolate chips in those?" was the question from Alex when I was sliding these into the oven. "Nope." "But I thought all blondies had chips or something in them." "Maybe the next round. This time I made them straight." About an hour after devouring half the pan, he said, "Never mind. These don't need a thing."

Blondies are perfect for people who don't love chocolate—and even for those who do. Much of their flavor comes from brown sugar, though we added peanut butter to this version. The process of creaming the sugar in the beginning is what creates that crisp crackly crust on top. These blondies are moist and chewy, dense but not heavy, and the flavor of peanut butter permeates each bite.

recipe continues

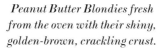

Peanut Butter Blondies fresh from the oven with their shiny, golden-brown, crackling crust.

8 tablespoons / 4 ounces / 113 grams unsalted butter, at room temperature

1¼ cups (packed) / 265 grams dark brown sugar

½ teaspoon / 3 grams fine sea salt

2 large eggs, at room temperature

1 teaspoon / 4 grams vanilla paste or pure vanilla extract

1 cup / 130 grams Gluten-Free Flour Blend (What IiF Flour 3.0, page 29,
    Batch-3 Flour, page 30, or Aki's Low-Allergy Blend, page 31)

¼ cup / 68 grams creamy peanut butter

Preheat the oven to 350°F. (180°C.). Butter an 8-inch square baking pan.

Put the butter, brown sugar, and salt in the bowl of stand mixer fitted with the paddle attachment (or use a hand mixer) and mix on low until light and creamy, 2 to 3 minutes. Beat in the eggs one at a time, making sure the first egg is fully incorporated before adding the second one. Mix in the vanilla. Add all of the flour and mix on low until fully blended, about 20 seconds. Add the peanut butter and let the paddle rotate a couple of times to swirl it into the batter without mixing it in completely; there should still be some streaks of peanut butter.

Pour the batter into the prepared pan and use a small offset spatula to spread it evenly into the corners. Bake for 35 minutes or until the blondie is just set: it won't jiggle when you shake the pan, and the top will be shiny and slightly crackled. Let cool completely before cutting.

ginger madeleines

makes about 3 dozen madeleines

Madeleines are French tea cakes. You can recognize them immediately because of their scalloped shape. Their texture is like a sponge cake, and they are tender and sweet. Here we've given them a little spice to liven them up. Fresh ginger has a pungent kick that softens and becomes rounded and warming when partnered with cane syrup and butter.

Cane syrup is a traditional American sweetener made in the South by extracting the juice from sugar cane stalks and boiling it down into syrup. It has a clean sweet flavor with a touch of astringency and a hint of burnt caramel. It can be substituted for molasses or maple syrup in recipes. There are few artisinal cane syrup companies, like Poirier's and Fain's; the most readily available brand is Steen's.

You can make the Madeleine batter ahead of time and bake the madeleines off à la minute. *Eaten warm, they are a special treat, especially when paired with hot tea or cider.*

1 cup / 200 grams sugar

4 ounces / 113 grams fresh ginger, peeled and sliced

1 teaspoon / 6 grams fine sea salt

1 cup / 315 grams cane syrup

1 teaspoon / 4 grams vanilla paste or pure vanilla extract

16 tablespoons (2 sticks) / 8 ounces / 225 grams cold unsalted butter, diced

2 large eggs

3½ cups / 455 grams Gluten-Free Flour Blend (What IiF Flour 3.0, page 29, Batch-3 Flour, page 30, or Aki's Low-Allergy Blend, page 31)

1 teaspoon / 5 grams baking soda

Softened butter for the molds

recipe continues

Special Equipment: *Madeleine pan*

Put the sugar, ginger, and salt in a food processor and pulse to a fine paste. Add the cane syrup and vanilla and pulse 3 or 4 times, or until absorbed into the sugar mixture. Scrape down the bowl with a rubber spatula as needed. Add the butter and pulse 5 or 6 times; the mixture will still be somewhat chunky. Add the eggs one at a time, pulsing after each addition until fully incorporated. Add the flour and baking soda and pulse until a uniform dough forms. Scrape into a medium bowl or container, cover, and chill for at least 3 hours, or overnight.

Preheat the oven to 350°F. (177°C.). Use a pastry brush to generously butter a Madeleine pan.

Portion the dough into rounded tablespoons and press into the prepared molds. Bake for 10 minutes, or until the cakes are just set. Let cool for 5 minutes, then pop the cakes out onto a rack to cool completely. If you want to bake another batch (or two) now, cool and clean the pan and butter it again before using.

These Ginger Madeleines have a clean, sweet flavor with a hint of caramel that pairs perfectly with hot tea or cider.

layer cakes

After using a butane torch to brûlée the top of the Tres Leches Cake.

tres leches cake

makes one 9-inch layer cake

This is our twist on the classic tres leches cake. It is usually a one-layer cake made with three milks: evaporated milk, sweetened condensed milk, and heavy cream. Not surprisingly, we were unable to keep from playing with the idea of three milks, and so this recipe uses three actual milks: almond milk, coconut milk, and condensed milk to soak the cake, along with heavy cream for the frosting. We use a half sheet pan for the cake and then cut out the layers, a tip we learned from Christina Tosi's book, Momofuku Milk Bar: *you can fit together pieces of cake if you build it in a mold, allowing you to get three round layers out of one sheet cake. You can use a springform pan to build it—no need to buy a special cake ring. This makes for a tall, beautiful cake that tastes as good as it looks.*

vanilla cake

4 large eggs, at room temperature

2 cups / 400 grams sugar

2¾ cups / 357.5 grams Gluten-Free Flour Blend (What IiF Flour 3.0, page 29, Batch-3 Flour, page 30, or Aki's Low-Allergy Blend, page 31)

1 cup / 260 grams whole milk, at room temperature

¾ cup / 170 grams peanut or vegetable oil

2½ teaspoons / 7.5 grams baking powder

¾ teaspoon / 4.5 grams fine sea salt

1 teaspoon / 4 grams vanilla paste or pure vanilla extract

soaking liquid

1 cup / 230 grams almond milk

1 cup / 240 grams unsweetened coconut milk

1 cup / 320 grams sweetened condensed milk

½ cup / 150 grams Bourbon Caramel Sauce (page 244)

3/8 teaspoon / 2.25 grams fine sea salt

recipe continues

1¼ cups + 2 tablespoons / 330 grams heavy cream

½ cup / 60 grams powdered sugar

¼ teaspoon / 1.5 grams fine sea salt

Preheat the oven to 325°F. (165°C.). Lightly grease a 13-by-18-inch baking sheet with neutral oil or nonstick cooking spray and line with parchment paper.

To make the cake, put the eggs and sugar in the bowl of a stand mixer fitted with the whisk attachment (or use a hand mixer) and beat on medium-high until light and lemon colored, about 5 minutes. Switch to the paddle attachment, add the flour, whole milk, oil, baking powder, salt, and vanilla, and mix on low until a smooth, uniform batter forms, 2 to 3 minutes.

Pour the batter into the prepared pan cake and spread it evenly. Bake for 20 to 25 minutes, until the cake just begins to pull away from the sides of the pan; the internal temperature should be 190° to 195°F. (88° to 91°C.).

Use a toothpick to poke holes all over the surface of the cake. Invert the cake onto a large cutting board. Remove the parchment paper. Use the bottom of a 9-inch springform pan and a paring knife to trace 2 full circles and 2 semicircles then cut them out. The remaining pieces can be trimmed to fit in the bottom of the springform pan. Assemble the pan, cut a parchment circle the size of the pan bottom, and put it in the pan.

To make the soaking liquid, whisk together the almond milk, coconut milk, sweetened condensed milk, caramel sauce, and salt in a medium bowl. Use a pastry brush to brush the mixture over the tops and bottoms of all the cake rounds and pieces. Arrange the semicircles and trimmed pieces of cake in one layer in the bottom of the springform pan. Then pour about one-third of the remaining soaking liquid over the cake so it covers the layer. Let the liquid soak into the cake.

Meanwhile, make the whipped cream: Put the cream, powdered sugar, and salt in the bowl of the stand mixer fitted with the whisk attachment (or use a hand mixer) and whip on medium-high until the cream just holds stiff peaks.

To assemble the cake, put half of the whipped cream in the center of the bottom cake layer and spread it out, leaving a ½-inch circumference of cake bare around the edges. Lay the second layer of cake on top of the cream, pressing gently so it lies flat. Spoon half of the remaining soaking liquid over the layer and let the liquid soak in for 5 minutes.

Spread the remaining whipped cream over the cake, leaving a ½-inch circumference of cake bare around the edges. Lay the remaining cake layer on top of the cream, pressing gently so it lies flat. Use a chopstick to poke about 50 holes straight down through the cake. Slowly pour the remaining soaking liquid over the top of the cake. This may need to be done in stages as it slowly sinks into the cake through the holes. When the liquid has all been absorbed, cover the edge loosely with plastic wrap and refrigerate until it has firmed up and the top layer is set, at least 2 hours, or for up to 24 hours.

Remove the cake from the refrigerator. Remove the springform ring from the cake. Use a butane torch to brûlée the top of the cake: the goal is a light, even caramelization, not charring the surface. Serve immediately, or return to the refrigerator for up to 6 hours.

For the best results, let the refrigerated cake sit at room temperature for at least 30 minutes before serving.

Use the bottom of a spring-form cake pan to trace circles into the baked vanilla cake layer with a knife.

You can maximize your yield by using whole and half circles of cake.

Fit the bottom layer of the cake into a springform cake pan, using the leftover pieces to fill in the gaps between the semicircles.

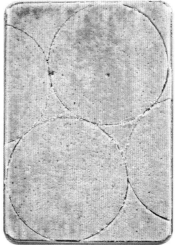

photographs continue

Allow the bottom layer to soak for 5 minutes. A pastry brush will help spread the soaking liquid over the surface of the cake.

Coat the top layer of the Tres Leches Cake with the remainder of the soaking liquid. The parchment paper below will catch any overflow.

bourbon caramel sauce

makes about 5 cups

We love caramel sauce. Yes you can buy it, but we prefer to make our own. We store it Mason jars in the pantry, so we have some whenever we want it—and it makes a wonderful gift. Distilled alcohol is considered gluten-free as long as there are no other flavorings added after distilling. Bourbon is our favorite alcohol here, but you can substitute any fruit juice, cider, or clear fruit-flavored liqueur that suits your fancy. The caramel has a tendency to separate in the jar, but all you have to do is give it quick stir and everything will come back together. It makes a fabulous dipping sauce for warm Doughnuts (page 105), or drizzle it over the top of a Banana Butterfinger Cream Pie (page 290). It adds depth of flavor to the Tres Leches Cake, and we're sure you can think of many more ways to enjoy it.

3¾ cups / 750 grams sugar

⅔ cup / 150 grams water

2½ tablespoons / 50 grams corn syrup

1½ cups + 1 tablespoon / 375 grams heavy cream

8 tablespoons / 4 ounces / 113 grams unsalted butter, sliced

5 teaspoons / 20 grams vanilla paste or pure vanilla extract

1½ teaspoon / 9 grams fine sea salt

½ cup + 1 tablespoon / 125 grams bourbon (see headnote)

Put the sugar, water, and corn syrup in a medium heavy-bottomed pot and stir the mixture together until it resembles wet sand. Put the pot over medium-high heat, put a lid on it, and cook the mixture for 10 minutes. (Let it cook undisturbed—stirring increases the likelihood of crystallization.) Remove the lid and take a look at the sugar syrup. It should be clear and boiling. Put the lid back on and cook for 5 more minutes.

Remove the lid. The sugar should be just beginning to caramelize. Continue to cook, swirling the pot occasionally to blend the caramelizing sugar into the rest of the syrup until the caramel is dark amber. We don't use a candy thermometer, because it increases the possibility of crystallization, but if you prefer to use one, a dark caramel occurs from 360° to 370°F. (182° to 188°C.).

Remove the pot from the heat and slowly and carefully pour the heavy cream into the hot caramel; it will boil and spurt, and there will be lots of steam. The caramel may seize and solidify—if so, just set it over low heat and stir until the hardened caramel melts into the sauce. Add the butter, vanilla paste, and salt and stir until the butter is melted. Stir in the bourbon; it will sputter and boil. Let the caramel sauce cool. Pour the caramel sauce into jars, label, and share with only those you love.

The perfect slice of luscious Triple-Chocolate Cake.

triple-chocolate cake

makes one 9-inch layer cake

This is a chocolate cake for serious chocolate lovers. It's tall and beautiful, and it makes a great birthday cake—it can be decorated with sprinkles or nuts if you like. Just one bite will tell the recipient how much you love him or her.

It may seem like a big batch of frosting, but Alex's pet peeve is skimpy frosting between cake layers. That said, our guests never leave anything on their plates, so the recipe must make the right amount. Use your favorite brand of chocolate and hang the expense, because this makes a cake that is better than any store-bought cake you've ever tasted.

This recipe makes more bourbon chocolate syrup than you will need to soak the cake; the extra syrup can be used to make chocolate milk or hot chocolate or to top ice cream sundaes. It's useful stuff to have in the fridge and so much better than mass-produced syrup.

chocolate cake

8 tablespoons / 4 ounces / 113 grams unsalted butter, sliced

4 ounces / 113 grams bittersweet chocolate, chopped

2 cups / 400 grams sugar

2¼ cups / 292.5 grams Gluten-Free Flour Blend (What IiF Flour 3.0, page 29, Batch-3 Flour, page 30, or Aki's Low-Allergy Blend, page 31)

¾ cup + 2 tablespoons / 210 grams natural cocoa powder

2 teaspoons / 12 grams baking powder

1 teaspoon / 6 grams fine sea salt

½ teaspoon / 2.5 grams baking soda

1¼ cups / 300 grams buttermilk, at room temperature

½ cup / 113 grams peanut or vegetable oil

4 large eggs, at room temperature

recipe continues

bourbon chocolate syrup

1¾ cups + 1 tablespoon / 375 grams sugar

1 cup / 225 grams water

½ cup + 1 teaspoon / 125 grams natural cocoa powder

¼ teaspoon / 1.5 grams fine sea salt

Scant tablespoon / 15 grams light corn syrup

1 tablespoon / 16 grams vanilla paste or pure vanilla extract

6 tablespoons / 85 grams bourbon, rum, or heavy cream

chocolate frosting

2 cups / 480 grams heavy cream

16 tablespoons (2 sticks) / 8 ounces / 225 grams unsalted butter, sliced

⅔ cup / 132 grams sugar

½ cup / 113 grams water

¼ cup / 80 grams light corn syrup

½ teaspoon / 3 grams fine sea salt

2 pounds / 910 grams bittersweet chocolate, finely chopped

Position the racks in the middle and upper third of the oven and preheat the oven to 350°F. (180°C.). Butter two 9-inch round cake pans and line the bottoms with ungreased parchment paper circles.

To make the cake, put the butter and chocolate in a small saucepan and heat over medium heat, stirring, until the butter and chocolate melts. Set aside to cool.

Put the sugar, flour, cocoa powder, baking powder, salt, and baking soda in a medium bowl and whisk to blend. Add the buttermilk, oil, and eggs and whisk together. Add the cooled butter mixture and whisk to blend, then whisk vigorously for 1 minute, or until the batter is smooth and shiny.

Divide the batter equally among the prepared cake pans and use a small offset spatula to spread it evenly and smooth the tops. Bake for 25 to 30 minutes, until the cake is just beginning to pull away from the sides of the pans; the internal temperature should be 190° to 195°F. (88° to 91°C.). Cool in the pans on a rack for 15 minutes.

Meanwhile, make the bourbon chocolate syrup: Put the sugar, water, cocoa, and salt in a medium saucepan and bring to a boil over medium heat, stirring constantly with a silicone spatula to keep the cocoa from scorching. Add the corn syrup and vanilla and stir to blend. Remove from the heat and stir in the bourbon. Let cool; the syrup will thicken as it cools. (The extra syrup can be kept in a jar or covered container in the fridge for up to 3 months.)

Set two wire racks, each large enough to hold two cake layers, over two separate sheet pans. Turn the cakes out of their pans, remove the parchment paper from the bottom of each layer, and use a serrated knife to split them in half horizontally. Lay the two halves of one cake layer, split side up, on one rack and the two halves of the other cake layer, split side up, on the second rack. Spoon ¼ cup of warm bourbon chocolate syrup over each layer, and then use a pastry brush to spread it from edge to edge. Let the cake layers cool completely and absorb the syrup, about 30 to 45 minutes. Cover loosely with plastic wrap and refrigerate until you are ready to assemble the cake.

To make the frosting, put the cream, butter, sugar, water, corn syrup, and salt in a medium saucepan and bring to a bare simmer, stirring, over medium heat. Remove from the heat and stir until the butter has completely melted. Add the chocolate, and whisk until all of the chocolate has melted and the mixture is glossy and smooth. Transfer to a bowl and refrigerate for 1½ to 2 hours, stirring occasionally, until the frosting is a spreadable consistency.

To assemble the cake, use the bottom half of one of the cut cakes as your first layer. Put it on a cardboard cake circle, if you have one, on a large plate or turntable. Put about ¾ cup of frosting on top of the first layer and use an offset spatula to spread it evenly, leaving a border of about ¼-inch around the circumference. Place the second layer on top of the first and spread with ¾ cup of frosting as you did the first layer. If the frosting starts to cool and stiffen up, use a hair dryer to gently warm it up again, until it spreads easily. Repeat with the third layer, and then lay the fourth layer on top. Spread about ¾ cup frosting over the top of the cake, letting it come down the sides. Clean off your spatula every so often to remove excess crumbs. Don't worry about making it look perfect; just coat the cake with frosting. This is the crumb coat so the important thing is to create a smooth surface and fill any holes.

Scrape off any excess frosting, rinse your spatula under warm water, and wipe it dry. Warming it will make it easier to spread the final coat of frosting. Frost the cake and use any remaining frosting to swirl onto the cake in pretty patterns, or use to pipe small rosettes around the top edge or to decorate it however you choose. Refrigerate the cake for at least 30 minutes so the frosting can set.

Bring the cake to room temperature before serving.

See process photographs on the following page

Whisk the frosting until it's glossy and smooth, then let it cool in the fridge for 1 to 2 hours until it's spreadable.

Cut the cake layers in half and soak each half with ¼ cup of warm bourbon chocolate syrup.

Ribbons of rich chocolate frosting adorn the top of the Triple Chocolate Cake (page 247).

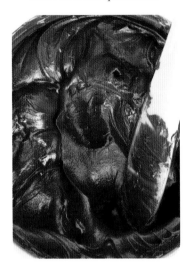

Layers of moist, snowy white Coconut Cake (page 252), and rich chocolate mousse.

coconut cake

makes one 9-inch layer cake

Most coconut cakes put the coconut on the outside of the cake. Our goal was to get as much coconut into the cake as possible. You may have noticed that we soak most of the cake layers in the recipes in this chapter. There are two reasons for this. One, the liquid adds flavor and that is always a good thing. Two, it adds moisture to the cake, which makes it more fun to eat and helps it remain fresh for a little longer—though if your family is like ours, your cake will disappear long before it can even think of drying out. We've frosted this cake with milk chocolate mousse, which adds another dimension of flavor and balances the coconut. If you prefer dark chocolate, you can substitute 12 ounces (340 grams) bittersweet chocolate for the milk. You use a little bit less because the flavor is stronger and the chocolate firms up in the mousse more. This is a cake that surprises many people, who don't often think of combining milk chocolate and coconut. After they taste it, though, they will never forget.

milk chocolate mousse

6 large egg yolks

½ cup / 115 grams unsweetened coconut milk

⅓ cup / 66 grams sugar

14 ounces / 400 grams high-quality milk chocolate, melted and still warm

1¼ cups / 300 grams heavy cream

½ cup / 120 grams sour cream

¼ teaspoon / 1.5 grams fine sea salt

coconut cake

3 cups / 390 grams Gluten-Free Flour Blend (What IiF Flour 3.0, page 29,
    Batch-3 Flour, page 30, or Aki's Low-Allergy Blend, page 31)

2 cups / 400 grams sugar

1 cup / 56 grams unsweetened flaked coconut

1 tablespoon / 18 grams baking powder

1 teaspoon / 6 grams fine sea salt

8 tablespoons / 4 ounces / 113 grams unsalted butter, at room temperature, sliced

½ cup / 113 grams peanut or vegetable oil

4 large eggs, at room temperature

1 cup / 256 grams unsweetened coconut milk, at room temperature

1 teaspoon / 4 grams vanilla paste or pure vanilla extract

soaking liquid

6 tablespoons / 96 grams unsweetened coconut milk

2 tablespoons / 36 grams Bourbon Caramel Sauce (page 244)

1 tablespoon / 12.5 grams sugar

4 cups / 224 grams unsweetened flaked dried coconut

To make the milk chocolate mousse, put the egg yolks, coconut milk, and sugar in a heat-proof bowl and set it over a saucepan of gently simmering water. Cook, whisking constantly (or use a hand mixer), until the mixture turns light yellow, has approximately tripled in volume, and falls in a ribbon when you lift the whisk, 10 to 15 minutes.

Transfer the mixture to the bowl of a stand mixer fitted with the whisk attachment (or use a hand mixer) and beat on medium-high until cool, about 10 minutes.

Slowly pour the warm melted chocolate into the yolk mixture and beat until fully incorporated.

Put the heavy cream, sour cream, and salt in a clean bowl and whip to firm peaks. Fold one-third of the whipped cream into the chocolate mixture, incorporating it completely, then fold in the remaining whipped cream. Cover and refrigerate for at least 4 hours, or, preferably, overnight.

Preheat the oven 350°F. (180°C.). Butter two 9-inch round cake pans and line the bottoms with parchment paper circles.

To make the cake, put the flour, sugar, coconut, baking powder, and salt in a food processor and pulse 4 or 5 times to grind the coconut to a fine powder. Add the butter, oil, eggs, coconut milk, and vanilla and process until completely smooth and silky, 1 to 2 minutes.

recipe continues

Divide the batter equally between the prepared cake pans and use a small offset spatula to spread it evenly and smooth the tops. Bake for 30 to 35 minutes, until the cake is just beginning to pull away from the sides of the pans; the internal temperature should be 190° to 195°F. (88° to 91°C.). Cool for 15 minutes in the pans on a rack, then turn the cake layers out onto a rack, remove the parchment, and let cool completely.

Once the layers are completely cool, using a serrated knife, split them horizontally in half. Lay the layers cut side up on two parchment-lined baking sheets.

To make the soaking liquid, whisk together the coconut milk, caramel sauce, and sugar in a small bowl until the sugar dissolves. Brush one-quarter of the soaking liquid onto each cake layer. Cover loosely with plastic wrap and refrigerate for at least 2 hours, and up to 24 hours.

To assemble the cake, put the first layer cut side up on a cardboard cake circle if you have one, or on a plate. Put about ¾ cup chocolate mousse on top of the layer and use an offset spatula to spread it evenly over the cake, leaving a border of about ¼ inch around the circumference. Put the next layer rounded side down on top of the mousse, and gently press on the cake layer to settle it. Add another ¾ cup mousse and spread it over the top as before. Add the next layer cut side up, and repeat. Put the top layer on the cake, cut side down, and spread about ¾ cup mousse over it so it goes slightly past the edges. Don't worry about making it perfect, just concentrate on covering the top of the cake. Clean off your spatula every so often, scraping excess mousse back into the bowl. Then spread a thin layer of mousse around the sides of the cake. This is the "crumb coat," so you just want to make everything smooth and even and fill in any gaps in the sides.

Scrape off any excess frosting, rinse your spatula under warm water, and wipe it dry. Warming it will make it easier to spread the final coat of frosting. Then spread the remaining mousse evenly over the top and sides of the cake.

Sprinkle about a cup of the flaked coconut over the top of the cake. Take handfuls of the remaining coconut and gently press them onto the sides of the cake, coating the entire surface. Refrigerate the cake for at least 30 minutes so the frosting can set up.

Bring the cake to room temperature before serving.

Pressing the coconut flakes against the milk chocolate mousse on the outside of the Coconut Cake.

A slice of Strawberries-and-Cream Cake, showing off the layers of tender white cake, sweet cream, and red berries.

strawberries-and-cream cake

makes one 9-inch layer cake

This is one of Aki's favorite cakes: soft white cake layers with fragrant straw-berries and freshly whipped cream. White cakes are made with only egg whites (you could use the leftover yolks to make the Agnolotti dough on page 148 on the same day). They have a light, fluffy texture and a fine crumb. This is the upscale version of strawberry shortcake, but it is still homey enough to satisfy the kid in us all. It goes without saying that this should be made when straw-berries are in season. Or you could substitute your favorite fruit: raspberries sliced in half, slices of ripe peaches, juicy orange suprêmes.

white cake

8 tablespoons / 4 ounces / 113 grams unsalted butter, at room temperature

1½ cups / 300 grams sugar

1 tablespoon / 18 grams baking powder

1 teaspoon / 6 grams fine sea salt

1 teaspoon / 4 grams vanilla paste or pure vanilla extract

9 large egg whites (put 3 in one small bowl and 6 in another bowl), at room temperature

2 cups / 260 grams Gluten-Free Flour Blend (What IiF Flour 3.0, page 29, Batch-3 Flour, page 30, or Aki's Low-Allergy Blend, page 31)

1 cup / 260 grams whole milk, at room temperature

strawberries and cream

2 quarts ripe strawberries

3 cups / 720 grams heavy cream

1⅓ cups / 150 grams powdered sugar

½ teaspoon / 3 grams fine sea salt

recipe continues

Preheat the oven to 350°F. (175°C.). Butter three 9-inch round cake pans. Dust them lightly with flour, flip them over, and tap the bottoms gently to remove any excess, then line with parchment circles.

Put the butter, 1¼ cups of the sugar, baking powder, and salt in the bowl of a stand mixer fitted with the paddle attachment (or use a hand mixer) and mix on low until the mixture is light and fluffy, 1 to 2 minutes. Add the vanilla and 3 egg whites and mix until the whites are fully incorporated. Add one-third of the flour and mix on low until it is absorbed. Add half the milk and mix until almost absorbed. Add half of the remaining flour mixture and mix in the same manner, followed by the remaining milk, and then the remainder of the flour. Then mix until the batter is completely smooth and silky, about 1 minute.

Put the remaining 6 egg whites in a large bowl and whisk until foamy (or use a hand mixer). Gradually add the remaining ¼ cup sugar and continue to whisk until the whites reach stiff peaks. Use a rubber spatula to fold the egg whites into the cake batter in 3 additions.

Divide the batter evenly among the prepared cake pans and smooth the tops with a spatula. Bake for 17 to 20 minutes, or until the cake is just beginning to pull away from the sides of the pans; the internal temperature should be 190° to 195°F. (88° to 91°C.). Let the cakes cool for 15 minutes in the pans on a rack, then turn them out onto a rack remove the parchment, and let cool completely.

Wash the strawberries and slice the stems off leaving each berry with a flat top. Reserve the 16 prettiest berries to decorate the top of the cake. Stand one of the remaining strawberries on its flat end and cut it vertically into 4 slices. Transfer to a bowl and repeat with the remaining berries.

When you are ready to build the cake, put the heavy cream, powdered sugar, and salt in the bowl of a stand mixer fitted with the whisk attachment (or use a hand mixer) and whip until the cream forms stiff peaks.

Put the first cake layer on a cardboard cake circle if you have one, or on a plate. Cover the top with sliced strawberries, leaving a ¼-inch border around the circumference. Cover the strawberries with about ¾ cup whipped cream and use an offset spatula to spread it evenly over the berries. Top with another cake layer and repeat. (You may have extra sliced berries which can be served alongside the cake.) Then frost the entire cake with the remaining whipped cream. Decorate the cake with the reserved strawberries.

Chill the cake for at least 30 minutes and up to 6 hours, before serving.

White cake batter beside whipped egg whites, ready to be folded together.

Build the Strawberries-and-Cream Cake by adding layers of cake, sweet berries, and softly whipped cream.

Add the top layer right-side up for a smooth surface for frosting.

Strawberries-and-Cream Cake, frosted with whipped cream and decorated with fresh berries.

A healthy slice of the best Carrot Cake you will ever eat (three-layer version).

carrot cake

makes one 6½-by-18-inch two-layer or one 9-inch three-layer cake

This is one of the best cakes we've ever made. We know this because everybody has told us so. Even people who don't normally like carrot cake devour it.

We use glazed walnuts in the recipe. First we steep them in sugar syrup to pull some of the tannins from the nuts, which reduces their natural bitterness. Then we roast them. The syrup still clinging to them candies as they bake, sealing the nuts and giving them a light, crunchy texture. These nuts are dangerously addictive—we've been known to pile them in a bowl and serve them with drinks. If you like, you can substitute an equal amount of any nut and give them the same treatment.

The ingredient list may look long, but everything works together. The warm spices in the cake balance the earthy sweetness of the carrots; the walnuts add richness; and the candied ginger and fresh orange zest brighten things up. The tangy but delicate cream cheese frosting provides the perfect creamy foil to the moist cake. Truthfully, we've been known to eat the leftovers for breakfast.

glazed walnuts

1 cup / 130 grams raw walnuts

¾ cup / 150 grams sugar

½ cup + 2½ tablespoons / 150 grams water

⅜ teaspoon / 2.25 grams fine sea salt

2 teaspoons / ⅓ ounce / 10 grams unsalted butter, sliced

cake

2⅓ cups / 300 grams Gluten-Free Flour Blend (What IiF Flour 3.0, page 29, Batch-3 Flour, page 30, or Aki's Low-Allergy Blend, page 31)

1 tablespoon / 18 grams baking powder

1¼ teaspoons / 6.25 grams baking soda

¾ teaspoon / 4.5 grams fine sea salt

recipe continues

1¼ cups (packed) / 260 grams light brown sugar

1 cup / 200 grams granulated sugar

4 large eggs

1½ cups / 337.5 grams vegetable oil

¼ cup / 60 grams heavy cream

1 tablespoon / 12 grams vanilla paste or pure vanilla extract

1 tablespoon / 11.5 grams finely chopped candied ginger

Grated zest of 2 large oranges

1½ teaspoons / 3 grams ground cinnamon

¾ teaspoon / 1.5 grams grated nutmeg

½ teaspoon / 0.5 grams ground cardamom

3 cups (firmly packed) / 300 grams shredded carrots (about 4 medium carrots)

cream cheese frosting

2 pounds 3 ounces / 1000 grams cream cheese, at room temperature

1½ cups / 360 grams heavy cream

2½ cups / 300 grams powdered sugar, sifted

½ teaspoon / 3 grams fine sea salt

½ teaspoon / 1 gram grated nutmeg

To make the glazed walnuts, put the nuts, sugar, water, and ¼ teaspoon of the salt in a small saucepan and bring to a boil over medium-high heat, then reduce the heat and simmer for 5 minutes. Remove from the heat, cover, and let the nuts steep for 20 minutes.

Preheat the oven to 350°F. (180°C.).

Drain the nuts, discarding the syrup, and transfer them to a medium bowl. Toss them with the butter and the remaining ⅛ teaspoon salt. Spread the nuts out on a baking sheet lined with parchment paper. Roast for 15 to 20 minutes, rotating the pan once, until the nuts are a deep golden brown. Remove from the oven and let cool completely; the nuts will crisp up as they cool. (The nuts will keep for up to 2 weeks in an airtight container at room temperature.) Leave the oven on.

Lightly butter a 13-by-18-inch baking sheet or three 9-inch round cake pans or spray with nonstick cooking spray and line with parchment paper.

To make the cake, whisk together the flour, baking powder, baking soda, and salt in a medium bowl.

Put the brown sugar, granulated sugar, and eggs, in the bowl of a stand mixer fitted with the paddle attachment (or use a hand mixer) and mix on medium-low until well combined.

Add the oil, cream, vanilla, candied ginger, orange zest, cinnamon, nutmeg, and cardamom and beat on low until just combined. Add the flour mixture and beat until just combined. Add the carrots and the glazed nuts and mix until just incorporated.

Pour the batter into the prepared baking sheet and smooth the top with a small offset spatula. If using 3 round cake pans, divide the batter evenly among them. There should be 610 to 620 grams of batter in each pan. Tap each pan lightly on the countertop a few times to help settle the batter. Bake the sheet cake for 25 to 30 minutes, until it is dark golden brown and a cake tester inserted in the center comes out clean. Round cake layers should be baked for 20 minutes; then rotate the pans and bake for an additional 10 minutes. The internal temperature should be 205°F. (96°C.). Cool in the pans on a rack for 15 minutes, then invert onto a rack, remove the parchment, and cool completely.

To make the frosting, put the cream cheese, cream, powered sugar, salt, and nutmeg in the bowl of a stand mixer fitted with the whisk attachment (or use a hand mixer) and beat on medium speed until light and fluffy.

To assemble a two-layer cake: Cut the cooled sheet cake lengthwise in half. Lay one layer on a serving platter. Use about one-quarter of the frosting to cover the top of the layer, leaving a ¼-inch border around the outside edges. Lay the second layer on top of the first, pressing down gently so it lies flat. Use the remaining frosting to cover the top and sides of the cake.

To assemble a three-layer cake: Turn the cake layers out onto wire racks. Put the first layer on a cardboard cake circle if you have one. With an offset spatula, evenly spread about ¾ cup frosting over the top, leaving a border of about ¼ inch around the circumference. Put the next layer on top, add another ¾ cup frosting, and spread it over the top as before. Put the final layer on top and spread about ¾ cup frosting over it, letting the frosting come to the edges and slightly past them. Don't worry about making it perfect. Clean off your spatula every so often, scraping excess frosting back into the bowl. Spread a thin layer of frosting around the sides of the cake. This is the crumb coat—you just want to make everything smooth and even and fill in any holes along the side. Scrape off any excess frosting, then rinse your spatula under warm water and wipe it dry. This will make it easier to spread the final coat. Swirl the remaining frosting onto the cake in pretty patterns or pipe small rosettes along the border.

Refrigerate the cake for at least 30 minutes so the frosting can set up. Bring the cake to room temperature before serving.

See process photographs on the following pages

Walnuts simmered in brown sugar syrup.

Drained walnuts with the butter added, ready for mixing.

Butter-glazed walnuts, ready to bake.

Roasted Glazed Walnuts.

Carrot Cake batter with oil blended into the eggs and sugar.

After adding flour to Carrot Cake batter.

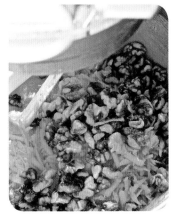

Adding the carrots and walnuts to the batter.

Fully blended Carrot Cake batter.

Weighing the Carrot Cake batter to create equal layers for the three-layer version.

Cream Cheese Frosting, ready to go.

Cooled Carrot Cake layers.

Fully assembled three-layer Carrot Cake.

An inside look at the Carrot Cake.

The first taste of tender Carrot Cake (page 261; two-layer version) and whipped cream cheese frosting.

boston cream pie

makes one 9-inch layer cake

This classic New England dessert is not a pie at all, but a sponge cake layered with vanilla pudding. Here the pudding is thickened with both cornstarch and tapioca starch—the blend of starches provides thickening power, silkiness, and elasticity. The cake is glazed with a rich chocolate ganache. We add some cornstarch to the ganache to help it set up nicely, along with touch of butter, because it makes it look and taste even better. We made this cake for Alex's Aunt Erica's birthday and we loved it so much that somehow it keeps reappearing on our table.

vanilla pudding

2 cups / 520 grams whole milk

1 cup / 240 grams heavy cream

1 cup + 2 tablespoons / 225 grams sugar

4 large egg yolks

3 tablespoons / 18 grams tapioca starch

1½ tablespoons / 10.5 grams cornstarch

1 teaspoon / 6 grams fine sea salt

8 tablespoons / 4 ounces / 113 grams unsalted butter, sliced

2 teaspoons / 8 grams vanilla paste or pure vanilla extract

sponge cake

1 cup + 2 tablespoons / 145 grams Gluten-Free Flour Blend (What IiF Flour 3.0, page 29, Batch-3 Flour, page 30, or Aki's Low-Allergy Blend, page 31)

1 teaspoon / 6 grams baking powder

¼ teaspoon / 1.5 grams fine sea salt

½ cup / 130 grams whole milk

4 tablespoons / 2 ounces / 56 grams unsalted butter, sliced

recipe continues

1 cup / 200 grams sugar

2 large eggs, at room temperature

½ teaspoon vanilla paste or pure vanilla extract

chocolate ganache

¼ cup / 60 grams heavy cream

2 tablespoons / 14 grams cornstarch

¼ teaspoon / 1.5 grams fine sea salt

8 ounces / 225 grams bittersweet chocolate, finely chopped

2 tablespoons / 1 ounce / 28 grams unsalted butter, cut into pieces

To make the pudding, put the milk, cream, sugar, egg yolks, tapioca starch, cornstarch, and salt in a medium saucepan and whisk together until well blended. Set the pan over medium heat and cook, stirring constantly with a silicone spatula, until the mixture comes to a boil and is as thick as pudding. Remove from the heat and stir in the butter and vanilla until the butter has melted and been absorbed.

Transfer the pudding to a bowl and cover with plastic wrap, pressing it directly on the surface to prevent a skin from developing. Refrigerate for at least 3 hours, or as long as overnight.

Preheat the oven to 325°F. (165°C.). Butter a 9-inch round cake pan and line the bottom with parchment paper.

To make the cake, put the flour, baking powder, and salt in a medium bowl and whisk to blend.

Put the milk and butter in a small saucepan and bring to a simmer over low heat.

Meanwhile, put the sugar and eggs in the bowl of a stand mixer fitted with the whisk attachment (or use a hand mixer) and until light and lemon colored, 3 to 5 minutes.

Add the vanilla to the egg mixture and mix to blend. Beat in the flour mixture on low speed until just incorporated. Beating on low speed, slowly pour in the hot milk and mix until just incorporated.

Pour the batter into the prepared pan and smooth the top. Bake for 20 to 25 minutes, until the cake is golden brown and is beginning to pull away from the sides of the pan; the internal temperature should be 190° to 195°F. (88° to 91°C.). Let cool for 15 minutes on a rack, then invert the cake onto a rack, remove the parchment, and let cool completely.

To assemble the cake, split the cake horizontally in half with a serrated knife. Lay the bottom half cut side up on a serving plate and top with the pudding. Spread the pudding in an even layer, leaving a ¼-inch border around the outside edges. Top with the top of the cake, cut side down, and press down gently to even the layers.

To make the ganache, put the cream, cornstarch, and salt in small saucepan and whisk to blend, set over medium heat, and bring to a simmer, stirring. Remove from the heat, add the chocolate, and whisk until the chocolate is melted and the ganache is smooth. Add the butter and whisk until the butter is melted and completely absorbed.

Pour the warm ganache onto the center of the cake and, working quickly, use an offset spatula to spread it evenly over the top. Letting it drip down the sides.

Refrigerate the cake for at least 30 minutes so the chocolate can set before serving.

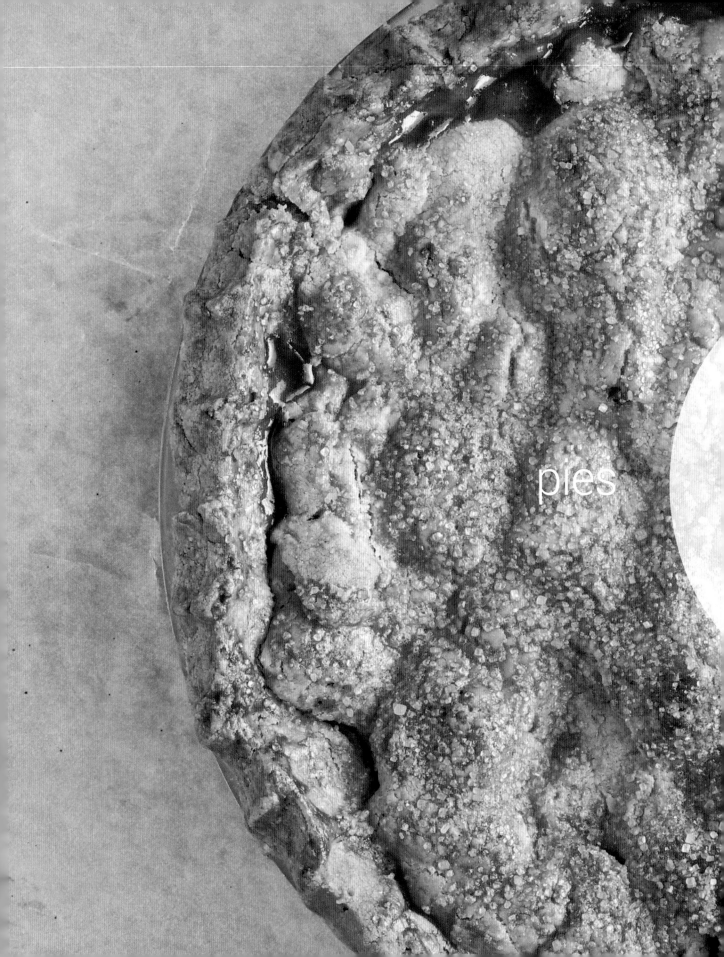

pies

all-butter pie dough

makes two 9-inch crusts

This is our classic pie dough. It has a rich flavor and a flaky texture. The food processor makes the dough simple to put together, and the gluten-free nature of the flour means you don't have to worry about a tough crust. The dough does tear easily, but you can simply pat it back together in the pie pan. Once it bakes, you'll never know the difference. We roll all of our piecrusts out on parchment paper to make it easier to move them from countertop to pie plate.

2½ cups + 2 tablespoons / 340 grams Gluten-Free Flour Blend (What IiF Flour 3.0, page 29, Batch-3 Flour, page 30, or Aki's Low-Allergy Blend, page 31)

2 tablespoons / 25 grams sugar

¾ teaspoon / 4.5 grams fine sea salt

16 tablespoons (2 sticks) / 8 ounces / 225 grams cold unsalted butter, diced

¼ cup / 55 grams ice water

Combine the flour, sugar, and salt in a food processor and pulse 4 or 5 times to blend. Add the butter and pulse 2 or 3 times, or until the mixture looks sandy. Add the ice water and run the processor for 5 to 10 seconds to bring the dough together. If it seems a little dry, add more ice water 1 tablespoon at time. The dough should resemble small pebbles and hold together when you squeeze it in your hand.

Turn the dough out onto a floured countertop in a pile. Sprinkle the top lightly with flour. Starting at one end, use the heel of your hand to smear a small amount of dough at a time against the countertop until you have smeared it into flakes of dough. Do this quickly, being sure not to work any sections of dough more than once. (This technique, known as *fraisage*, forms flaky layers of fat and flour.) Once all of the dough has been flattened, divide the flakes into 2 equal stacks and gently press into compact disks, no more than 2 inches thick.

You can roll the crust(s) out and bake immediately or roll them out, wrap them securely in plastic wrap, and freeze for up to 2 weeks. Or keep the dough, wrapped, in the refrigerator for up to a week. Let refrigerated dough rest at room temperature for at least 30 minutes before rolling.

Just mixed All-Butter Pie Dough turned out onto the countertop.

A light dusting of flour on the dough before fraisage begins.

Starting fraisage, *the smearing of the butter into the flour.*

Completed fraisage, *the pie dough is ready to be brought back together.*

All-Butter Pie Dough being shaped into disks.

Two All-Butter Pie Dough disks, ready to be rolled.

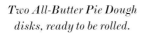

All-Butter Pie Dough rolled out on parchment paper for easy handling.

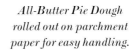

Using the pie pan to check the size of the pie dough.

Parchment paper makes it easy to invert the dough into the pie pan.

The pie dough ready to be trimmed and pinched.

Pinched pie dough, ready for action.

nut-butter pie dough

makes two 9-inch crusts

This is one of those recipes where a small change made a big difference. The addition of nut butter brings an entirely new dimension of flavor to piecrust. You can use any store-bought nut butter: peanut, almond, or SunButter, or even Nutella. You can also make your own peanut butter by grinding the nuts in a food processor. We add 0.5 percent salt by weight to roasted nuts and, if we're feeling sweet, a teaspoon or two of honey, then simply process them, scraping the bowl down occasionally, until smooth and creamy.

This crust is great when you want to add a hint of nuttiness to a pie without putting nuts in the filling. We especially like it with the Apple Grape Pie (page 282) and the Blueberry-Cheesecake Pie (page 286).

2½ cups + 2 tablespoons / 340 grams Gluten-Free Flour Blend (What IiF Flour 3.0, page 29, Batch-3 Flour, page 30, or Aki's Low-Allergy Blend, page 31)

1 tablespoon / 12.5 grams sugar

½ teaspoon / 3 grams fine sea salt

8 tablespoons / 4 ounces / 113 grams cold unsalted butter, diced

½ cup / 135 grams chilled nut butter

¼ cup / 55 grams ice water

Combine the flour, sugar, and salt in a food processor and pulse 4 or 5 times to blend. Add the butter and nut butter and pulse 2 or 3 times, or until the mixture looks sandy. Add the ice water and run the processor for 5 to 10 seconds to bring the mixture together. If it seems a little dry, add more ice water 1 tablespoon at time. The dough should resemble small pebbles and hold together when you squeeze it in your hand.

Turn the dough out onto a floured countertop in a pile. Sprinkle the top of the dough lightly with flour. Starting at one end, use the heel of your hand to smear a small amount of dough at a time against the countertop until you have smeared it into flakes of dough. Do this quickly, being sure not to work any sections of dough more than once. (This technique, known as *fraisage*, forms flaky layers of fat and flour.) Once all of the dough has been flat-tened, divide the flakes into 2 equal stacks and gently press into compact disks, no more than 2 inches thick.

You can roll the crust(s) out and bake immediately or roll them out, wrap them securely in plastic wrap, and freeze for up to 2 weeks. Or keep the dough, wrapped, in the refrigerator for up to a week. Let refrigerated dough rest at room temperature for at least 30 minutes before rolling.

Chocolate Pie Dough in a pan, ready for blind baking or filling.

chocolate pie dough

makes two 9-inch crusts

This chocolate crust is so rich and flaky that we save the scraps of dough and make small cookies out of them. The quality of the cocoa makes a huge difference in the dough. We like Cacao Barry, Valrhona, and Ghirardelli best. Chocolate piecrust is a great match for Banana Butterfinger Cream Pie (page 290) and Masa Harina Pie (page 293).

2 cups / 260 grams Gluten-Free Flour Blend (What IiF Flour 3.0, page 29, Batch-3 Flour, page 30, or Aki's Low-Allergy Blend, page 31)

½ cup + 2 tablespoons / 75 grams natural cocoa powder

2 tablespoons / 25 grams sugar

¾ teaspoon / 4.5 grams fine sea salt

16 tablespoons (2 sticks) / 8 ounces / 225 grams cold unsalted butter, diced

¼ cup / 55 grams ice water

Combine the flour, cocoa, sugar, and salt in a food processor and pulse 4 or 5 times to blend. Add the butter and pulse 2 or 3 times, or until the mixture looks sandy. Add the ice water and run the processor for 5 to 10 seconds to bring the mixture together. If it seems a little dry, add more ice water 1 tablespoon at time. The dough should resemble small pebbles and hold together when you squeeze a bit in your hand.

Turn the dough out onto a floured countertop in a pile. Sprinkle the top lightly with flour. Starting at one end, use the heel of your hand to smear a small amount of dough at a time against the countertop until you have smeared it into flakes of dough. Do this quickly, being sure not to work any sections of dough more than once. (This technique, known as *fraisage*, forms flaky layers of fat and flour.) Once all of the dough has been flattened, divide the flakes into 2 equal stacks and gently press them into compact disks, no more than 2 inches thick.

You can roll the crust(s) out and bake them immediately or roll them out, wrap them securely in plastic wrap, and freeze for up to 2 weeks. Or keep the dough, wrapped, in the refrigerator for up to a week. Let refrigerated dough rest at room temperature for at least 30 minutes before rolling.

summer peach pie

makes one 9-inch pie

Is there anything better than a fragrant, perfectly ripe peach? It is one of the last truly seasonal treasures to arrive on our table. In our house, unblemished peaches are devoured out of hand and the rest are set aside for pie. We cook the peaches before filling the pie for two reasons: the caramelized sugar adds a great depth of flavor and the initial cooking helps release the abundant juices and set them into a gel with the starches. We leave the skins on our fruit, but feel free to peel yours if you prefer. The sliced peaches become plump, tender, and silky in the filling. We like to serve this with our Sweet-and-Spicy Ginger Cream Ice Cream (page 25), but softly whipped cream or vanilla ice cream works equally well.

All-Butter Pie Dough (page 272) or Nut-Butter Pie Dough (page 274)

6 large peaches, halved, pitted, and cut into bite-sized pieces

¾ cup / 150 grams granulated sugar

½ teaspoon / 3 grams fine sea salt

2 tablespoons / 14 grams tapioca starch

1 tablespoon / 6 grams cornstarch

¼ cup / 56 grams cold water

1 large egg yolk

1 tablespoon / 16 grams whole milk

2 tablespoons / 28 grams raw sugar

Preheat the oven to 375°F. (190°C.). Lightly butter a 9-inch pie pan.

Roll out one piece of dough into a 12-inch circle on parchment paper or a silicone mat. Slide one hand underneath the parchment, slightly lifting the center of the dough, pick up the pie pan in your other hand, and invert it over the dough, pressing the center of the dough into the center of the pan, then carefully flip over the pie pan and the dough. Lift off the parchment paper and discard. Gently press the dough against the bottom and sides of the pan. Trim the edges, leaving a 1-inch overhang. Cover loosely with plastic wrap and refrigerate.

Put the peaches in a bowl, add ¼ cup of the granulated sugar and the salt, and mix gently to blend.

Put the remaining ½ cup sugar in a medium saucepan, set it over medium heat, and caramelize the sugar, tilting the pan as needed to mix. Once the sugar turns dark amber, carefully add the peaches, and any juices and stir gently. The caramel will bubble vigorously and steam when you add the fruit and then seize and harden. Turn the heat down to low and continue to cook until the caramel melts.

Mix together the tapioca starch, cornstarch, and cold water in a small bowl to make a slurry. Once the caramel melts, add the slurry and stir to blend. Bring the mixture to a simmer, stirring, and cook, stirring, until it thickens. Remove from the heat and let cool for 15 minutes, stirring occasionally.

Roll the second piece of dough out into a 12-inch circle on parchment paper or a silicone mat. Pour the peaches and their juices into the prepared piecrust. Lay the second crust over the top and trim it so that there is a 1-inch overhang all around. If the piecrust falls apart a bit, as gluten-free crusts sometimes do, just press it back together. Tuck the edges of the top crust over the edges of the bottom crust and fold them under, pinching them together gently all the way around.

Mix the egg yolk and milk together with a pastry brush and brush the egg wash over the top of the pie. Sprinkle the raw sugar evenly over the top.

Put the pie on a parchment-lined baking sheet and bake for 45 minutes. Rotate the pie (don't worry if some of the juices have bubbled over), lower the oven temperature to 350°F. (180°C.), and bake for 45 minutes more, or until the pie is a deep golden brown. Let cool for at least 1 hour before serving.

honey walnut pie

makes one 9-inch pie

This pie is for walnut lovers. The intense sweetness of the honey helps balance the slight natural bitterness of the walnuts and brings out their rich, buttery flavor. We like a flavorful honey, and we recommend that you find the best local honey you can get your hands on. The play between the delicate flaky crust, the sweet honey gel, and softly crunchy nuts is seductive and indulgent. Serve with vanilla ice cream or a dollop of Cinnamon Whipped Cream (page 296).

1 disk Chocolate Pie Dough (page 277) or All-Butter Pie Dough (page 272)

2½ cups / 200 grams walnut halves

1 cup / 260 grams high-quality honey, such as sourwood, orange blossom, or
  basswood

⅓ cup (packed) / 70 grams light brown sugar

¼ teaspoon / 1.5 grams fine sea salt

4 large eggs, at room temperature

¼ cup / 60 grams heavy cream

Preheat the oven to 325°F. (160°C.). Lightly butter a 9-inch pie pan.

Roll out the dough into a 12-inch circle on parchment paper or a silicone mat. Slide one hand underneath the parchment, slightly lifting the center of the dough. Pick up the pie pan in your other hand, and invert it over the dough, pressing the center of the dough into the center of the pan, then carefully flip over the pie pan and the dough. Lift off the parchment paper and discard. Gently press the dough against the bottom and sides of the pan. Trim the edges, leaving a 1-inch overhang. Tuck the overhang under the crust, forming a soft cylinder of dough all the way around the edge of the pie. Use your thumbs and forefingers to gently pinch and crimp this dough all the way around to form the border. Cover loosely with plastic wrap and refrigerate.

Put the walnuts in a large bowl and set aside.

Heat the honey and sugar in a medium saucepan over medium heat, stirring constantly with a silicone spatula, until the sugar dissolves. Add the salt and stir to blend, then remove from the heat and let cool for 15 minutes.

Add the eggs to the sugar syrup one at a time, stirring until each egg is fully incorporated before adding the next. Stir in the cream until fully blended. Pour the mixture over the walnuts and stir to thoroughly coat the nuts.

Using a slotted spoon, spoon the walnuts into the piecrust. Then slowly pour the remaining liquid into the crust; you may not need all of it to fill the pan. Bake for 45 to 55 minutes, until the filling is golden brown and just set. When you gently shake the pie pan, it will wobble a bit but should not seem liquid at all. Let cool completely before serving.

NOTE: *Do you remember tasting honeysuckle as a kid? Pulling the small threads from inside the yellow blossoms to taste the sweet nectar clinging to them? Bees use their tongues to harvest that nectar and then store it in their "honey stomach." Their honey stomach can hold up to 70 milligrams of nectar, which they carry back to the hive. The worker bees suck the honey from the carrier bees' stomachs and process them in their own bodies to break the nectar down into simple sugars. Then they spread it through the honeycombs, where the water evaporates out of it, thickening and concentrating the liquid. The bees use their wings to fan the combs and speed up the process. Once the honey reaches the right consistency, they plug the comb with wax to save it until they are ready to eat it. The honey gets its color and flavor from the type of flower nectar collected by the bees.*

apple grape pie

makes one 9-inch pie

Our favorite all-purpose apple is the Honeycrisp. As its name indicates, it is crisp and juicy, with a sweet, tangy flavor. It's actually a cross between the Macoun and the Honeygold varieties. These apple crosses are created by pollinating the blossoms of one apple variety with pollen from another. The resulting apples will look like the original apples from that tree, but their seeds will produce trees that have apples of a new variety, combining elements of the original apple and the one that supplied the pollen.

Apples and grapes may sound like a surprising combination, but they are delicious together. Last fall, huge beautiful grapes appeared in all the local markets just as apple season hit its peak. It only made sense to bring them together in a pie.

All-Butter Pie Dough (page 272) or Nut-Butter Pie Dough (page 274)

2 cups / 325 grams large, seedless grapes

3 large apples, preferably Honeycrisp

¾ cup / 150 grams granulated sugar

2 tablespoons / 14 grams cornstarch

1 tablespoon / 6 grams tapioca starch

¼ teaspoon / 1.5 grams fine sea salt

¼ teaspoon / 0.5 gram ground cinnamon

⅛ teaspoon / 0.25 gram ground mace

1 large egg yolk

1 tablespoon / 16 grams whole milk

2 tablespoons / 28 grams raw sugar

Preheat the oven to 375°F. (190°C.). Lightly butter a 9-inch pie pan.

Roll out one piece of dough into a 12-inch circle on parchment paper or a silicone mat. Slide one hand underneath the parchment, slightly lifting the center of the dough, pick up the pie pan in your other hand, and invert it over the dough, pressing the center of the dough into the center of the pan, then carefully flip over the pie pan and the dough. Lift off the parchment paper and discard. Gently press the dough against the bottom and sides of the pan. Trim the edges, leaving a 1-inch overhang. Cover loosely with plastic wrap and refrigerate.

Cut the grapes lengthwise in half and put them in a large bowl. Peel the apples and cut them into quarters. Lay each piece flat on the cutting board and slice away the stem, seeds, and core. Then split each quarter lengthwise in half and cut it crosswise into ½-inch pieces. Add them to the bowl, then add the granulated sugar, cornstarch, tapioca starch, salt, cinnamon, and mace and mix gently with a rubber spatula to blend well.

Pour the mixture into the prepared piecrust, gently spreading the fruit evenly over the bottom.

Roll the second piecrust out into a 12-inch circle on parchment paper or a silicone mat. Lay it over the top of the pie and trim it so that there is a 1-inch overhang all around. Tuck the edges of the top crust over the edges of the bottom crust and fold them under, pinching them together gently all the way around.

Mix the egg yolk and milk together with a pastry brush and brush the egg wash over the top of the pie. Sprinkle the raw sugar evenly over the top.

Put the pie on a parchment-lined baking sheet and bake for 45 minutes. Rotate the pie, lower the oven temperature to 350°F. (180°C.), and bake for 45 minutes more, or until the pie is a deep golden brown. Let cool for at least 1 hour before serving.

See process photographs on the following page

Apple Grape Pie filling (page 282) in the bottom crust.

Sprinkle flour over the top layer and brush with egg wash.

Cover the pie with a thin layer of raw sugar before baking.

Apple Grape Pie fresh out of the oven and cooling in the pan.

Sliced golden-brown Apple Grape Pie filled with sweet, juicy fruit.

A slice of Apple Grape Pie (page 282), bursting with juicy fruit surrounded by crunchy-tender crust.

blueberry-cheesecake pie

makes one 9-inch pie

This recipe brings together cheesecake and pie, two of our favorite things. One of the hardest things to get right about cheesecake is the crust. It's often indifferently made with store-bought graham crackers and is overly buttery and sweet. We had already turned that problem upside down by creating a streusel-topped cheesecake. One day Aki had an epiphany and decided to bake the streusel cheesecake in a piecrust, and just like that, we had a new favorite: cheesecake pie. The blueberry layer adds a sweet, tangy fruit flavor, without being gummy, like most blueberry toppings. Lavender flowers are sold in specialty supermarkets and most spice shops. If you can find them, their floral sweetness will heighten the flavors of the berries. Once you try this pie, you'll never look at cheesecake the same way again.

1 disk All-Butter Pie Dough (page 272) or Nut-Butter Pie Dough (page 274)

blueberry layer

2 pints / 620 grams blueberries

½ cup / 100 grams sugar

⅜ teaspoon / 2.25 grams fine sea salt

2 tablespoons / 12 grams tapioca starch

1½ teaspoons / 3.5 grams cornstarch

1 tablespoon / 14 grams water

cheesecake layer

¾ cup / 180 grams sour cream

⅓ cup / 75 grams sugar

¼ teaspoon / 1.5 grams fine sea salt

1 large egg

1 teaspoon vanilla paste or pure vanilla extract

½ pound / 225 grams cream cheese, diced, at room temperature

1 tablespoon / ½ ounce / 14 grams unsalted butter, melted

¾ cup / 150 grams sugar

1 cup / 130 grams Gluten-Free Flour Blend (What IiF Flour 3.0, page 29,
Batch-3 Flour, page 30, or Aki's Low-Allergy Blend, page 31)

⅛ teaspoon / 0.25 gram dried lavender flowers (optional)

⅛ teaspoon / 0.75 gram fine sea salt

8 tablespoons / 4 ounces / 113 grams cold unsalted butter, diced

Preheat the oven to 350°F. (180°C.). Lightly butter a deep 9-inch pie pan.

Roll out the dough into a 12-inch circle on parchment paper or a silicone mat. Slide one hand underneath the parchment, slightly lifting the center of the dough. Pick up the pie pan in your other hand, and invert it over the dough, pressing the center of the dough into the center of the pan, then carefully flip over the pie pan and the dough. Lift off the parchment paper and discard. Gently press the dough against the bottom and sides of the pan. Trim the edges, leaving a 1-inch overhang. Tuck the overhang under the crust, forming a soft cylinder of dough all the way around the pie. Use your thumbs and forefingers to gently pinch and crimp this dough all the way around to form the border.

Bake the crust for 30 minutes. Rotate the pan and bake for 10 more minutes, or until the crust is a deep brown. Put the pan on a wire rack and let cool completely.

To make the blueberry layer, put the blueberries, sugar, and salt in a medium saucepan and bring to a simmer over medium heat. Reduce heat to low and cook for 10 minutes, until the berries begin to burst and become juicy.

Meanwhile, put the tapioca starch, cornstarch, and water in a small bowl and stir to make a slurry. Increase the heat to medium, pour in the slurry, and cook, stirring constantly, until the mixture comes to a boil and thickens, about 5 minutes. Remove from the heat and let cool.

Preheat the oven to 350°F. (180°C.).

Meanwhile, make the cheesecake layer: Put the sour cream, sugar, and salt in a blender and blend on low until smooth. Add the eggs one at a time, blending just until incorporated. Add the vanilla and blend to incorporate. Add the cream cheese and blend until smooth. With the blender running, pour in the melted butter and blend until the butter has been absorbed. Set aside.

recipe continues

To make the streusel, put the sugar, flour, lavender, if using, and salt in a food processor and pulse to a fine powder, about 30 seconds. Add the butter and pulse until the mixture resembles coarse meal. Reserve in a covered container in the refrigerator.

Pour the blueberry layer into the baked piecrust, using a small offset spatula to spread it evenly on the bottom. Pour the cheesecake layer over the blueberry layer. Put the pie in the oven and bake for 15 minutes.

Remove from the oven and carefully sprinkle the streusel over the top of the pie. Return to the oven and bake for another 40 minutes, until the filling is just set but still wobbles slightly when shaken gently; the internal temperature of the cheesecake layer should be 150°F. (66°C.). Let the pie cool completely.

Transfer the pie to the refrigerator and chill for at least 3 hours before serving.

Lavender streusel ready to top the Blueberry-Cheesecake Pie.

Tapioca and cornstarch slurry added to the just-burst blueberries.

Thickened blueberries cooled in par-baked piecrust, ready for the cheesecake layer.

Baked streusel-topped Blueberry-Cheesecake Pie.

Sliced Blueberry-Cheesecake Pie.

banana butterfinger cream pie

makes one 9-inch pie

There's something about a Butterfinger: must be that light, layered, crispy, crunchy peanut butter filling. While we're not known to sit down and eat a whole Butterfinger, we love to use them as an add-in: swirled into ice cream, folded into cookie dough, or, in this case, crumbled over the top of a pie. We've taken the English approach to banana pudding, folding the fruit into the warm pudding to infuse its flavor throughout (as opposed to layering the fruit and cooled custard for the all-American version). We pour it into a baked piecrust and let it set up. Then we cover the top with a luscious layer of whipped cream and sprinkle a crushed Butterfinger bar over the top. The result is irresistible.

1 disk Nut-Butter Pie Dough (page 274), All-Butter Pie Dough (page 272), or Chocolate Pie Dough (page 277)

2½ cups / 650 grams whole milk

⅔ cup / 132 grams sugar

4 large egg yolks

¼ cup / 28 grams cornstarch

¼ teaspoon / 1.5 grams fine sea salt

2 tablespoons / 1 ounce / 28 grams unsalted butter, diced

3 medium bananas, diced

topping

1¾ cups / 420 grams heavy cream

¼ cup / 30 grams powdered sugar

⅛ teaspoon / 0.75 gram fine sea salt

1 original Butterfinger candy bar, chopped (see Note)

Preheat the oven to 350°F. (180°C.). Lightly butter a 9-inch pie pan.

Roll out the dough into a 12-inch circle on parchment paper or a silicone mat. Slide one hand underneath the parchment, slightly lifting the center of the dough. Pick up the pie pan in your other hand, and invert it over the dough, pressing the center of the dough into the center of the pan, then carefully flip over the pie pan and the dough. Lift off the parchment paper and discard. Gently press the dough against the bottom and sides of the pan. Trim the edges, leaving a 1-inch overhang. Tuck the overhang under the crust, forming a soft cylinder of dough all the way around the edge of the pie. Use your thumbs and forefingers to gently pinch and crimp this dough all the way around to form the border.

Bake the crust for 20 minutes. Rotate the pan and bake the crust for 10 more minutes, or until set and a deep brown. Put the pan on a rack and let cool completely.

Meanwhile, put the milk, sugar, egg yolks, cornstarch, and salt in a medium saucepan, set it over medium-high heat, and whisk to blend, then stir constantly with a silicone spatula as the mixture comes to a boil. Boil for 1 to 2 minutes, until the mixture thickens to the texture of mayonnaise. Remove from the heat and stir in the butter until it is melted and absorbed. Stir in the bananas. Remove from the heat and let the pudding cool for 20 minutes, stirring occasionally to make sure that all the bananas are completely submerged.

Pour the pudding into the pie shell and smooth the top, being sure that all bananas are submerged. Cover with plastic wrap, pressing the wrap against the surface of the filling, and refrigerate for at least 4 hours, until completely cool and set.

To make the topping, put the heavy cream, sugar, and salt in the bowl of a stand mixer fitted with the whisk attachment (or use a large bowl and a handheld mixer) and whip on medium-high speed until the cream forms stiff peaks.

Pipe or spread the cream over the top of the pie. Sprinkle the crushed Butterfingers over the cream. Refrigerate for at least 1 hour, and up to 6 hours, before serving to let the cream set.

NOTE: *As of this writing, only the original Butterfinger bar is guaranteed-gluten free.*

Banana cream pie smothered in crushed Butterfingers.

Sliced Banana Butterfinger Cream Pie (page 290), showing layers of buttery piecrust, creamy banana pudding, softly whipped cream, and crunchy Butterfingers.

masa harina pie with coffee cream

makes one 9-inch pie

This pie was inspired by a budino at Charcoal BYOB, one of our favorite local restaurants in Yardley, PA. The filling, which includes maple syrup, is reminiscent of Indian pudding, but instead of cornmeal we use masa harina to give it a complex corn flavor. It's smooth and silky and rich. The chocolate and coffee cream provide an edge of sweetness and a hint of bitterness. Made with ingredients available year-round, it's a four-season pie.

1 disk Chocolate Pie Dough (page 277)

2 cups / 470 grams Masa Harina Puree (page 13)

3 large eggs

¾ cup / 150 grams sugar

2 tablespoons / 12 grams tapioca starch

1 tablespoon / 7 grams cornstarch

¾ teaspoon / 4.5 grams fine sea salt

1 teaspoon / 4 grams vanilla paste or pure vanilla extract

¼ cup + 1 tablespoon / 75 grams pure maple syrup, preferably Grade B

1½ cups / 360 grams heavy cream

coffee cream

1½ cups / 360 grams heavy cream

¾ cup / 90 grams sifted powdered sugar

2 teaspoons / 6 grams instant coffee

¼ teaspoon / 1.5 grams fine sea salt

Preheat the oven to 350°F. (180°C.). Lightly butter a 9-inch pie pan.

Roll out the dough into a 12-inch circle on parchment paper or a silicone mat. Slide one hand underneath the parchment, slightly lifting the center of the dough. Pick up the pie pan in your other hand, and invert it over the dough, pressing the center of the dough into the center of the pan, then carefully flip over the pie pan and the dough. Lift off the parchment paper and

recipe continues

discard. Gently press the dough against the bottom and sides of the pan. Trim the edges, leaving a 1-inch overhang. Tuck the overhang under the crust, forming a soft cylinder of dough all the way around the edge of the pie. Use your thumbs and forefingers to pinch and crimp this dough to form the border. Cover loosely with plastic wrap and refrigerate.

Put the masa puree, eggs, and sugar into a food processor and pulse 3 times to break up the masa. Scrape down the sides of the bowl and process for 30 seconds. Add the tapioca starch, cornstarch, salt, vanilla extract, and maple syrup and process for 30 seconds. Add the cream and process for 10 seconds or until smooth.

Strain the filling through a fine-mesh strainer into a 1-quart measuring cup or a pitcher. Pour the filling into the prepared crust and bake for 30 minutes.

Turn the oven down to 300°F. (150°C.) and bake for 1 hour, or until the filling is set, with a slight jiggle when you gently shake the pan. Remove the pie from the oven and let it cool on a rack for 1 hour. Refrigerate, uncovered, for at least 3 hours, until it is completely chilled.

Meanwhile, make the coffee cream: Put the heavy cream, powdered sugar, instant coffee, and salt in the bowl of a stand mixer fitted with the whisk attachment (or use a hand mixer) and whip starting on low and slowly increasing the speed to medium, until the cream forms soft peaks. Transfer the coffee cream to a covered container and refrigerate for up to 8 hours. Gently rewhip the cream before serving if it begins to fall or separate. Slice the pie and serve each slice with a healthy dollop of coffee whipped cream.

Chocolate Pie Dough in a pan, ready for blind baking or filling.   *Chocolate Pie Dough with Masa Harina Pie filling, ready to be baked.*

Slice of silky Masa Harina Pie with a chocolate crust and Coffee Cream.

flavored whipped cream

makes about 2¾ cups

Flavored whipped cream is an easy way to make any dessert special. Heavy cream comes in two versions these days, pasteurized and ultrapasteurized. Pasteurized cream is heated to 167°F. (75°C.) for 15 seconds and then chilled. Ultrapasteurized cream is heated to 280°F. (138°C.) for 2 seconds, which gives it a longer shelf life and a distinctly cooked flavor. It doesn't whip well, and we avoid using it whenever possible.

We make our whipped cream with powdered sugar because it dissolves easily and the cornstarch in helps stabilize the cream. These flavored whipped creams will keep in a covered container in the refrigerator for several days. On the off chance that they start to fall or separate they can simply be whipped back together by hand. We also add a touch of salt, which brings out the natural flavors of the ingredients. You can use a hand mixer and a large bowl if you don't have a stand mixer.

cinnamon whipped cream

1½ cups / 360 grams heavy cream

¾ cup / 90 grams sifted powdered sugar

1 teaspoon / 2 grams ground cinnamon

¼ teaspoon / 1.5 grams fine sea salt

Put the heavy cream, powdered sugar, cinnamon, and salt in the bowl of a stand mixer fitted with the whisk attachment and whip, starting on low and slowly increasing the speed to medium, until the cream forms soft peaks.

maple whipped cream

1½ cups / 360 grams heavy cream

3 tablespoons / 45 grams pure maple syrup, preferably Grade B

1 tablespoon / 7.5 grams powdered sugar

¼ teaspoon / 1.5 grams fine sea salt

Put the heavy cream, maple syrup, powdered sugar, and salt in the bowl of a stand mixer fitted with the whisk attachment and whip, starting on low and slowly increasing the speed to medium, until the cream forms soft peaks.

caramel whipped cream

1½ cups / 360 grams heavy cream

¼ cup / 145 grams Bourbon Caramel Sauce (page 244)

¼ teaspoon / 1.5 grams fine sea salt

Put the heavy cream, caramel sauce, and salt in the bowl of a stand mixer fitted with the whisk attachment and whip, starting on low and slowly increasing the speed to medium, until the cream forms soft peaks.

cocoa whipped cream

¾ cup / 90 grams powdered sugar

½ cup / 60 grams natural cocoa powder

1½ cups / 360 grams heavy cream

¼ teaspoon / 1.5 grams fine sea salt

Whisk together the powdered sugar and cocoa powder in the bowl of a stand mixer; push the mixture through a fine-mesh strainer if it seems lumpy.

Fit the mixer with the whisk attachment, add the heavy cream and salt, and whip, starting on low and slowly increasing the speed to medium, until the cream until forms soft peaks.

cookies

An inside look at the Classic Chocolate Chip Cookie.

classic chocolate chip cookies

makes about 3 dozen cookies

Two chocolate chip cookie recipes? Yes. It was absolutely necessary to include both kinds: one soft and cakey, the other chewy. These are our riff on the classic Tollhouse cookie. We've been making these cookies with wheat flour for years. Made with our gluten-free blend, they are still soft and cake-like, with a delicate chew. We use a combination of light and dark brown sugar to get the flavor just right. The secret is letting this dough rest in the refrigerator for at least an hour before baking the cookies. This lets the flours hydrate and gives the flavor of the vanilla a chance to develop. Cold dough spreads less in the oven, so you get a thicker cookie. We're happy to say that no one has been able to tell the difference between these and the originals, and people still ask for the recipe all the time. Great cookies make people happy.

16 tablespoons (2 sticks) / 8 ounces / 225 grams unsalted butter, at room temperature

3 tablespoons / 12 grams Toasted Milk Powder (page 15; optional)

1 teaspoon / 6 grams fine sea salt

1 teaspoon / 5 grams baking soda

1 cup (packed) / 213 grams light brown sugar

½ cup (packed) / 107 grams dark brown sugar

2 large eggs, at room temperature

1 teaspoon / 2 grams vanilla paste or pure vanilla extract

2½ cups + 1 tablespoon / 335 grams Gluten-Free Flour Blend (What IiF Flour 3.0, page 29, Batch-3 Flour, page 30, or Aki's Low-Allergy Blend, page 31)

1½ cups / 255 grams premium chocolate chips (we use Ghirardelli bittersweet chocolate chips)

Put the butter, toasted milk solids, if using, salt, and baking soda in the bowl of a stand mixer fitted with the paddle attachment (or use a hand mixer) and mix on low. Add the sugars ½ cup at a time and then mix until light and fluffy, 2 to 3 minutes. Add the eggs one at a time,

recipe continues

making sure that the first egg is thoroughly incorporated before adding the second one. Add the vanilla and blend well. Add all of the flour and mix on low until the dough just comes together.

Remove the bowl from the mixer, add the chocolate chips, and fold in by hand. Turn the dough out onto a piece of plastic wrap, wrap, and chill in the refrigerator for at least 1 hour.

Position the racks in the upper and lower thirds of the oven and preheat the oven to 375°F. (190°C.). Line two baking sheets with parchment paper.

Use a ¾-ounce ice cream scoop or a tablespoon to portion the dough into 1½-tablespoon balls and place them about 2 inches apart on the baking sheets. Bake for 7 to 9 minutes, rotating the pans halfway through, until the cookies are golden brown and just set. Let cool on the pans for 10 minutes, then transfer to a wire rack to cool completely.

The cookies can be stored in an airtight container for up to 1 week.

Just-mixed Classic Chocolate Chip Cookie dough.

Scoops of Classic Chocolate Chip Cookie dough on a baking sheet, ready to be baked.

Classic Chocolate Chip Cookies cooling on a wire rack.

A plate of Chewy Chocolate Chip Cookies (page 304) ready to be devoured

chewy chocolate chip cookies

makes about 3 dozen cookies

Chocolate chip cookies range from thin and flat to thick and chewy. Everybody has a preference, and for years we were partial to one recipe (see page 301). But sometimes Aki craved something a little bit chewier. So when we read about a recipe using melted butter that made super-chewy sugar cookies, it made perfect sense to adapt it to chocolate chip cookies. And once you're melting the butter, it's a small step to brown it, which adds a great depth of flavor to the cookies. Then, because browning the butter removes the liquid from the fat, we added a bit of milk. Adding the milk to the hot butter causes it to turn brown and curdle, but although it looks alarming, the cookies have an addictive butterscotch flavor that keeps you reaching for just one more. We guarantee these will be some of the best chocolate chip cookies you've ever tasted.

The dough is quickly stirred together and then chilled overnight. If you like, you can scoop the cookies before chilling, laying them out on a single baking sheet. We like to bake one pan of these at a time and keep the extra in the freezer for when a craving hits.

16 tablespoons (2 sticks) / 8 ounces / 225 grams unsalted butter, sliced

2 tablespoons / 33 grams whole milk

3 tablespoons / 12 grams Toasted Milk Powder (page 15; optional)

3 cups / 390 grams Gluten-Free Flour Blend (What IiF Flour 3.0, page 29, Batch-3 Flour, page 30, or Aki's Low-Allergy Blend, page 31)

1 teaspoon / 5 grams baking soda

1 teaspoon / 6 grams fine sea salt

1 cup / 200 grams granulated sugar

1 cup (packed) / 213 grams dark brown sugar

1 teaspoon / 4 grams vanilla paste or pure vanilla extract

2 large eggs, at room temperature

1 large egg yolk, at room temperature

3 cups / 510 grams premium chocolate chips

(we use Ghirardelli bittersweet chocolate chips)

Put the butter into a medium saucepan and cook over medium-high heat, stirring constantly, until it melts, begins to turn golden brown, and gives off a nutty aroma. Remove from the heat and stir in the milk and toasted milk solids, if using. The mixture will be a deep golden liquid with a mass of milk solids on the bottom; it will look curdled and slightly broken. Let cool to room temperature.

Put the flour, baking soda, and salt in a large bowl and whisk to blend.

Add the granulated sugar, brown sugar, vanilla, eggs, and yolk to the pan of melted butter and stir to blend. Pour into the flour mixture and stir with a rubber spatula or wooden spoon until about halfway blended. Add the chocolate chips and fold the mixture together until fully blended.

Transfer the dough to a covered container and refrigerate overnight. Alternatively, use a ¾-ounce scoop or small spoon to portion the dough into generous 1½-tablespoon balls and lay them out on a parchment-lined baking sheet. Cover and chill overnight; or portion and freeze on the baking sheet until frozen solid. Frozen cookie dough may be kept in a covered container for up to 1 month.

Position the racks in the upper and lower thirds of the oven and preheat oven to 350°F. (180°C.). Line two baking sheets with parchment paper.

If you haven't already done so, use a ¾-ounce scoop or spoon to portion the dough into generous 1½-tablespoon balls. In either case, lay the cookies out on the parchment-lined pans, leaving about 2 inches between them. (If the cookies are frozen, let them defrost at room temperature for 30 minutes before baking.)

Bake the cookies for 10 minutes, then rotate the pans and bake for an additional 5 to 7 minutes, until the cookies are set and golden brown. Let cool on the pans for at least 10 minutes before serving.

The cooled cookies can be stored in an airtight container for up to 1 week.

See process photographs on the following page

*Just-mixed Chewy
Chocolate Chip Cookie
dough (page 304).*

*Scoops of Chewy Chocolate
Chip Cookie dough on
a baking sheet, ready to
be baked.*

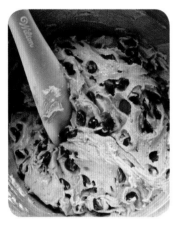

*A tray of Chewy Chocolate
Chip Cookies, hot out of
the oven.*

*A broken Chewy Chocolate
Chip Cookie.*

snickerdoodles

Snickerdoodles are a holiday favorite in our house. While their cinnamon-sweetness can be appreciated at any time of year, our Christmas cookie tin is never without them. Although it may seem strange to put the butter, sugar, eggs, and vanilla in the mixer all at the same time, and it will look like a mess in the beginning, it comes together beautifully. Our original family recipe used a combination of butter and shortening, but shortening leaves a funny aftertaste, so our snickerdoodles are 100-percent butter, and all the more flavorful for the change.

1½ cups / 300 grams sugar

16 tablespoons (2 sticks) / 8 ounces / 225 grams unsalted butter, at room temperature

2 large eggs, at room temperature

½ teaspoon / 2 grams vanilla paste or pure vanilla extract

3 cups / 390 grams Gluten-Free Flour Blend (What IiF Flour 3.0, page 29, Batch-3 Flour, page 30, or Aki's Low-Allergy Blend, page 31)

1 tablespoon / 18 grams baking powder

¾ teaspoon / 4.5 grams fine sea salt

coating

¼ cup / 50 grams sugar

2 teaspoons / 4 grams ground cinnamon

Position the racks in the upper and lower thirds of the oven and preheat the oven to 400°F. (205°C.). Line two baking sheets with parchment paper.

Put the sugar, butter, eggs, and vanilla in the bowl of a stand mixer fitted with the paddle attachment (or use a hand mixer) and mix on low until well blended.

Whisk together the flour, baking powder, and salt in a bowl and stir into the butter mixture.

Mix the sugar and cinnamon for rolling in a small bowl.

recipe continues

Use a ¾-ounce scoop to portion the dough into generous 1½-tablespoon balls, roll each one in the cinnamon sugar, and lay out on the prepared pans, leaving 2 inches between them. Bake for 10 minutes, rotating the pans halfway through, or until just set and turning golden brown around the edges.

Let the cookies cool for 10 minutes on the pans, then transfer to a wire rack to cool completely.

The snickerdoodles can be kept in an airtight container for up to 1 week.

Roll the balls of Snickerdoodle dough in cinnamon sugar before laying them out on sheet pans.

Baked Snickerdoodles fresh from the oven.

*A plate of tender-crisp Snickerdoodles
with a slightly crunchy coating of cinnamon sugar.*

Cooling Peanut Butter Cookies on a sheet pan.

peanut butter cookies

makes about 3 dozen cookies

These are addictive cookies. The peanut butter gives them body and richness, but they have a tender texture as you sink your teeth into one, and the peanut butter flavor lingers with a haunting sweetness on the back of your palate. If you are a chocolate lover, these are easily enriched with chocolate chips, chopped Cadbury Mini Eggs, or Heath Bar bits, if that's how you roll.

16 tablespoons (2 sticks) / 8 ounces / 225 grams unsalted butter, diced, at room temperature

1¼ cups / 250 grams granulated sugar

1¼ cups (packed) / 258 grams dark brown sugar

1 teaspoon / 6 grams fine sea salt

1 teaspoon / 5 grams baking soda

1 cup / 270 grams creamy peanut butter, preferably organic

1 teaspoon / 4 grams vanilla paste or pure vanilla extract

3 large eggs, at room temperature

2½ cups / 325 grams Gluten-Free Flour Blend (What IiF Flour 3.0, page 29, Batch-3 Flour, page 30, or Aki's Low-Allergy Blend, page 31)

Position the racks in the upper and lower thirds of the oven and preheat the oven to 325°F. (163°C.). Line two baking sheets with parchment paper.

Put the butter, both sugars, salt, and baking soda in the bowl of a stand mixer fitted with the paddle attachment (or use a hand mixer) and mix on low until well blended. Add the peanut butter and vanilla and mix until well blended. Add the eggs one at a time, mixing until each is fully incorporated. Add the flour and mix on low until fully absorbed.

Use a ¾-ounce scoop to portion the dough into generous 1½-tablespoon balls and place them on the prepared pans, leaving about 2 inches between them. Use a wet fork to gently press down on each one, creating a crisscross pattern on the top of the cookie.

Bake for 15 to 18 minutes, rotating the pans halfway through, until the cookies are just set and the edges are golden brown. Let cool for 5 minutes on the pans before transferring to a rack to cool completely. The cookies can be stored in an airtight container for up to 1 week.

Baked Jam Cookies, cooling on a sheet pan.

jam cookies

These cookies are reminiscent of the jam-filled cookies made by Pepperidge Farm. They are buttery and sweet and utterly addictive. You can use your favorite jam. We like to make these with a variety of flavors around the holidays, so they are one cookie that is guaranteed to appeal to almost everyone.

16 tablespoons (2 sticks) / 8 ounces / 225 grams unsalted butter, at room temperature

1 cup / 200 grams sugar

½ teaspoon / 3 grams baking powder

½ teaspoon / 3 grams fine sea salt

1 large egg

1 teaspoon / 4 grams vanilla paste or pure vanilla extract

2¾ cups / 360 grams Gluten-Free Flour Blend (What IiF Flour 3.0, page 29, Batch-3 Flour, page 30, or Aki's Low-Allergy Blend, page 31)

1 cup / 340 grams fruit jam

Position the racks in the upper and lower thirds of the oven and preheat the oven to 300°F. (150°C.). Line two baking sheets with parchment paper.

Put the butter, sugar, baking powder, and salt in the bowl of a stand mixer fitted with the paddle attachment (or use a hand mixer) and beat on low until light and creamy. Add the egg and mix until it is fully incorporated. Add the vanilla and mix to incorporate. Add all of the flour and mix on low until it is fully absorbed, about a minute; the dough will be stiff.

Use a ¾-ounce scoop to portion the dough into generous 1½-tablespoon balls and place them on the prepared pans, leaving 2 inches of space between them. Use the back of a round ¼-teaspoon measuring spoon to press down the center of each cookie, forming a small well for the jam. Put ¼ teaspoon jam in the center of each cookie.

recipe continues

Bake for 20 to 22 minutes, rotating the pans halfway through, until the cookies are just set and golden brown around the edges. Let cool on the pans for 10 minutes, then transfer to a rack to cool completely.

The cookies can be stored in an airtight container for up to 1 week.

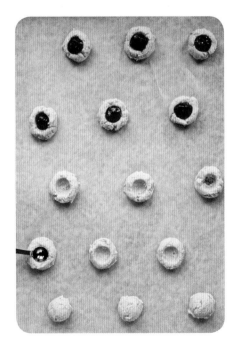

Shaping Jam Cookies: Use the back of a round measuring spoon to make the indentation and then use the front to scoop the right amount of jam for filling.

Stroopwafels (page 316) take on a cake-like texture around the chewy maple filling

stroopwafels

makes about 15 cookies

These are very special cookies, native to the Netherlands. Their name translates as "syrup waffles," and they are traditionally made by sandwiching two wafer cookies around a caramel filling. You will need a stroopwafel, krumkake, or Belgian cookie iron for these; pizzelle makers result in cookies that are too thick. You can find krumkake irons and Belgian cookie irons at specialty kitchen stores and online.

We make our caramel with maple syrup, and we add a bit of corn syrup, an invert sugar, to prevent crystallization, along with some cream, so that finished caramel is smooth and spreadable. As the cookies sit, they soften into a cake-like texture around the chewy filling. These are large cookies, so you only really need one per person.

cookie dough

2¼ cups / 295 grams Gluten-Free Flour Blend (What IiF Flour 3.0, page 29,
    Batch-3 Flour, page 30, or Aki's Low-Allergy Blend, page 31)

½ cup (packed) / 105 grams light brown sugar

⅜ teaspoon / 2.25 grams fine sea salt

¼ teaspoon / 0.5 gram ground cinnamon

8 tablespoons / 4 ounces / 113 grams unsalted butter

1 large egg

½ cup / 112.5 grams water

maple caramel filling

1 cup / 240 grams pure maple syrup, preferably Grade B

1 tablespoon + 1 teaspoon / 25 grams light corn syrup

4 tablespoons / 2 ounces / 56 grams cold unsalted butter, diced

¼ teaspoon / 1.5 grams fine sea salt

¼ cup / 60 grams heavy cream

Special Equipment: *Stroopwafel or krumkake iron*

To make the dough, put the flour, brown sugar, salt, and cinnamon in a food processor and pulse to blend. Add the butter and pulse a few times, until the mixture looks like coarse meal.

Whisk together the egg and water in a small bowl, then pour into the flour mixture and pulse until the mixture just comes together into a dough.

Turn it out onto a clean countertop and knead it 2 or 3 times. Put the dough in a bowl, cover with plastic wrap, and let rest for 30 minutes at room temperature. (The dough can also be wrapped in plastic wrap and refrigerated overnight.)

To make the caramel, put the maple syrup, corn syrup, butter, and salt in a 2-quart sauce-pan, set over medium heat, and cook, without stirring, until it reaches 245°F. (118°C.). The bubbles will look thick and viscous.

Remove the pan from the heat and whisk in the cream. Transfer the caramel to a heatproof bowl and let cool to room temperature.

Preheat your stroopwafel, krumkake, or Belgian cookie iron according to the manufacturer's instructions.

Weigh out 40-gram portions (about 2 tablespoons) of the dough and roll them into small balls.

Bake the cookies in the iron following the manufacturer's directions. (Our krumkake iron takes 1½ minutes to cook the stroopwafels to a uniform golden brown.) While the cookies are still warm from the iron, use a serrated knife to split each one in half. Spread the cut of one half with a thin layer of caramel and top with the other half. Then use a 4-inch round cutter to punch out each cookie into a neat circle. (Use the scraps for snacks or ice cream mix-ins.) Let the cookies cool completely on racks. Repeat until all of the cookies are made.

The cookies can be stored in an airtight container for up to 3 days.

See process photographs on the following page

Shape the Stroopwafel dough (page 316) by rolling portions into balls on a cutting board.

Baked Stroopwafels on a wire rack, stuffed and ready to be trimmed.

Use a round cookie cutter to trim the Stroopwafels. Save the trimmings for snacks.

arnhem biscuits

makes about 4 dozen cookies

We first encountered a recipe for Arnhem biscuits in John Thorne's book Pot on the Fire. *His description led Aki to seek out Roald Dahl's book* Memories with Food at Gipsy House. *His description of a book signing in Holland and the special cookies delivered by a local baker made us itch to try them out. We have no doubt that these gluten-free cookies are different from the ones Dahl consumed so long ago. Still, there are similarities. These cookies are thin and crunchy, made with a flaky unsweetened dough coated in caramelized sugar. The overnight fermentation of the yeast gives them a deep, haunting flavor. Most important, the cookies are addictive and your fingers will stray back to the cookie plate again and again. That's the mark of a great cookie.*

1¾ cups / 225 grams / Gluten-Free Flour Blend (What IiF Flour 3.0, page 29, Batch-3 Flour, page 30, or Aki's Low-Allergy Blend, page 31)

¼ teaspoon / 1.5 grams fine sea salt

1 teaspoon / 3 grams instant yeast

½ cup + 1 tablespoon / 150 grams whole milk

8 tablespoons / 4 ounces / 113 grams unsalted butter, sliced, at room temperature

About ½ cup / 100 grams raw sugar for rolling out the dough

Put the flour and salt in the bowl of a stand mixer fitted with the paddle attachment (or use a hand mixer).

Stir the yeast into the milk in a small bowl until dissolved. Pour into the flour and mix on medium-low until the mixture comes together. Increase the speed to medium and begin adding the butter 1 or 2 pieces at a time, making sure that each piece is absorbed before adding another. When all of the butter has been incorporated, transfer the dough to a covered container and let rise at room temperature for 4 hours.

Put the dough on a 13-by-18-inch piece of parchment paper and top with another sheet of parchment paper. Roll out to a rectangle about 10 by 12 inches and about ⅛ inch thick.

recipe continues

Slide the dough onto 13-by-18-inch baking sheet and refrigerate overnight.

Remove the top piece of parchment and sprinkle raw sugar generously over the dough. Put the paper back on and flip the dough over. Remove the parchment paper and scatter raw sugar over this side as well. Replace the paper and roll out the dough a few times to press the sugar into the dough.

Using a fluted pastry cutter, cut the dough into 1-by-2-inch rectangles. Transfer the cookies to the lined pans, leaving about 1 inch of space between them.

Cover with plastic wrap and let the cookies proof for 1 hour. They will be slightly puffy, but they will not rise very much.

Position the racks in the upper and lower thirds of the oven and preheat the oven to 275°F. (135°C.). Line two baking sheets with parchment paper.

Remove the plastic wrap and bake the cookies for 60 to 75 minutes, rotating the pans halfway through, until the cookies are a very deep golden brown; this caramelization is a big part of the flavor development. Let the cookies cool for 10 minutes, then loosen them from the paper and enjoy, or cool completely on racks.

The cookies can be stored in an airtight container for up to 1 week.

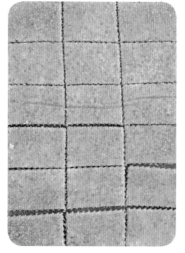

Arnhem Biscuit dough, rolled out, covered with raw sugar, and cut with a fluted cutter.

Caramelized, sugar-crusted Arnhem Biscuits, cooling on a sheet pan.

Crunchy, flaky, sugar-coated Arnhem Biscuits.

Decorated Cut-Out Sugar Cookies in a tin for sharing.

cut-out sugar cookies

makes about 5 dozen 2- to 3-inch cookies

This is a great recipe to make with kids. The dough is mixed together and kneaded by hand. After a brief rest in the refrigerator you roll out the dough, cut out shapes, and decorate them with colored sugar, or whatever suits your fancy. The cookies mature overnight—the texture softens and the vanilla flavor intensifies—so they taste even better the second day, making them perfect for classroom bake sales and gifts. During the holidays, you can cut out the centers and fill them with crushed hard candy to make stained glass cookies, or top them with chopped peppermints. Plain cookies can be frosted or dipped in chocolate. The sugar or frosting on top adds most of the sweetness to create the perfect crisp/tender cookie.

3¼ cups / 422.5 grams Gluten-Free Flour Blend (What IiF Flour 3.0, page 29, Batch-3 Flour, page 30, or Aki's Low-Allergy Blend, page 31)

1 teaspoon / 6 grams baking powder

1 teaspoon / 5 grams baking soda

½ teaspoon / 3 grams fine sea salt

16 tablespoons (2 sticks) / 8 ounces / 225 grams unsalted butter, at room temperature

2 large eggs, at room temperature

¾ cup / 150 grams sugar

1 teaspoon / 4 grams vanilla paste or pure vanilla extract

Colored sugar, crushed candy, nuts, or sprinkles, for decorating

Put the flour, baking powder, baking soda, and salt in a large bowl and whisk to blend. Use a fork to cut in the butter until the mixture is coarse and crumbly.

Whisk together the eggs, sugar, and vanilla in a medium bowl until light. Make a well in the center of the flour mixture and pour in the egg mixture. Mix with your fingers, working from the center outward, until a slightly sticky dough forms.

recipe continues

Turn the dough out onto a clean countertop and knead a few times, until smooth. Wrap in plastic wrap and refrigerate for at least 1 hour, and up to 2 days.

Position the racks in the upper and lower thirds of the oven and preheat the oven to 375°F. (190°C.). Line two baking sheets with parchment paper.

Divide the dough into thirds. Roll out one piece at a time, keeping the remaining dough in the refrigerator. Roll the dough out on a lightly floured surface until it is rough rectangle, about ⅛ inch thick. Cut out shapes with cookie cutters and lay them out on the prepared baking sheets, leaving 1 inch of space between them. Decorate with colored sugar, candy, nuts, or sprinkles.

Bake for 8 to 11 minutes, rotating the pans halfway through, until the cookies are puffed, pale, and just set, with golden brown edges. Transfer to wire racks to cool.

The cookies can be stored in an airtight container for up to 1 week.

Chocolate Snaps (page 326) can be enjoyed as is, or used to make Cookie Crepe Cake (page 329).

chocolate snaps

makes about 4 dozen cookies

As a kid, Aki was very fond of the small boxes of chocolate cookies that she could buy at the candy store. They were dry, unfrosted, and crunchy, and they tasted intensely of chocolate. Over the years, the cookies disappeared (the closest substitute was Oreos without their cream filling), and it became her mission to re-create them. These chocolate snaps are the culmination of that mission. They have a deep chocolate flavor and are perfect as is, though you could sand-wich them together with buttercream or layer them with whipped cream for an icebox cake. They are also perfect for cookie crumb crusts.

1¼ cups / 165 grams Gluten-Free Flour Blend (What IiF Flour 3.0, page 29,
    Batch-3 Flour, page 30, or Aki's Low-Allergy Blend, page 31)

1½ cups /300 grams sugar

½ cup / 60 grams natural cocoa powder (use Dutch-process or King Arthur black cocoa
    if you want darker cookies)

1 tablespoon / 5 grams baking soda

¼ teaspoon / 1.5 grams baking powder

¼ teaspoon /1.5 grams fine sea salt

10 tablesoons / 5 ounces / 142 grams cold unsalted butter, diced

1 large egg

1 teaspoon / 4 grams vanilla paste or pure vanilla extract

Position the racks in the upper and lower thirds of the oven and preheat the oven to 375°F. (190°C.). Line two baking sheets with parchment paper.

Put the flour, sugar, cocoa, baking soda, baking powder, and salt in the bowl of a food pro-cessor and pulse to blend. Add the butter and pulse until the mixture resembles coarse meal, about 10 seconds. Add the egg and vanilla and pulse until a crumbly dough forms.

Turn the dough out onto a lightly floured countertop and knead a few times to make sure everything has come together. Using a small scoop or a measuring spoon, portion the dough into teaspoon-sized balls and lay them out on the parchment-lined baking sheets, leaving 2 inches of space between them. Use the bottom of a glass or the palm of your hand to gently flatten each ball into a round approximately ½ inch thick.

Bake for 10 minutes, rotating the pans halfway through, or until the cookies are completely set and the tops have acquired a network of cracks. Let cool completely on a rack.

The cookies can be stored in an airtight container for up to 1 week.

Chocolate Snap dough just mixed in the food processor.

Use a 1 tablespoon ice-cream scoop to portion the cookie dough onto a sheet pan lined with parchment paper.

Flatten the cookies slightly before baking.

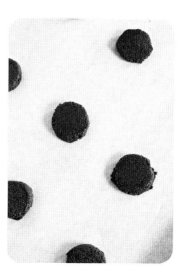

Chocolate Snap Cookie Crepe Cake, layered with whipped cream and chocolate cookie curls.

cookie crepe cake

makes one 8-inch cake

Crepe cakes are thing of beauty: many layers of crepes separated by whipped cream. As they sit in the refrigerator, the flavors and textures slowly meld, creating one fabulous whole. We blend some of the cookies with melted butter to make cookies curls for garnishing the top of the cake. We like to use our Chocolate Snaps for this recipe, but you can substitute any favorite cookie. We've tried this with everything from Oreos to peanut butter cookies and they all work. Depending on the cookie you choose, you can also flavor the whipped cream, choosing the variation on pages 296–97 that best suits your cake. No matter what, this is an impressive cake but it is easily put together even by those who have a fear of frosting.

cookie curls

14 ounces (just over ½ batch)/ 400 grams Chocolate Snaps (page 326)

8 tablespoons / 4 ounces / 113 grams unsalted butter

crepes

12¼ ounces (just under ½ batch) / 350 grams Chocolate Snaps

1¾ cups / 400 grams whole milk

3 large eggs

½ cup / 75 grams Gluten-Free Flour Blend (What IiF Flour 3.0, page 29, Batch-3 Flour, page 30, or Aki's Low-Allergy Blend, page 31)

whipped cream

2½ cups / 600 grams heavy cream

½ cup + 2 tablespoons / 120 grams granulated sugar

¼ cup / 30 grams powdered sugar

½ teaspoon / 3 grams fine sea salt

recipe continues

To make the curls, put the cookies into a blender. Melt the butter in a small saucepan over medium heat, then continue to cook it until it stops sizzling and the butter solids begin to brown.

Pour the hot butter into the blender. Turn the blender on low, gradually increase the speed to medium-high, and blend until smooth, about 3 minutes. Pour the cookie mixture into a small shallow plastic storage container.

Freeze the cookie mixture for at least 4 hours, until frozen solid.

Pop the cookie mixture out of the container. Set a mandoline over a chilled bowl and use it to shave the frozen block into curls, or shave the block with a vegetable peeler. Cover and reserve in the freezer.

To make the crepes, put the cookies, milk, eggs, and flour into a blender. Turn on low, gradually increase the speed to high, and blend until the batter is a deep, dark gray and smooth. Stop occasionally and use a rubber spatula to scrape the batter off the sides of the blender.

Pour the batter into a small deep bowl. Heat an 8-inch nonstick crepe pan or skillet over medium heat until hot. Using a 2-ounce ladle, pour batter into the pan and tilt the pan so the batter coats the bottom evenly. Put the pan back on the heat and cook until the crepe is set, about 10 seconds. Flip the crepe and cook for 2 to 3 seconds more, until just set, then flip it out onto a rack. Repeat with the remaining batter; you should have about 20 crepes. Once cool, the crepes can be stacked on a plate and covered with plastic wrap until ready to use.

To make the whipped cream, put the cream, granulated sugar, powdered sugar, and salt in the bowl of a stand mixer fitted with the whisk attachment (or use a hand mixer) and whip until the cream just holds stiff peaks.

To assemble the cake, place one crepe on a large plate. Put a large spoonful of whipped cream on the crepe and use an offset spatula to spread the cream evenly in a thin layer over the crepe. Put another crepe on the cream and repeat. Continue until all the crepes are used, reserving one large spoonful of whipped cream to decorate the cake. Be sure to keep the layers as even as possible, and do not top the last crepe with cream. Cover the cake loosely with plastic wrap and refrigerate for at least 4 hours, and up to 24 hours, so the cake can set up.

When ready to serve, remove the crepe cake from the refrigerator. Spread the reserved spoonful of cream over the top of the cake. Decorate the top generously with the cookie curls. Serve immediately, using a serrated knife to cut the cake. Any leftovers can be kept, covered, in the refrigerator for up to 5 days.

A bowl full of chocolate snap curls.

Place the whole cookies and crepe ingredients in a blender.

The crepe batter should be dark gray, smooth, and a little less viscous than pancake batter.

Chocolate Snaps pureed into crepe batter, and cooked into crepes for the Cookie Crepe Cake.

maple oatmeal-raisin cookies

makes about 1 dozen cookies

These are soft, chewy oatmeal raisin cookies. The surprise is the maple flavor. It gives them a little something special. We let the batter rest for 30 minutes before baking so that the flour hydrates and the oats soften. These cookies have a moist, tender texture with random bursts of sweetness from the raisins. We like to eat them still warm from the oven with warm apple cider or straight out of the cookie jar with coffee for breakfast on the run.

8 tablespoons / 4 ounces / 113 grams unsalted butter, sliced

½ cup / 120 grams pure maple syrup, preferably Grade B

½ cup / 85 grams raisins

½ cup / 75 grams Gluten-Free Flour Blend (What IiF Flour 3.0, page 29, Batch-3 Flour, page 30, or Aki's Low-Allergy Blend, page 31)

½ cup / 50 grams rolled oats

¼ teaspoon / 1.5 grams fine sea salt

Put the butter in a large glass measuring cup or microwave-safe bowl and microwave for 1 minute, or until it melts completely. Add the maple syrup, raisins, flour, oats, and salt and stir to blend. Set the batter aside to hydrate for 30 minutes at room temperature; it will thicken to the texture of peanut butter.

Position the racks in the upper and lower thirds of the oven and preheat the oven to 350°F. (180°C.). Line two baking sheets with parchment paper.

Use a ¾-ounce scoop or a measuring spoon to portion the dough into generous 1½ tablespoon balls and place them approximately 2 inches apart on the prepared baking sheets. Bake for 7 to 9 minutes, rotating the pans halfway through, until just set and brown around the edges. Let cool for 5 minutes, then transfer to a wire rack to cool completely.

The cookies can be stored in an airtight container for up to 1 week.

oatmeal lace cookies

makes about 3 dozen cookies

These are "the other" oatmeal cookies—they are as elegant as the Maple Oatmeal-Raisin Cookies (page 332) are homespun. They are basically a layer of toasted oats held together by a lacy web of caramelized butter and sugar. We use them to garnish ice cream or to serve alongside coffee. If you work quickly, you can lift them from the pan while they are still hot and wrap them around the handle of a wooden spoon to make "cigarettes," or lay them over a rolling pin, and let them harden in those shapes. You can dip them in chocolate or stuff them with whipped cream. The broken ones are delicious scattered over ice cream, or you could what we do and save them for a cook's treat.

12 tablespoons (1½ sticks) / 6 ounces / 170 grams unsalted butter, melted and cooled

1½ cups / 150 grams rolled oats

1¾ cups / 175 grams sugar

¾ tablespoon / 7 grams Gluten-Free Flour Blend (What IiF Flour 3.0, page 29, Batch-3 Flour, page 30, or Aki's Low-Allergy Blend, page 31)

¼ teaspoon / 1.5 grams fine sea salt

1 teaspoon / 4 grams vanilla paste or pure vanilla extract

1 large egg

Position the racks in the upper and lower thirds of the oven and preheat the oven to 325°F. (165°C.). Line two baking sheets with parchment paper.

Put the melted butter, oats, sugar, flour, salt, and vanilla in large bowl and mix with a rubber spatula to blend well. Add the egg, mixing well.

Use a ¾-ounce scoop to portion the dough into generous 1½-tablespoon balls and place them on the prepared baking sheets, leaving 2 inches of space between them. Flatten them gently with a small offset spatula to a thickness of about ¼ inch.

recipe continues

Bake for 10 minutes, then rotate the pans and bake for an additional 8 minutes, or until the cookies are golden brown. Let cool for 5 minutes, then use a spatula to transfer the cookies to a rack to cool completely.

The cookies can be kept in an airtight container for up to a week.

NOTE: *If you want curved cookies, bake only one sheet of cookies at a time. As soon as they come out of the oven, use an offset spatula to slide the hot cookies off the baking sheet and drape them over a rolling pin or wine bottle to cool. Or wrap them up around a wooden spoon handle or a cannoli mold to make cylinders. They will firm up and hold their shape once cool.*

Baked Lemon Sablés (page 336) cooling on a sheet pan.

lemon sablés

makes 3 dozen cookies

This recipe was inspired by cookbook author and cookie expert Dorie Green-span. She makes amazing sablés that inspired us to make our own gluten-free version. These are like shortbread cookies, only better. They have a fine, sandy texture and a delicate crunch. We love their simplicity. The flavors of butter and vanilla are clear and strong, with just a hint of nuttiness from the gluten-free blend. The toasted milk solids help amplify the butter, giving it the essence of browning while preserving its sweet flavor. It's a small accent that makes all the difference.

16 tablespoons (2 sticks) / 8 ounces / 225 grams unsalted butter, at room temperature

½ cup / 100 grams granulated sugar

¼ cup / 30 grams powdered sugar

½ teaspoon / 3 grams fine sea salt

1 large egg

3 tablespoons / 45 grams heavy cream

1 teaspoon / 5 grams vanilla paste or pure vanilla extract

1½ tablespoons / 6 grams Toasted Milk Powder (page 15)

2¼ cups + 1 tablespoon / 300 grams Gluten-Free Flour Blend (What IiF Flour 3.0, page 29, Batch-3 Flour, page 30, or Aki's Low-Allergy Blend, page 31)

⅔ cup / 150 grams raw sugar

Grated zest of 4 lemons

Put the butter, granulated sugar, powdered sugar, and salt in a the bowl of a stand mixer fitted with the paddle attachment (or use a hand mixer) and mix on low to blend, then increase the speed to medium and mix until the mixture is fluffy and light in color. Add the egg, heavy cream, and vanilla paste and mix until incorporated. Add the toasted milk solids and flour and mix on low, gradually increasing the speed to medium, until the flour is absorbed. Increase the speed to high and beat until the dough is smooth.

Put a 24-inch-long piece of plastic wrap on the counter. Spoon the dough down the center of the plastic wrap. Using the plastic wrap, form the dough into a cylinder approximately 18 inches long and 2 inches in diameter, then wrap it in the plastic, twist the ends to seal, and refrigerate for at least 4 hours to firm up.

Put the raw sugar and lemon zest into a bowl and stir to distribute the lemon zest evenly. Cover and set aside.

Put a 20-inch-long piece of parchment paper on the counter and sprinkle the lemon sugar over the paper. Unwrap the chilled dough and roll the dough over the sugar, pressing firmly so the sugar adheres to it and it is completely crusted in lemon sugar. Wrap the log tightly in the plastic wrap and refrigerate for at least 1 hour.

Position the racks in the upper and lower thirds of the oven and preheat the oven to 350°F. (180°C.). Line two baking sheets with parchment paper.

Unwrap the cookie dough and cut the cylinder into ½-inch slices. Arrange the cookies approximately 2 inches apart on the prepared baking sheets. Bake for 20 minutes, until they are just set and golden brown around the edges. Remove the cookies from the oven and let them cool completely on the pans.

The sablés can be stored in an airtight container for up to 1 week.

Just mixed Sablé dough, ready to be rolled into logs.

Roll the logs of Sablé dough in lemon sugar to create crunchy edges.

Lemon Sablé dough rolled in sugar, ready to be sliced.

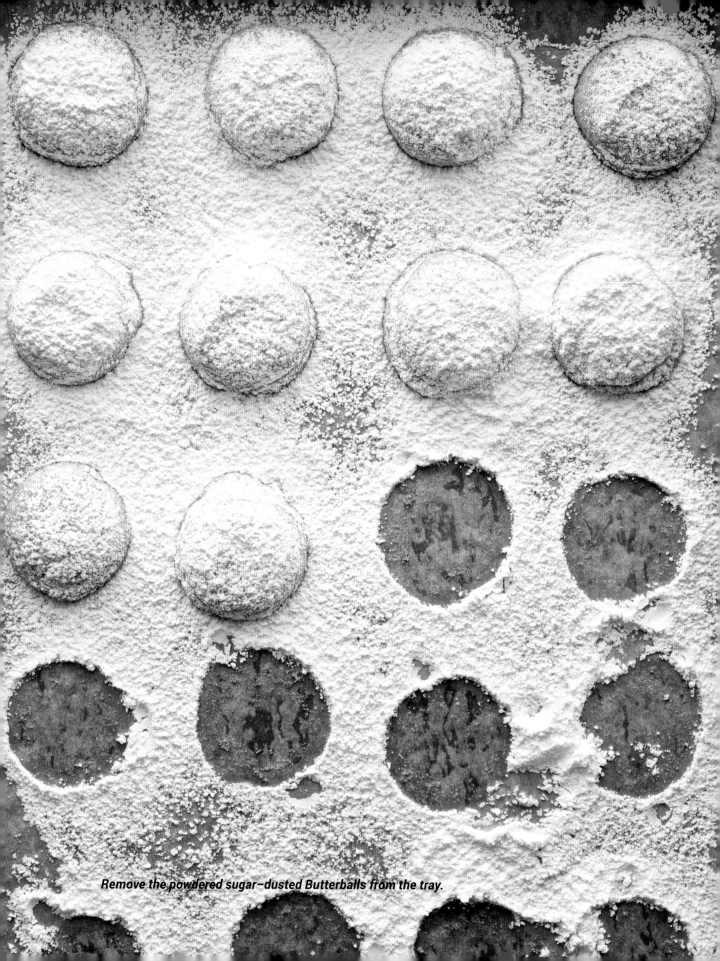

Remove the powdered sugar–dusted Butterballs from the tray.

butterballs

These are Aki's mom's favorite cookies. Aki's Italian aunts in Pittsburgh made them every Christmas and Easter. They belong to a large family of rich nut cookies, including Mexican wedding cakes, almond or pecan crescent cookies, and kourabiedes, that are rolled in powdered sugar. The dough is very similar to a shortbread dough, with the addition of ground walnuts. These cookies are soft and delicate, prone to crumbling if held too tightly. The original recipe rolled the warm cookies in powdered sugar; Alex likes them with a lighter dusting of powdered sugar. Both methods are included below, so you can choose the one you prefer. These cookies are slightly messy to eat, which induces people to laugh, lick their fingers, and have fun with their dessert.

1 cup / 80 grams walnuts, toasted and cooled

2⅓ cups / 300 grams Gluten-Free Flour Blend (What IiF Flour 3.0, page 29, Batch-3 Flour, page 30, or Aki's Low-Allergy Blend, page 31)

¾ teaspoon / 4.5 grams fine sea salt

¼ teaspoon / 0.25 gram ground mace

16 tablespoons (2 sticks) / 8 ounces / 225 grams unsalted butter, at room temperature

½ cup / 56 grams powdered sugar

2 teaspoons / 8 grams vanilla paste or pure vanilla extract

2 cups / 240 grams powdered sugar for rolling

Put the walnuts, flour, salt, and mace in a food processor and pulse to grind the nuts to a fine powder. Pour out onto a sheet of parchment or into a bowl. Put the butter and powdered sugar in the food processor and pulse 4 or 5 times, until fully combined. Add the vanilla and pulse 2 or 3 times to blend. Add the flour mixture and pulse until a dough forms.

Transfer the dough to a covered container and refrigerate for at least 1 hour.

Position the racks in the upper and lower thirds of the oven and preheat the oven to 325°F. (160°C.). Line two baking sheets with parchment paper.

recipe continues

Use a ¾-ounce scoop to portion the dough into generous 1½-tablespoon balls and place them on the prepared baking sheets, leaving approximately 2 inches between them. Bake for 18 minutes, or until the cookies are set and just golden brown around the very edges. Remove from the oven and transfer to a rack to cool for 10 minutes.

Lay the cookies out on a cool baking sheet and either roll them in a bowl of the powdered sugar or sift the powdered sugar over the warm cookies. Cool completely.

The cookies will keep in an airtight container at room temperature for up to a week.

Caramelized, roasted walnuts for Butterballs.

Portion the Butterballs with an ice cream scoop.

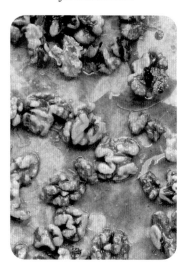

lemon angeletti

makes about 5½ dozen cookies

When we were testing recipes for this book, Aki was working on a chewy lemon cookie. Instead, she ended up with these small soft cookies, rich with lemon and vanilla. She liked these even better than her original vision because they resemble bites of frosted cake. They are the ultimate Italian angeletti, soft domes of sweet, cakey cookies coated in white icing, but they are filled with bright lemon flavor. Try them, and they just might become one of your favorite cookies too.

cookies

2 cups / 400 grams sugar

16 tablespoons (2 sticks) / 8 ounces / 225 grams unsalted butter, at room temperature

1 tablespoon / 18 grams baking powder

1 teaspoon / 6 grams fine sea salt

3 large eggs, at room temperature

½ teaspoon / 2.5 grams lemon oil or lemon extract

½ teaspoon / 2 grams vanilla paste or pure vanilla extract

5 cups / 650 grams Gluten-Free Flour Blend (What IiF Flour 3.0, page 29, Batch-3 Flour, page 30, or Aki's Low-Allergy Blend, page 31)

1 cup whole milk, at room temperature

lemon frosting

2 cups / 225 grams powdered sugar

Grated zest of 1 lemon

2 tablespoons / 28 grams fresh lemon juice

4 tablespoons / 2 ounces / 56 grams unsalted butter, sliced, at room temperature

recipe continues

Position the racks in the upper and lower thirds of the oven and preheat the oven to 375°F. (190°C.). Line two baking sheets with parchment paper.

To make the cookies, put the sugar, butter, baking powder, and salt in the bowl of a stand mixer fitted with the paddle attachment (or use a hand mixer) and beat on low until light and creamy, 2 to 3 minutes. Add the eggs one at a time, making sure each egg is fully incorporated before adding the next. Scrape down the sides of the bowl as needed. Add the lemon oil and vanilla and mix to incorporate. Add all of the flour and mix on low until it is absorbed, then slowly drizzle in the milk, with mixer running, until incorporated. Remove the bowl from the mixer and use a rubber spatula to give the dough a final mix.

Use a ¾-ounce scoop to portion the dough into generous 1½-tablespoon balls and place them on the prepared pans, leaving approximately 2 inches between them. Bake for 12 minutes, or until the tops are set but still pale and the bottom edges are golden brown.

While the cookies are in the oven, make the frosting: Put the powdered sugar, lemon zest, lemon juice, and butter in a small bowl and mix with a whisk or rubber spatula until smooth.

When the cookies come out of the oven, put a small dollop of frosting on top of each one, then go back as it softens and spread it gently over the top of the cookie. Let cool completely on a rack.

The cookies will keep in an airtight container at room temperature for up to a week.

Lemon Angeletti, soft little cake cookies, frosted and cooling.

Crunchy Biscotti with Pistachios and Dried Cherries in the cookie jar.

biscotti with pistachios and dried cherries

makes about 3 dozen cookies

Aki learned how to make biscotti one summer when we worked on Martha's Vineyard. The owner of the restaurant was Italian, and it was one Aki's duties as pastry chef to be sure that the biscotti jar was filled at all times. This was not an easy task, because the employees loved them as much as the guests. Good biscotti are light and dry, made for dunking. They should crumble slightly and never be tough or chewy. Gluten-free flour is perfect for biscotti, and here the combination of dried sour cherries and pistachios is a match made in heaven.

16 tablespoons (2 sticks) / 8 ounces / 225 grams cold unsalted butter, diced

1½ cups / 300 grams sugar

1 teaspoon / 6 grams fine sea salt

4 large eggs, cold

1 teaspoon / 4 grams vanilla paste or pure vanilla extract

4 cups / 520 grams Gluten-Free Flour Blend (What IiF Flour 3.0, page 29, Batch-3 Flour, page 30, or Aki's Low-Allergy Blend, page 31)

1 tablespoon / 18 grams baking powder

1 cup / 120 grams salted roasted pistachios

½ cup / 65 grams dried sour cherries

Preheat the oven to 350°F. (180°C.). Line a baking sheet with parchment paper.

Put the butter, sugar, and salt in a food processor and pulse just to blend; the mixture should still look somewhat chunky. Add the eggs one at a time, pulsing after each addition until fully incorporated. Add the vanilla and pulse to blend. The mixture will look somewhat light and fluffy.

Whisk together the flour and baking powder, add to the food processor, and pulse until the mixture comes together as uniform dough. Turn it out onto a lightly floured counter and sprinkle the pistachios and dried cherries over the top. Use a bench scraper to fold the nuts and fruit into the dough until evenly distributed.

recipe continues

Divide the dough in half. Form each half into a log about 12 inches long and 1½ inches in diameter. Put the logs on the parchment-lined pan and bake for 30 minutes, or until golden brown and completely set.

Remove from the oven, transfer the logs to a cutting board, and immediately cut each log into 1-inch-thick slices on the diagonal, using a serrated knife. Be gentle, as the cookies tend to be a little bit crumbly.

Arrange the slices flat side down on the baking sheet, return to the oven, and bake for 10 minutes. Remove from the oven, flip the cookies over, and bake for 10 to 15 minutes, until they are golden brown and completely dry. Let cool completely on the baking sheet.

The biscotti can be stored in an airtight container at room temperature for up to 1 month.

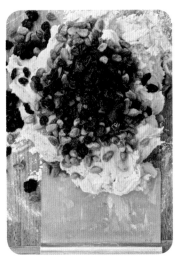

Gently fold fruit and nuts into the biscotti dough with a bench scraper.

Mixed biscotti dough, studded with fruit and nuts, ready to be shaped into logs.

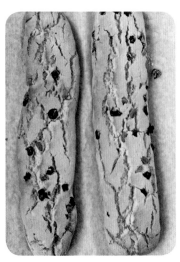

Baked logs of Biscotti with Pistachios and Dried Cherries, hot and ready for slicing.

cookie crumb streusel / petit beurre-scotti

makes about 2 dozen

Here's the thing about making biscotti, especially if they contain nuts or chocolate chunks: they have a tendency to break when you slice them, and sometimes they fall apart. The end pieces are not so beautiful, and they get knocked around in the cookie jar. Because people tend to reach for the perfect cookies, we set aside the discards and use them to make something new. You could put them into a Cookie Crepe Cake (page 329), or you could make cookie crumb streusel or Petit Beurre-scotti. Petit beurres are classically made by baking butter cookies, crushing them into crumbs, adding more butter, and baking them again. They are rich and delicate treats. No one will ever guess that these cookies originated in the discard pile.

7 ounces / 200 grams broken biscotti pieces (or substitute your favorite cookie)

6 tablespoons / 75 grams light brown sugar

½ cup / 65 grams Gluten-Free Flour Blend (What IiF Flour 3.0, page 29, Batch-3 Flour, page 30, or Aki's Low-Allergy Blend, page 31)

⅛ teaspoon / 0.75 gram fine sea salt

8 tablespoons / 4 ounces / 113 grams unsalted butter, at room temperature

Put the biscotti pieces, brown sugar, flour, and salt into a food processor and pulverize into fine crumbs. Add the butter and pulse 15 to 20 times to blend it into the crumbs. Put the mixture into a bowl and squeeze it together to make larger streusel-style chunks.

For streusel, use the crumbs immediately or transfer to a zip-top bag and refrigerate for up to 3 days or freeze up for to a month.

For Petit Beurre-scotti, turn the mixture out onto a 13-by-18-inch piece of parchment paper. Gently press and push it together to form a flat rectangle of dough. Top with a second piece of parchment. Roll the dough into a rough rectangle approximately 10 inches by 15 inches. Put the dough on a large baking sheet and refrigerate for at least 1 hour.

recipe continues

Preheat the oven to 325°F. (165°C.).

Remove the top piece of parchment paper. Bake the sheet of cookie dough for 15 minutes, or until it is browning on the edges and bubbling lightly in the center.

Remove the dough from the oven and use a cookie cutter to cut shapes in the hot dough; let the cut cookies cool completely on the pan before removing them. The cookies are for serving; the scraps are great broken up and sprinkled on ice cream. Alternatively, cut the warm cookie into bars and avoid any trim.

The cookies can be stored in an airtight container for up to 1 week.

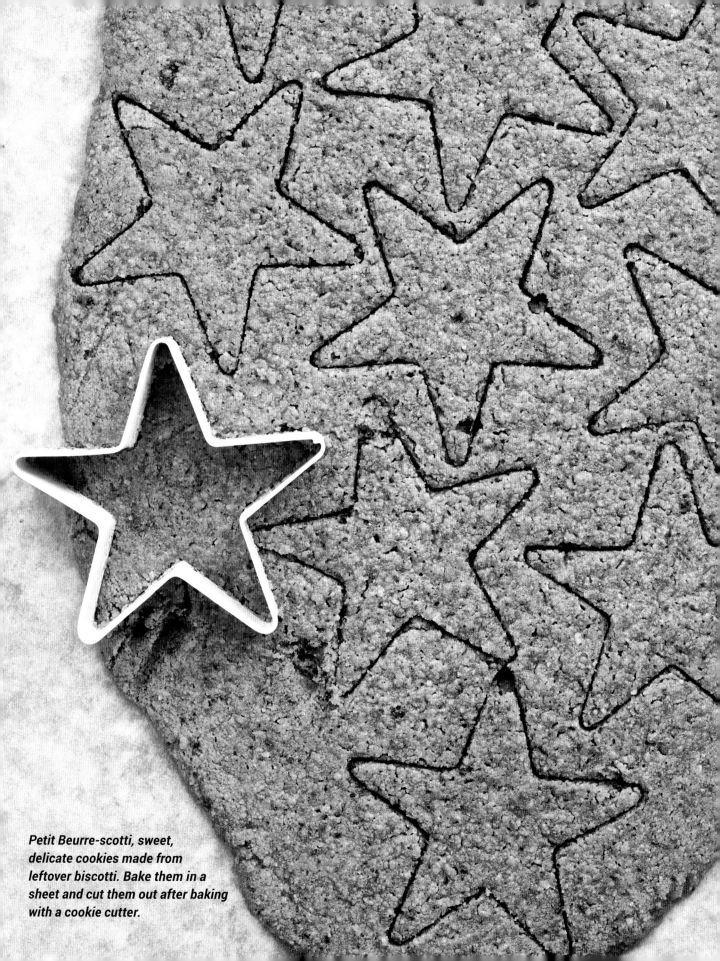

Petit Beurre-scotti, sweet, delicate cookies made from leftover biscotti. Bake them in a sheet and cut them out after baking with a cookie cutter.

acknowledgments

everything we do is a collaboration, and this book is no exception. We'd like to thank our exacting and inspiring editor, Maria Guarnaschelli; her assistant, Mitchell Kohles; the art director, Ingsu Liu; the designer, Jean Orlebeke; the production manager, Anna Oler; the project editor, Susan Sanfrey; and the entire team at Norton for welcoming us into the fold and helping us create this book. A special thank-you to our agent, Sharon Bowers, who has been with us from the beginning of our publishing careers. A big thank-you to our daughter, Amaya, our favorite kitchen assistant; to our friends and family, for their tireless taste-testing and support; to all of the chefs and cooks who tested our recipes and offered their feedback; and to all of our readers, who make our books possible. We couldn't have done it without you.

sources

Amazon
www.amazon.com
A source for anything you can't find at your local stores, including sodium citrate, copper cannelé molds, organic beeswax, cocoa powders, and parchment paper sheets for lining baking sheets.

Bob's Red Mill
www.bobsredmill.com
Good source of gluten-free flours and other baking products.

Boyajian
www.boyajianinc.com
Citrus and other flavored oils, vinegars, and extracts.

Cacao-Barry
www.cacao-barry.com
High-quality chocolates and cocoa powder.

Fain's Honey
www.fainshoney.com
Ribbon cane syrup, molasses, and honeys.

Fantes
www.fantes.com
Specialty cookware, including pasta equipment, meat grinders, whipped cream canisters and chargers, bakeware, and krumkake irons.

Fentiman's
www.fentimans.com
Ginger beer and other soft drinks and cocktail mixers.

Fever Tree
www.fever-tree.com
Ginger beer and other soft drinks and cocktail mixers.

Ghirardelli

www.ghirardelli.com

Our favorite supermarket-brand chocolate chips.

King Arthur Flour

www.kingarthurflour.com

Great source for gluten-free flours, baking supplies, black cocoa, cookware, and storage containers, among other products.

Lodge Cast Iron

www.lodgemfg.com

Cast-iron combo cooker, skillets, pizza pans, grills, and bakeware.

Nielsen-Massey

www.nielsenmassey.com

Vanilla paste and extracts.

Poirier's Pure Cane Syrup

(337) 254-8758

Old-fashioned cane syrup from Louisiana.

Reed's

www.reedsinc.com

Original Ginger Brew and other ginger sodas.

Regatta Ginger Beer

www.regattagingerbeer.com

Steen's Cane Syrup

www.steensyrup.com

Valrhona

www.valrhona-chocolate.com

High-quality chocolates and cocoa powder.

index

Note: Page references in *italics* indicate recipe photographs.